LEARNING TO TEACH IN SOUTH AFRICA

LEARNING TO TEACH IN SOUTH AFRICA
WALLY MORROW

HSRC
PRESS

Published by HSRC Press
Private Bag X9182, Cape Town, 8000, South Africa
www.hsrcpress.ac.za

First published 2007

ISBN 978-0-7969-2186-4

Copyedited by Peter Lague
Typeset by Stacey Gibson
Cover design by Fuel Design
Print management by comPress

Distributed in Africa by Blue Weaver
Tel: +27 (0) 21 701 4477; Fax: +27 (0) 21 701 7302
www.oneworldbooks.com

Distributed in Europe and the United Kingdom by Eurospan Distribution Services (EDS)
Tel: +44 (0) 20 7240 0856; Fax: +44 (0) 20 7379 0609
www.eurospangroup.com/bookstore

Distributed in North America by Independent Publishers Group (IPG)
Call toll-free: (800) 888 4741; Fax: +1 (312) 337 5985
www.ipgbook.com

Contents

Abbreviations

ABET	Adult Basic Education and Training
AIDS	Acquired Immune Deficiency Syndrome
ANC	African National Congress
BEd	Bachelor of Education (Now known as the BEd Hons)
BSc	Bachelor of Science
CASS	Continuous Assessment
CIEP	Centre International d'Etudes Pedagogiques (Paris)
CORDTEK	Committee of Rectors and Deans of Teacher Education in KwaZulu-Natal
COTEP	Committee on Teacher Education Policy
CPTD	Continuing Professional Teacher Development
CUP	Committee of University Principals
DEd	Doctor of Education
HIV	Human Immunodeficiency Virus
INCLASS	International Network for Class Size Study
INSET	In-service Education of Teachers
IPET	Initial Professional Education of Teachers
MEd	Master of Education
MST	Maths, Science and Technology
NCHE	National Commission on Higher Education (SA 1996)
NECC	National Education Crisis Committee
OBE	Outcomes-Based Education
OBET	Outcomes-Based Education and Training
PhD	Doctor of Philosophy
PRESET	Pre-service Education of Teachers
SADTU	South African Democratic Teachers' Union
S-G	Superintendent-General
SRHE	The Society for Research into Higher Education (UK)
TIMSS	Third International Mathematics and Science Study
UNAIDS	(Joint) United Nations Programme on HIV and AIDS

UNESCO	United Nations Educational, Scientific and Cultural Organisation
UWC	University of the Western Cape
WCED	Western Cape Education Department
Wits	University of the Witwatersrand

The essays in context

Significant events		Essays
	— 1989	Aims of education in South Africa
Nelson Mandela released from prison	— 1990	
UNESCO World Declaration on Education for All		
	— 1991	
	— 1992	Teaching large classes in higher education
		A picture holds us captive
The National Education Policy Investigation (NEPI) Report	— 1993	
First democratic election in South Africa	— 1994	Teacher Education: reconstruction and challenges
The South African Qualifications Authority Act (SAQA)	— 1995	
The National Commission on Higher Education Report	— 1996	What is Teacher Education?
The Constitution of the Republic of South Africa Act		Teacher Education, pluralism and the ugly lines of segregation in South Africa
The National Education Policy Act		The politics of difference in South African education
The South African Schools Act		
Official launch of Curriculum 2005	— 1997	
Higher Education Act		
	— 1998	Multicultural education in South Africa
Second democratic election in South Africa	— 1999	The practice of organising systematic learning
		Scripture and practices
Norms and Standards for Educators	— 2000	
Curriculum 2005 is reviewed		
UNESCO World Education Forum – *Dakar Framework for Action, Education for All*		
South African Council for Educators (SACE) Act		
National Plan for Higher Education	— 2001	
Qualifications for Educators in Schooling: Standards Generating Body for Educators in Schooling, Report to SAQA		
Implementation of the Revised National Curriculum Statement (RNCS)	— 2002	
	— 2003	
Ten years of democracy in South Africa	— 2004	
Third democratic election in South Africa		
	— 2005	The rubber hits the tar
		What is teachers' work?

Introduction

> ...when jargon might abate, and here and there some genuine
> speech begin...

Thomas Carlyle, *Past and Present*

The earliest of these essays was written in 1989, prior to the unexpected release of Nelson Mandela, the latest in 2005, 11 years after the first democratic election in South Africa. During this period I taught and, for some of the time, was the Dean of Education at the Universities of the Western Cape and Port Elizabeth[1]. From 2003, I was the Chair of the Ministerial Committee on Teacher Education.

This background explains why these essays address a web of issues that has emerged in the practical, institutional and political dimensions of our professional lives as we try to transform education in South Africa. It can also explain the three main interweaving themes that run through the book. The first is teaching and the ways in which financial, conceptual, institutional and other constraints set boundaries around what is possible, and seen as possible. The second is an ongoing struggle with relativism and multiculturalism. Relativism was at the root of Apartheid[2] and continues to lead an insidious life in thinking about education in South Africa. The third is Teacher Education, which overlaps with the other two themes and depends heavily on them.

Nobody seriously doubts that teaching is at the heart of, and essential to, anything that could be called education or schooling. But, paradoxically, in our policies and plans we think very little about teaching. Perhaps we assume that we all know what teaching is, having experienced it for many years of our lives in schools and other institutions of learning; perhaps we think that it is better to talk of 'facilitation' or 'instruction'; perhaps we think that if only we could improve the 'management' of educational institutions then teaching would automatically improve; and perhaps we think that teaching is no longer needed because we now have 'learner-centred education'. A striking feature of the recent Western Cape Education Department Strategic Plan[3] is its silence about teaching (Essay 12). Perhaps this silence is due to the fact that in South Africa we no longer have any teachers but, instead, now have 'classroom educators'. Under the impact of workerist modes of thinking and managerialism the fragile professional status of teachers has been undermined

(Essays 2, 5 and 6) and we increasingly reach for curriculum 'reform' and shallow notions of 'accountability'[4] in our desperate attempt to accomplish the much-to-be-desired 'transformation' of education, which does not yet seem to be at hand.

These issues are not merely symptoms of the ways in which language sets communication traps in a multilingual society; they indicate frames of thinking that shape not only what we do but how we understand what we are doing. They might also indicate either a sheer ignorance of debates in the fields of teaching and education (Essay 7) or simply an attempt to duck those debates that are, after all, 'merely theoretical'. In the light of the fact that teaching is essential in any schooling or education, these tendencies are regrettable and likely to hinder the project of educational transformation in our country; we need to retrieve a sense of the centrality of teaching.

Teaching is never an easy task, and its difficulties are compounded where resources shrink and learner–teacher ratios escalate under the pressure for greater access, and where we promulgate policies and regulations that might be an outcome of 'stakeholder negotiations'[5] but are, in fact, based on unsatisfactory theoretical foundations.

Where human, financial and other material resources for education shrink, as they have (and not only in South Africa), there is a tendency to think that 'standards are declining' and the only solution is to demand more resources so that the job can be properly done. Such a situation prompted Essays 1 and 3, in which I try to push the boundaries of our usual concept of teaching. Starting from the idea that teaching is conceptually linked to the idea of access, these essays argue that there are two distinct kinds of access – formal and epistemological – not commonly distinguished from each other. Formal access is a matter of access to the institutions of learning, and it depends on factors such as admission rules, personal finances, and so on; epistemological access, on the other hand, is access to knowledge[6]. While formal access is important in the light of our history of unjustifiable institutional exclusions, epistemological access is what the game is about. One way of characterising teaching is to say that it is the practice of enabling epistemological access. In Essays 1 and 3 the argument is made that because we have a restricted concept of teaching, we cannot see how to tackle the problem of maintaining the quality of teaching as resources shrink – the problem of how to increase formal and epistemological access simultaneously.

The issue of policies based on unsatisfactory theoretical foundations is taken up elsewhere in these essays, and particularly in Essays 6 and 7. In Essay 6 the problem of the definition of teaching is addressed in terms of different ways of understanding how to define a concept. If we think that concepts are 'names', we run into problems (this issue is also addressed in Essay 3 in the section called 'The concept of teaching'). We should think of concepts not as names but as rules for practical thinking. Essay 6 shows how the *Norms and Standards for Educators*[7] defines teaching as if it is the name of roles and responsibilities of teachers employed in the schooling system. Due to this way of defining teaching, the *Norms and Standards* generates an understanding of teachers as civil servants rather than as members of a profession, it inflates the work of schoolteachers and, despite its expressed intention, forecloses on the possibility of other ways of teaching.

In spite of the establishment of an all-inclusive National Qualifications Framework and the efforts of the South African Qualifications Authority to establish a system to recognise every kind of learning, the question remains whether we have halted the deterioration of 'the culture of teaching and learning'[8]. Essay 2 addresses this question and introduces the idea that the task of professional teachers is, centrally, to organise systematic learning[9]– that kind of learning which leads to epistemological access. In pre-ICT ages much of the work of teachers might have been to transmit information, but that task has become more or less redundant in a world saturated with various forms of mass media and that has seen unimagined developments in electronic technologies[10]. The idea of teaching as the organising of systematic learning echoes through many of the subsequent essays.

In Essays 1 and 3 teaching is defined as an activity guided by the intention to promote learning, and it is shown how this definition can enable us to think more flexibly about the activity of teaching. This is already a step away from understanding teaching as the name for some observable features of our world, but one of its weaknesses is the weight carried by the word 'intention'. In Essay 3 I try to avoid this weakness by talking of 'embodied intention', although this is not much of an improvement. The definition provided in Essay 2 (namely that teaching is the organising of systematic learning) throws stronger emphasis on to learning and the specific activity of *organising* learning. The next step is to add the idea of teaching as a practice (dealt with in Essay 4) and we land up with a powerful definition of teaching as the practice of organising systematic learning. The power of this definition is demonstrated in Essay 5, in a context of showing how it can be used as the basis in the reconceptualisation of Teacher Education.

The shrinking of resources for education[11] and a clearer concept of teaching prompt us to reconsider the traditional model of a school, and the responsibilities of schoolteachers. The traditional model of a school assumes that the full range of teachers is appointed in each school and that teachers are expected to do many things in addition to teaching. But good teachers are in short supply[12], yet they are the most essential and precious resource in any education system. The traditional model of schools restricts the distribution of this resource. While a school in Rondebosch (an affluent suburb of Cape Town) might have five or six excellent teachers of English or Mathematics, there might be a dozen schools a mere five kilometres away in Khayelitsha (a sprawling township on the outskirts of Cape Town) with not a single excellent English or Mathematics teacher among them. At the same time we expect schoolteachers not only to teach but also to run the hockey and netball teams, to act as security guards, to undertake 'pastoral' responsibilities such as identifying children in distress, and to organise cultural events such as choir festivals and inter-school debates.

Because of widespread poverty, the disruption of family life and community safety nets, not to mention the HIV and AIDS pandemic, the caring functions of schools need to be dramatically expanded in the South African context. But to expect schoolteachers to undertake this responsibility is to squander the essential resource of our education system. If we are serious about the right to quality education for all, we will have to reconsider our traditional model of schools and the functions of the teachers in them. This is a major issue for the future of education in South Africa, but it remains undeveloped in these essays. It is mentioned in the final paragraph of Essay 4, discussed in the last two sections of Essay 6 and referred to in Essay 12, in the context of a comment about the promising idea that schools might become the sites for the delivery of a whole range of social services for the young.

During the 1990s one of the debilitating tendencies in debates about how to achieve the transformation of education was the assumption that everything that had happened in education under Apartheid was bad and should be rejected without question. This stance has its roots in a form of relativism based on the view that 'it is all a matter of power'. It is a stance that does not distinguish between merely rejecting a claim and refuting it (by appeal to evidence and argument) or between mere counter-suggestibility (reject everything said by the authorities or some other person or group) and critical thinking, and it is a stance entirely inhospitable to education[13]. Two of the essays in this book challenge this assumption. Essay 2 addresses it directly, while Essay 7 discusses it in the opening section, showing how it inhibits critical thinking, paradoxically one of the critical cross-field outcomes of the National Qualifications Framework.

Essay 2 argues that a mere rejection of how Teacher Education was constructed under Apartheid does not provide us with a recipe for how to reconstruct Teacher Education in a post-1994 South Africa. It claims that there has been a loss of a sense of the significance of systematic learning and, although this might be placed at the door of Apartheid policies and resistance to them, the recovery of a sense of the significance of systematic learning will depend on the retrieval of the ideals of the teaching profession. The ideals of the teaching profession need to be built into Teacher Education for a 'new' South Africa.

The main agenda of Essay 7 is to demonstrate the unsatisfactory theoretical foundations of Outcomes-Based Education (OBE). OBE is sometimes said to be the 'philosophical underpinning' of the transformed education system of South Africa, and it was commonly introduced by contrasting it point by point with 'Apartheid education'. Perhaps it was felt that this kind of rhetoric was needed to get buy-in from the huge number of people involved – but it is very much in the style of mere rejection and simple counter-suggestibility. Essay 7 digs around the theoretical roots of OBE and provides a pessimistic prognosis. OBE has indeed had a profound impact on education in South Africa. It stands behind the National Qualifications Framework and has become a main pillar in the national curricula for schooling and the reconstruction of the official work of teachers. It has also penetrated the thinking of many people in influential positions in our public life. However, whether it has been beneficial to the project of transforming education is a moot point. It is now so deeply embedded in the foundations of educational policies and structures that it has become something like an immovable dogma, immune to mere argument. And it is relativism that is the chief enemy of the use of argument.

As Susan Haack points out[14], relativism is a *family* of theories related in terms of their claim that 'something is relative to something else'. A radical form of relativism will try to claim that there are no universal concepts (or truths) –

that all concepts are relative to particular socio-historical contexts. But in this form relativism is self-refuting[15]; it undermines not only itself but also the possibility of the resolution of disagreements by the use of argument and evidence. This form of relativism also underlies the view that power is ubiquitous and that therapy (including some forms of negotiation) is the royal road to the resolution of conflict[16].

A main difficulty in the struggle with relativism[17] is that in some of its versions it makes plausible claims. For instance, some kinds of constructivism (inspired largely by theories that emerge out of the sociology of knowledge) are obviously true, and highly illuminating in the sphere of education. Two of the essays in this book, 4 and 8, consequently express some sympathy for a particular strand in relativism.

Essay 4 is a discussion about whether profound changes in the contemporary world entail that we should reconsider the 'content and methods' of basic education. It is argued that the fundamental goal of basic education is to enable access to the modern world, which has become universal. However, how this goal might be accomplished (in other words, the 'content and methods' of basic education), it is suggested, is to be determined in the light of particular socio-historical conditions in different societies. For example, the situation is different in affluent industrialised societies with long traditions of basic education for all and relatively high levels of literacy, and in those, such as South Africa, still trying to establish basic education for all, and in which levels of literacy are comparatively low.

A related argument is made in Essay 8. Here it is argued that any significant discussion of the aims of education, one which might have some purchase on schooling policy and educational practice, presupposes particular historical conditions and, in particular, a 'shared moral discourse'. This essay – written prior to the release of Mandela in February 1990 – in its argument that there was no point hoping for a significant discussion of the aims of education in South Africa at that time, concedes one of the elements of a relativist stance, namely that the significance of a discussion of aims of education depends on (is relative to) particular socio-historical conditions – especially a shared moral discourse, which is a characteristic of a cohesive society. These conditions can, by and large, be met in affluent industrialised societies with long histories of democratic politics, but they were not met in South Africa in the late 1980s[18].

In Essays 9, 10 and 11, I make use of a conceptual distinction drawn by Charles Taylor[19] between the politics of equal dignity and the politics of difference. The politics of equal dignity is the form of politics for which impartial treatment of all persons and opposition to discrimination are the central regulative ideals; it emphasises the similarities between all human beings and assumes that all are potential participants in the discourses of reason. The politics of difference, by contrast, is a kind of politics that demands discrimination in favour of identified groups on the grounds that they have been, and are, systematically disadvantaged by the hegemonic system.

Essay 9 argues that multiculturalism (including multicultural education as its reproductive organ) is a form of the politics of difference, but that the politics of difference is no stranger in South Africa. Apartheid was a form of the politics of difference in that it deliberately prevented the development of social cohesion and hindered the development of a shared moral discourse. This leads to the conclusion that we should not welcome multicultural education in South Africa, nor think of it as a possible dimension of our schooling or Teacher Education. But this conclusion is counter-intuitive in a society so manifestly characterised by all the forms of diversity, highlighted in debates about multicultural education.

Thus Essay 10 revisits the idea of multicultural education. The question is here posed about in what ways multicultural education would have to be interpreted to distance it from the politics of difference and, by implication, from Apartheid. Two key differences are identified: multicultural education would need to reject the view that cultural groups are stable and permanent, and it would need to distance itself definitively from the relativism which is so central to the politics of difference. Reinterpreted in this way, which runs against the current of much of the debate about multicultural education, multicultural education can be understood as having an important role in schooling and Teacher Education in South Africa.

But this is not the end of the struggle with relativism. It keeps on rearing its head in various disguises in our thinking. It appears in some versions of affirmative action, radical feminism and the call for the 'Africanisation' of curricula, all of which, of course, have implications for schooling and Teacher Education. Essay 11 takes up the cudgels again, once more using Taylor's distinction between the politics of equal dignity and the politics of difference as the conceptual tool. This essay focuses on the key concept of discrimination, and shows how there is a form of discrimination, in respect to degrees of epistemological access, which is necessary in education. To reject this form of discrimination would, in effect, be to reject education. Given our project of transforming education we should remain wary of the various versions of the politics of difference and adhere firmly to the politics of equal dignity, while recognising that it is not opposed to discrimination per se but only to unjustifiable discrimination.

The theme of Teacher Education emerges in many essays in this book. From these it is clear that Teacher Education presupposes a concept of teaching and, in many cases, a model of a school and the functions of schoolteachers as well. It should also be clear that any programme of Teacher Education presupposes a particular epistemology, and thus that the struggle with relativism, and the ways in which some versions of relativism can compromise the whole enterprise of education, is highly relevant to Teacher Education.

Essay 5 addresses Teacher Education head-on, but others – particularly Essays 2 and 9 – draw out the implications for Teacher Education from the arguments being developed. Impoverished views of Teacher Education, which see it as nothing more than training for a role in the current schooling system, might seem entirely 'practical', but such views are disastrous if we are serious about wanting to transform education in South Africa.

Notes

1   Now merged with the Port Elizabeth Technikon, and renamed the Nelson Mandela Metropolitan University.

2   See Wally Morrow, ' "Philosophies of Education" in South Africa' (1984) and 'Education as an "own affair" ' (1986) in *Chains of Thought*, Johannesburg: Southern Book Publishers, 1989, for earlier struggles with relativism in South Africa. The struggle continues.

3   *Education 2020: A Human Capital Development Strategy for the Western Cape*, 5 September 2004.

4   See Wally Morrow, 'Accountability and the idea of a profession' (1980) in *Chains of Thought*, Johannesburg: Southern Book Publishers, 1989.

5   See Wally Morrow, 'Stakeholders and senates: The governance of higher education institutions in South Africa', in *Cambridge Journal of Education*, Vol. 28 No. 3, 1998, pp. 385–405.

6 'Knowledge' must here be understood as encompassing all kinds of knowledge, including how to weld a steel structure to support the roof of a shopping centre, how to care for the chronically ill, how to read, how to solve problems in mathematics, how to conduct research in microbiology, etc.

7 DoE (Department of Education), *Norms and Standards for Educators*, Government Gazette #20844, 4 February 2000, which remains the ruling policy for teaching and Teacher Education in South Africa.

8 The phrase comes from the decade of the 1990s, during which there was much concern about the ways in which this 'culture' had unravelled in the years of resistance to Apartheid.

9 This kind of learning typically takes some time to accomplish, and involves learning how to become a participant in any complex practice – such as reading and writing, distinguishing between history and propaganda, competently cooking pastry, identifying fraudulent accounting practices, building houses, or analysing legal texts.

10 Breathtaking developments of information and communication technologies, which make vast stores of information available, seem to promise universal access to 'knowledge' without any teaching. But the accessibility of this information remains limited for many people because of lack of basic print literacy and other appropriate cognitive capacities in terms of which to understand it. (See Essay 4.)

11 The key resource, of course, is good teachers. See UNESCO Institute for Statistics, *Teachers and Educational Quality: Monitoring Global Needs for 2015*, 2006; and SAHRC, *Report of the Public Hearing on the Right to Basic Education*, 2006, '…teachers were identified as the most important role-players within the education system.' (p. 3)

12 As even affluent countries such as Switzerland and the UK have discovered.

13 See Wally Morrow, 'To gather the living flower: Some problems about critical thinking and education' (1986) in *Chains of Thought*, Johannesburg: Southern Book Publishers, 1989.

14 ' "Relativism" refers, not to a single thesis, but to a whole family. Each resembles the others in claiming that something is relative to something else; each differs from the others in what it claims is relative to what.' Susan Haack, 'Reflections on relativism: From momentous tautology to seductive contradiction' in *Manifesto of a Passionate Moderate*, Chicago: University of Chicago Press, 1998, p. 149.

15 See Wally Morrow, *Chains of Thought*, Johannesburg: Southern Book Publishers, 1989, p. 61.

16 Some 'conflicts' are disagreements.

17 '...modern relativism has complex relations to colonialism.' Bernard Williams, 'Human rights and relativism' in *In the Beginning was the Deed*, Oxford, N.J.: Princeton University Press, 2005, p. 68.

18 This essay is not merely of historical interest as we still worry about how cohesive South African society is.

19 The Canadian philosopher – not to be confused with the erstwhile President of Liberia. The philosopher draws this distinction in Charles Taylor, 'The politics of recognition' in Amy Gutmann (ed.), *Multiculturalism and 'The Politics of Recognition'*, Oxford, N.J.: Princeton University Press, 1992.

1 *Teaching large classes in higher education*

(Address at the University of the North[1], 14 October 1992)

I have gradually come to the conviction that it is important for us to reflect systematically on the topic of teaching large classes in higher education. It was surprisingly difficult for me to get my conviction into sharp focus and, until a few months ago, I had the arrogant impression that I was a kind of a trailblazer, trying to find a path through a tangled and unmapped territory. I am sure of the rightness of my conviction that the topic is important; I was quite wrong to think that I was a trailblazer.

In early 1992 a British Council pamphlet came my way announcing a course to be run at Leeds University in England about English language teaching in large classes. I started to make some enquiries and soon discovered that out in the big world there is a flourishing debate about teaching large classes. I discovered that there were people in Holland and Germany who research this field professionally, that Graham Gibbs and his colleagues at Oxford Polytechnic have published a range of books and booklets about teaching large classes in higher education[2], that Hywel Coleman of Leeds University has a flourishing research project focused on language teaching in large classes, a project which has drawn participants from a staggering range of countries across the world, and that there is an International Network for Class Size Study (INCLASS), founded to facilitate the sharing of knowledge about large class teaching across international boundaries.

One reason Coleman gives for INCLASS not having an explicit reference to 'large classes' built into its title is that there is breathtaking diversity in what different teachers in different circumstances think of as a 'large class'. In some of the research reports published by Coleman and his collaborators people speak of a class of 40 as a 'large class' while, at the other extreme, at a university in Bangkok, it is only when the class reaches about 2 000 that it is seen as a 'large class'. This variability in perception is both interesting and important, and it is connected to our concept of teaching.

There are many places in the world where teaching in crowded classes is a constant daily task for countless teachers at all levels of the schooling system from pre-primary to tertiary. What my discoveries revealed to me was something that in retrospect should have been obvious: there is a considerable body of people trying to reflect critically and professionally on this situation. Another myth that was exploded for me was the myth that it is mainly developing countries that face this problem. In the United States of America there is a long tradition of very large undergraduate classes, a tradition that is an outcome of the political project of providing higher education for a high proportion of the population. It is true that resource-impoverished countries such as Thailand, India, Indonesia, Pakistan, Botswana, Nigeria, Kenya and Uganda face this problem in a more acute form, but it is also an increasingly urgent problem in countries such as Portugal, Poland, Singapore, Taiwan, and even Japan and England, in which education budgets are progressively under pressure. The World Bank reports that one of the major problems in tertiary education in sub-Saharan Africa is overcrowded classes.

At one level of analysis it is quite straightforward to understand why this is becoming an international problem. Across the world, budgets for education, especially for higher education, have become less generous, and they continue to shrink. Education systems everywhere are being forced to run on leaner funding. Furthermore, in any schooling system (including tertiary schooling) a major part of the cost (estimates range from 75 to 90 per cent) is teachers' salaries. The most effective way, thus, to reduce the cost of any schooling system is to employ fewer teachers. The number of students, however, does not decline; on the contrary, especially in developing countries, it is rapidly increasing. The result is obvious: fewer teachers, more students and bigger class sizes.

We have seen this in our own higher education institutions. For example, in the Faculty of Education at the University of the Western Cape (UWC), the number of students in the one-year diploma course expanded from 200 in 1986 to 1 000 in 1992, an increase of 500 per cent; the numbers in our Bachelor of Education[3] course grew from 125 in 1986 to over 500 in 1991, an increase of 400 per cent, and it was only our insisting strictly on the closing date for applications that prevented that number from being about 800 in 1991. Needless to add in this audience, the number of academic staff expanded by only some 25 per cent over the same period. Of course, the same kinds of stories can be told about your university, and about Venda, Zululand, Unitra, Unibop, Durban-Westville and Fort Hare.[4] In all these universities, class sizes have exploded with little, if any, expansion in the size of the staff. Heroic members of the academic teaching staff have struggled to cope with what seems to be an overwhelming situation, while others have become so demoralised that they cynically step away from their professional responsibilities since they see the situation as hopeless.

This situation has been growing amongst academic teaching staff and it has become an urgent problem to address, as our overcrowded institutions hover precariously on the edge of breakdown. And yet no one that I knew of at UWC or elsewhere in our university system had had the courage, wit or inclination to name the beast or to reflect systematically on it and how we were learning to live with it; all we did was more or less cope or not cope with it in daily practice. It was as if we were suffering from a collective professional block.

Once I had named the issue of large class teaching in my own thinking, I realised that although I had never thought about it systematically, I had been interested in the issue, in my practices as a teacher and as a learner, for a very long time. This realisation had an echo when I read a comment recorded by Coleman at a workshop in the Ivory Coast. One participant thanked the organisers for '…making me aware of large classes, which I had not been aware about before'. Here was a teacher who had struggled with the situation in practice but had never had his practices organised around the name 'large class teaching'. Let me briefly note three of many experiences that linked up for me under the name.

In my very first year at the University of the Witwatersrand (Wits) almost 35 years ago, as the first of my family ever to get to university, I chose to do maths on the grounds that it was the matric subject that I had most enjoyed and for which I had achieved the best symbol in my mediocre matric results. I found myself in a class of about 400, many of whom were there because maths 1 was a compulsory course for engineers, architects, medical students, etc. Within the first weeks of the course I was completely lost. The lecturers of the course would come into the crowded venue, start talking at a rapid pace, scribble complex and obscure formulae and fragments of sentences on the chalkboard, and at the end of the period gather up their notes and leave. What I was supposed to do as a Maths I student was a complete mystery to me. I hardly understood a word of what was said in the textbook or the lectures and I had no idea where I could get help. I struggled hopefully for the whole year – perhaps I was expecting some magic to rescue me – and managed to get about 6 per cent in the final exam.

While I was training to be a teacher of English it had somehow been conveyed to me that an essential aspect of the job was to get to know my pupils well, engage in rich conversation with each and every one of them, and give them regular essay-writing – at least once a week – to be individually and carefully responded to by me, the teacher. Nothing that I was taught during my training prepared me for the situation I found myself in when I started my career as a schoolteacher. At Jeppe Boys' High School in Johannesburg I had to teach seven classes with an average size of 35 (the Standard Six classes had 40 in them), ranging from Standard Six to Ten, and I was timetabled for 35 periods a week. The picture of teaching conveyed to me in my training generated a suicidal project. The intense personal contact it demanded was exorbitant given that I had some 250 pupils, and the marking load took up many hours every night and most of the weekends. My personal life shrank to nil and, although I was young and healthy, my physical condition declined alarmingly. One of the most depressing things about this memory is that now, more than 30 years later, we still run teacher training courses that assume that the ideal teaching situation is to have about 20 pupils with whom one can have close contact and each of whom needs his or her contributions, written or otherwise, individually and carefully responded to.

My third memory is of an Academic Diploma class I found myself in, at London University in 1967. The class was made up of about 1 200 students from an amazing range of countries across the world. One common feature of the student body was that they all had a first degree from some university and some formal qualification as a teacher. They could all thus be assumed to be fairly mature students, who knew something about how to read and had some proven ability to write academic texts. This course also had a number of outstanding features: it was superbly organised with clear and definite instructions to students about what they needed to do; the lectures – delivered to the whole group, in a huge hall with a good sound system – were inspiring; and it comprised a carefully constructed reading programme and a series of written assignments as well as regular tutorials run by higher degree students, who marked the assignments of their group. In retrospect, this strikes me as an example of successful large class teaching in a higher education context.

Now, here is the problem: given that many of us in fact teach large classes in our universities, and that many of us handle this situation on a daily basis, why is it that none of us, no one that I know of anyway, has tried to get to grips with thinking systematically, and with practical intent, about this issue?

Why don't we address the problem?

This is the problem I am going to try to address in the rest of this essay. Why is it that we seem to have a professional and institutional inability to face the problem head-on, and think intelligently about how we might cope with it? Why was it so difficult for me, as a teacher at UWC, to get this problem into sharp focus? We might talk here about our *reluctance* to think about large class teaching in our institutions, but I think it might be more accurate to say that we *resist* thinking about this matter. What, then, are the sources of this resistance?

One possibility, which I shall simply mention, then pass by, is that most of what we know about Faculties of Education – and others in the business of trying to tell people how to teach – makes us skeptical about the possibility that theorising about a teaching problem is going to make anything like a practical contribution to how we handle it. Theorising about teaching has a low reputation among practising teachers. I understand clearly why teacher training courses generally have such a low reputation, but I do not believe that theorising – if it is understood as reflecting critically and intelligently on the practice of teaching – is useless. On the contrary, I hold the view that the theory and practice of teaching are two sides of the same coin, and the right sort of theorising about teaching is one of the principal ways of improving the practice. I will therefore leap over this possible source of our resistance to thinking about large class teaching.

An emblematic experience I had at UWC a few months ago could begin to help us acknowledge some deeper sources of our resistance. A colleague from the Academic Development Centre at UWC, a centre founded to contribute to the quality of teaching and learning at the university, came to see me about the possibility of writing a Doctor of Education thesis. His idea was to investigate small group teaching in a university setting in South Africa. I mildly suggested to him that he would have a better chance of making a contribution to the future of university education if he turned his topic on its head and thought in terms of investigating large group teaching. He left, has not come back to me, and I subsequently heard that he said that the Dean of the Faculty of Education shows little interest in what potential students are interested in and is determined to impose his own private agendas on students he might supervise.

The interesting question here is why this person, *employed explicitly to think about teaching and learning in our university*, should think that it is more important to investigate small rather than large group teaching, and see as an affront my suggesting that he should turn his topic on its head.

One possibility is that he, along with many of us, holds a political position that encourages the thought that large classes in our institutions are the product of the Apartheid government's evil policies, and are merely a temporary aberration, a crisis situation, which will disappear in the new democratic South Africa. In that utopia the cosy and intimate virtues of small group teaching will, again, achieve their rightful and central role in our higher education, and his research will achieve its just recognition.

A second possibility is that his thinking is constructed around the image of the ideal teaching situation as a small face-to-face group with rich, intensely individual interaction among the participants. It might be that his thinking about the *quality* of higher education, the *standards* that it should strive for, is closely connected with this image of the ideal teaching situation.

What I am suggesting here is that there are both political and conceptual reasons why we resist thinking about large class teaching. Let me note that these two kinds of reasons are closely entangled with each other and there is not a sharp distinction between them.

At the heart of our political resistance to thinking about large class teaching in our universities lies the fact that historically white universities have, by and large, been well funded over a long period of time and are more richly endowed than historically black universities. These differences in financial standing account for – in general terms – smaller classes in historically white than in historically black universities. To allow ourselves to think carefully about large class teaching is thus, in a sense, to admit defeat in the struggle against the injustices of Apartheid education. There is an echo here of a comment, again recorded by Coleman, made this time by a participant in a workshop in Senegal: 'Has our government asked you to come and tell us to tolerate a state of affairs which we all know should not be tolerated?'

But this, in a sense, is to take too simple a view of the political issues involved since it raises another political problem that we cannot ignore. Let me introduce this with a story.

Some months ago I was at a meeting and saw a member of the South African Democratic Teachers' Union (SADTU) wearing a button pronouncing the demand: 'Down with class sizes.' In my discussion with him he said that he thought that a normal class size should be about 20. Now while we all have sympathy for those thousands of teachers faced with classes of up to 75 or even more learners, as a policy the idea that the overall norm for class sizes should be say, 20, is not a real option.

Short of an economic miracle – which does not look likely – funds for education, especially higher education, are likely to remain more or less as they are, or perhaps even decline. The reasons for this are that even in the best possible economic scenario, and with a democratic government in place[5], there are urgent social projects on our agenda, from a revision and expansion of public health and medical facilities, to housing, welfare services, and the upgrading of our urban and rural environments. Because of the limited size of the national financial cake and other legitimate, urgent calls on public funds, a reduction in class sizes would probably have to be bought at the cost of the number of school places available, a consequence we can hardly accept.

Of course, what we need is a redistribution of resources across our education system, including at tertiary level. Some schools and universities are much more privileged in class sizes and in many other ways than others, and the resources within the system will have to be redistributed to overcome these injustices. But we are probably going to have to settle on a class size of about 40, not 20 or 25, in our primary and secondary schools in South Africa. It is also likely that a university like UWC is much more typical, in respect to class sizes, of what a university will be like in a future South Africa, than are the historically white universities.

It is, in part, for this reason that UWC can legitimately claim to be making an important contribution to our collective experience about the future of university education in South Africa. On a lean budget it has persistently pursued the ideal of providing access to higher education to sectors of the population previously excluded on academically irrelevant grounds. But there are problems, and one of them is the problem of large classes.

We might articulate this problem in the following terms: given scarce resources, there is a conflict between our desire to reduce class sizes and our commitment to providing access to education, including higher education. I shall now try to get this problem into manageable shape.

Access to higher education

Let us think about the idea of access. Access to higher education has two dimensions, one more obviously a matter of institutional policy and the other more obviously a matter of teaching practice. The former is formal access to the institution; the latter is teaching and learning strategies that enable our students, many from a background of schooling that has not prepared them well for university study, to learn the kinds of things universities teach. This latter kind of access is access to the knowledge that universities distribute, what might, for convenience, be called 'epistemological access'. Let us first focus briefly on formal access and then consider epistemological access.

Our commitment to formal access to higher education for a significant proportion of our population is grounded in two arguments. One is an argument about high-level skills required in a modernising society. We do not need to go into all the issues raised by this argument; we need simply to note that in a sense we have little option but to ensure access to higher education for as significant a proportion of our population as possible. But a second, and deeper, argument revolves around our political and moral ideals of a democratic society. The longer-term sustainability of a democratic society depends on an educated citizenry, and we therefore have to be committed to the ideal of the greatest possible cultural and educational development across the whole population.

In any case, if we look at what has happened in countries across the world, especially in the case of our neighbours to the north, we can see that the political pressure for formal access to higher education is likely, if anything, to increase. In a sense we need to change our mindset; we need to come to see that learning how to cope responsibly with the pressure for greater access to higher education can be one of our major contributions to the future of higher education in South Africa. But we are not likely to be able to do that as long as we continue to resist thinking systematically about the teaching of large classes.

We need urgently to change our shared self-understanding of the situation we are in as well as our perception of our political location in debates about the future of higher education in South Africa. We need to come to accept that large undergraduate classes are not a temporary aberration, a crisis situation, which we must somehow cope with until the new utopian South Africa arrives. We need to accept that the teaching of large undergraduate classes will be the norm in the future university system in South Africa, and that all universities in the system will be under strong pressure to move in that direction. We are collectively well placed to make a major contribution to the future of university education in South Africa, provided, that is, we can overcome our resistance to thinking rigorously about the teaching of large classes.

The main argument against large classes is that such classes inevitably lead to inferior education. In the case of higher education the thought might be that the quality of education is sacrificed in situations of large class teaching, that the standards will be 'lower'. The two forms of access, formal access and epistemological access, are in direct conflict with each other; the more we satisfy the former, the less we can satisfy the latter; to pursue the former is to betray the latter. We admit large numbers into our undergraduate programmes at the cost of offering them an inferior kind of higher education. In order to investigate this argument, let us turn our attention now to the concept of epistemological access.

The concept of teaching

The argument as I have presented it above reveals the conceptual sources of our resistance to thinking about large class teaching, and it also brings out the link between the political and conceptual sources of our resistance. If our concept of teaching is constructed around the image that the ideal teaching situation is one in which there is a teacher–student ratio of about 1:15 with plenty of opportunity for rich face-to-face discussion, the detailed marking of students' scripts and so on, then we will see any departure from this 'ideal' as deficient, a degenerate version of teaching. Large class teaching is thus *defined* as a degenerate version of teaching and, at the extreme, we might be unable to see it as 'real' teaching at all. The interesting point about this way of describing this stance is that it reveals lucidly how a particular concept of teaching, constructed on the basis of a highly specialised image of the material conditions of an 'ideal teaching situation', holds our thinking fixed in one cramped position – it paralyses our professional intelligence.

If our concept of teaching is constructed around the image of a 1:15 teacher–student ratio, with all the rich opportunities and possibilities such a situation offers, then we have an explanation for the despair and guilt of many teachers teaching larger classes. It is simply not possible for them to satisfy the professional responsibilities implied in this concept of teaching, and the despair and demoralisation we see in some of our colleagues might be explained in this way.

We can note further that in our institutions there are many projects that are founded on the ideal of trying to replicate the demands of such a concept of teaching in a resource-starved environment. If I seem to be overplaying my hand here, I can note that I have vivid experiences in my own faculty of the power of this concept of teaching – seldom, of course, clearly articulated or defended – in distorting and restricting my colleagues' thinking about the practical tasks of teaching.

The formal element of the concept of teaching is that it is an activity guided by the intention to promote learning. There is, of course, much more work needed to defend this concept of teaching and to spell out what this formula means. But here we can note just the following.

The concept of learning is hardly transparent and, unfortunately, the work of generations of psychologists, many driven by impoverished concepts of knowledge, has muddied the field considerably without contributing much to our understanding. Furthermore, the word 'intention' in the formula needs elaboration. Perhaps here we can say that at least it implies a realistic intention, which implies that it is an intention that takes seriously into consideration the current epistemological condition of the learners (all teaching begins from the current state of knowledge of the learners) as well as the possibilities of success of various kinds of teaching strategies. This is one reason the phrase 'epistemological access' might be illuminating. The teacher's job is to give learners access to knowledge.

But, most importantly, to characterise teaching as an activity guided by the intention to promote learning, does not tie the concept of teaching to any particular situations. On the contrary, it releases us from the prison of particular images of teaching. It opens the door on the possibility that the situations and conditions of teaching can be hugely various and it – at least – contributes to undermining our conceptual resistance to seeing large class teaching as a possibly genuine kind of teaching, enabling us to take a fresh and imaginative view of our professional tasks in a variety of situations. It unlocks the possibility that we can think flexibly and intelligently about how we might teach in large classes.

An example

I think I might usefully conclude this reflection with an example of what can happen once we take the lid off the precious, we might almost say 'hothouse', concept of teaching that still provides the organising framework of many of the practices in our universities.

I have already noted that our BEd course expanded fourfold over a period of five years – from 125 in 1986 to 500 in 1991. The BEd is an honours-level course and a colleague and I were responsible for the research methods semester module, compulsory for all BEd students, which we called 'Metatheory'. In earlier years, we had taught this course in a conventional face-to-face mode, supplemented with reading (which we soon discovered was far too ambitious for most of the students) and essays marked by us. But two developments disrupted our labour-intensive, but familiar and comfortable, teaching procedures. One, as I have noted, was a dramatic increase in the number of students in the course, but the other – familiar to historically black universities across the country – was frequent and unpredictable class boycotts.

We could, I suppose, have continued 'normally', accepting that the circumstances had overtaken us and provided a plausible excuse for our increasing lack of success in enabling our students to attain the kind of epistemological access it was the purpose of the course to achieve. But we decided that we needed to reconsider our teaching procedures. Part of our inspiration came from an analysis of the Open University (in the UK) way of teaching. What drew us in this direction was the thought that this was a way of teaching which, although it might have included some face-to-face contact, was not *dependent* on that for its success; its success rested more on clarity of both conceptual and practical organisation. The 'coursebooks' for each module provided a model of how to enable students to study effectively. At the heart of each of these texts was a clear and definite conceptual structure, and each text included advice to students about how they should manage their study time.

We decided to reconfigure the Metatheory course, guided by three main principles derived from our experience and our analysis of the Open University procedures:

- the achievement of epistemological access should not be *dependent* on contact-time;
- the conceptual and practical organisation of the course should be strong, unambiguous and explicit; and
- students should not be faced with tasks that would simply defeat them. (Most of our students are full-time schoolteachers and we aimed to make sure that everything we asked them to do for this course was sharply focused on what we were trying to teach them.)

We compiled a core text in which the main line of *argument*[6] was systematically outlined, avoiding unnecessary qualifications and complications while maintaining its logical and epistemological integrity. We tried to ensure that this text was as accessible as possible in style: short sentences, a minimum of qualifying clauses, straightforward vocabulary with any even marginally unusual words introduced with great care, etc. This text consists of 93 numbered points organised in terms of three main blocks – one for each of the research paradigms involved – each with five units. Some of the points are very brief – a sentence or two – and others include diagrams to illustrate conceptual relationships and the use of the key terminology, as well as slogans and acronyms, to enable students to remember the main elements of the argument. This core text provides the conceptual framework in terms of which students can locate other reading they are required to do, the essays they write, their discussions with others in the course (we encourage students to form study groups) and, if they take place, the contact sessions.

Once we began to understand the core text as providing the basic conceptual structuring of the course, our view of the purpose and use of contact-time changed radically: contact-time became a supplement to the course rather than its heart – nice to have but not essential to its success. Contact-time was no longer needed systematically to develop the overall conceptual structure of the course, which meant that it could be used to focus on particular key hinges of the overall argument, or sticking points identified by the students themselves. Contact-time was not 'lectures'. In preparation for each contact session, we advise the students to read the relevant unit in the core text, and think about what they want to ask about it.

A typical contact session begins with brief introductory remarks, but their mode is basically that of *discussion* with the participation of students. Contrary to our initial expectations, the students take to this mode with ease (perhaps because they are teachers and are used to talking in public). We think of contact-time not only as bringing the material vividly to life and showing how important the arguments are for our understanding of education and research, but also as providing students with a supportive context in which to practise the kind of language into which the course is trying to provide access. Our assumption is that even if there are 500 students in the venue, the issues raised by a few of the students will echo what many of the others are thinking, provided everyone can hear.

There are many other aspects of this course that I could describe, but let me add just three that are relevant to large class teaching.

One is that we require students to write only three brief essays, each about three or four pages, one for each main part of the course. The rationale for this is that we are trying to encourage students to understand that the quality of their writing is much more important than its quantity, and also that it is better to have shorter pieces more critically marked than longer pieces with a few anodyne comments at the end. The essay topics are given to students in the form of well-developed handouts, some five or six pages long, contextualising the topic within the conceptual structure of the course, explaining how it is related to other issues and problems in education and research in education, providing detailed references to particular points in the core text and particular readings to be done, and step-by-step procedures for how to write the essay. Over time we have established a team of reliable markers, and have constructed 'marking sheets' with additional criteria added for the second and third essay. Students are invited to rate their essay on each of the criteria prior to handing them in for official assessment and, when their marked essay is returned, to compare their own assessment with that of the marker. Each year we choose a new overall theme for the three essays, both to avoid students' handing in essays copied from previous years and also, over time, to show how the conceptual core of the course generates unexpected ways of understanding the practices and study of education[7].

A second is that we have stripped down the additional reading required to a minimum since we realise that the volume and sophistication of the reading we previously required was way beyond the time and capacities of the majority of students in the course. We constructed a Reader with precisely selected readings from elsewhere, some only brief extracts (a mere page or two). The core text refers to these other readings and provides the conceptual scaffolding for students to be able to understand how to read them, and how they fit in to the overall picture.

A third is that we communicate with students on a weekly basis through brief handouts, displayed on notice boards and available for collection at the faculty offices. The main purpose of these handouts is to remind students about what they should be doing in relation to the course, week by week, and to try to help them manage their study time effectively. A further purpose of the handouts is to counteract the kind of anomie students can suffer in a situation in which contact-time is limited.

I would not like to pretend that we have solved all the problems, but we have found a way of coping responsibly with an increasing number of students, in a volatile and unpredictable environment, and without increasing costs. And we manage to do this without losing sight of our professional responsibility to enable a particular kind of epistemological access. I do not want to claim that what we do is an unalloyed success, but I do think that we can reasonably claim that the quality of the epistemological access we provide is not deficient, and that we have developed a web of procedures that enables us to cope with a rapidly growing number of students without either committing suicide or betraying our students or what we are teaching them.

The moral of this story – every story has a moral – is that here is one instance I know of, of how a concept of teaching not tied to a particular material image released our professional intelligence and enabled us to think imaginatively about how to provide epistemological access simultaneously to a large group of students. We didn't think of ourselves as teaching a large class, but that is what we were doing; and we did not resist doing so through failing to think through both our political and professional commitments.

Notes

1   Became University of Limpopo in July 2001.

2   See, for instance, Graham Gibbs & Alan Jenkins (eds) *Teaching Large Classes in Higher Education: How to Maintain Quality with Reduced Resources,* London: Kogan Page, 1992.

3   Subsequently renamed BEd (Hons).

4   The University of Transkei (Unitra) became Walter Sisulu University in July 2005, and the University of Bophuthatswana (Unibop) merged with Potchefstroom University to become North-West University in January 2004.

5   This essay was written in 1992, prior to the democratic transition in South Africa.

6   An argument is not merely a list of points.

7   We know that there are students from previous years who run informal 'seminars' for current students in the communities and we see ourselves as contributing to the ongoing education of such groups.

2 Teacher Education: reconstruction and challenges

(Talk given at the CORDTEK Conference, Springfield College of Education, August 1994)[1]

Revolution and mirror images

Near the beginning of *Emile*, Rousseau, one of the fathers of the French Revolution, tells us that things are so bad in the society and education of his day that the best recipe for change is to do the opposite of everything that was previously done.

Such a sentiment has been at the root of much revolutionary fervour – slaves must become masters, masters must become slaves – but it is a conservative trap; it encourages us to think in terms of polar opposites and to think of revolution as simply favouring the alternative of each pair. If the hated regime prioritised facts, the revolution must prioritise values; if the oppressive regime overrode wants, we must celebrate wants.

In our historical situation I do think we need something like a revolution in the ways we think about schooling and, consequently, Teacher Education. But we will not accomplish such a revolution if we merely do the opposite of whatever was done in the past, even if we could. A revolution would consist rather in escaping from the framework that generates the polar opposites.

Let us remind ourselves of two polar opposites that can prevent our seeing what we need to do, and that we have inherited from Apartheid and the struggle against it.

The unjust and divided education systems of Apartheid, with the 'white' system massively and persistently better resourced than the 'black' systems, have fostered a deep conviction that whatever the 'white' system did and had provides the model for what all should do and have. If the 'whites' had an 18:1 pupil–teacher ratio and a four-year initial teachers' diploma, we should all have an 18:1 pupil–teacher ratio and a four-year diploma; anything else will, obviously, be inferior.

But we can also consider what is, in a sense, an opposing tendency: to conceive of democratic education as the opposite of Apartheid education. Many people can say little about what democratic education is other than that it must be the opposite of Apartheid education. But most of us here will acknowledge that we have run into some serious problems in our institutions and practices, and that some of our problems revolve around confusions about how we can give body to the ideals of democratic education.

Polar opposites such as these trap us into the frameworks that constructed them, and it is the framework itself that hinders our search for viable solutions.

Causes and remedies

Our schooling system is in a far from healthy condition. Indeed, in some regions and sectors, the system is close to total collapse. Most of us get a shock of recognition when we read Elizabeth de Villiers's *Walking the Tightrope*[2], with its descriptions of the deep malaise that pervades many of our schools – overcrowded, violent, and suffused with frustration and dashed hopes. Many teachers, overwhelmed by despair and cynicism, defeated by the numbers of learners they are expected to teach and embittered by what they see as their poor levels of payment, do the absolute minimum, devoting their energies to other pursuits. They do not see themselves in terms of the ideals of the teaching profession; they have ceased to care.

Most of us here, I think, will acknowledge that the main causes of this deterioration have been political. But it would be an error for us to assume that because the causes were political that therefore the remedies will be political, at least in some facile sense of 'political'. The educational struggle in this country was at its heart a *political* rather than an educational struggle, and whatever else it might be claimed to have brought about, it has not brought about an educational utopia. My main claim in this essay is that a large part of the remedy is going to have to be professional.

I am not claiming that the idea of a profession is not political in some deeper sense, nor that there are no political dimensions to finding a remedy for our ills. It is quite clear that the educational policies – which will be put into effect by the democratically elected government of this country, including the administrative structures put in place, funding decisions taken, and so on – will provide some of the remedy. My claim is rather that it would be an error for us to think that such political measures are going to be a sufficient remedy.

Key agents in the success of any schooling system are the professional teachers who work in it. Even the most perfect political arrangements will not enable us to put Humpty Dumpty together again. The commitment, competence and quality of the teachers in any schooling system are necessary ingredients for its success.

Loss of a sense of the significance of systematic learning

Many people talk about a breakdown in the culture of learning. Another, and more explanatory, way of referring to this phenomenon is in terms of a loss of a sense of the significance of systematic learning. This phrase also provides a focus in terms of which to try to understand many of the current ills of our education system, and how we might remedy them.

A sense of the significance of systematic learning is necessarily a shared good, maintained by and within communities of practitioners and the institutions in which they work. Where, such as in our situation, this good has been lost sight of, the blame cannot be pinned to any particular individuals, classes of individuals or institutions.

Sometimes when people think about these things, they think in terms of a deterioration of standards; however, a much less misleading way of talking is in terms of the concept of caring. A community which has a sense of the significance of systematic learning cares about learning; it understands it as having value that stretches beyond whatever value it might have in the market-place of employment, or the competition for social status, for example, and is offended by fraudulent simulacra.

If we now ask how we might recover a sense of the significance of systematic learning, then we can see that there can be no simple answer. Although institutional arrangements might enable and encourage a sense of the significance of systematic learning, no administrative dictates can guarantee this achievement; it depends crucially on the cumulative efforts of individuals who understand what it involves and what its cultural and political significance is.

There are forms of theorising about education that undermine a sense of the significance of systematic learning. In general such theorising revolves around the issues of the arbitrariness of 'official knowledge', the idea that knowledge and power are simply two sides of the same coin, and relativist or subjectivist epistemologies that tell us that knowledge is merely the common convictions of this or that local group, or the subjective beliefs of particular individuals. In these ways of thinking systematic learning is nothing other than an arbitrary imposition (Who decides?), and resistance to systematic learning comes to be seen as critical thinking.

Such skepticism does not seem to have reached two countries I have recently visited, Malaysia and South Korea. In these countries there is a widely shared sense of the significance of systematic learning. A skeptic might say that I am here confusing a sense of the significance of systematic learning with market forces. In our situation, the skeptic might continue, with our high levels of unemployment, we can hardly expect a recovery of a sense of the significance of systematic learning. My view about this is that we here have a chicken and egg problem. Although market forces and a sense of the significance of systematic learning might be in some ways linked to each other, there seems no particular reason to accord either explanatory priority – especially in a phase of reconstruction.

The challenge for professional teachers

If a main problem for us is a loss of a sense of the significance of systematic learning, what can we do about it? I would here like to claim that professional teachers have – at least – a key role in the recovery of a sense of the significance of systematic learning. Indeed, I regard this as one of the principal challenges currently facing the teaching profession in South Africa. The reconstruction of our country depends on a reconstruction of the education system, and professional teachers are the main agents in this task.

One obstacle here is the shallow way in which the notion of the teaching profession has been politicised. That kind of politicisation has led to the concept of the profession having been located in the discourse of the right so that there is a tendency for professional associations to be contrasted with teacher unions, with all the forces of political correctness encouraging us to align ourselves with the unions. In my view it would be a bad error to abandon the concept of a teaching profession to the reactionary discourses of the right. What we need to do is to relocate the concept of the profession in the discourses of the left, those discourses that have the interests of the poor, exploited and excluded members of society at their heart.

The concept of a profession encapsulates the idea of expertise and knowledge to be deployed in the service of communities and individuals. The benefits of a profession are not merely to individual members of the profession but to the communities they serve. This is a reason to have some reservations about how the policy of affirmative action is to be implemented in the realm of Teacher Education. If we admit someone to the teaching profession on affirmative action grounds, we might benefit this person, but the question that needs to be pressed is how that benefit is to be weighed against the possible benefits or harms to those he or she will teach, perhaps over many years.

One thing I am committed to in putting forward these views is that it is a mistake, in pursuit of a form of democratic egalitarianism, to repudiate the special expertise of teachers in contributing to the quality of life in a society. Such egalitarianism is based on misplaced political commitment and is as much a betrayal of the aspirations of learners as is any authoritarian imposition.

Indeed, this point needs to be taken further. One of the aspects of the situation we find ourselves in is a serious disintegration of professional authority. If the teaching profession is going to make an effective contribution to a retrieval of a sense of the significance of systematic learning, we will have to recover a proper understanding of the nature of professional authority, how it differs from authoritarianism and from political authority, and the ways in which it is enabling rather than restrictive. We will need to take into account the ways in which professional authority depends on respect for professional judgement and on institutional and community support and encouragement.

Professional authority *constitutes* the sphere of learning. What this implies is that the idea of service, which is central to the concept of a profession, is not subservient to the current whims, wants and beliefs of those served. A profession does not serve a society by making itself into its servant.

The teaching profession has the political responsibility to constitute the sphere of learning in society, and to enable access to it. One way of describing our present malaise is to say that a central reason we have collectively lost a sense of the significance of systematic learning, is that too many members of the teaching profession have, for whatever justifiable or unjustifiable reasons, failed to fulfil their public responsibility to contribute to the constitution of the sphere of learning. We need to discover, or rediscover perhaps, a culture of professional teaching, and at the heart of this stands the idea of professional practices.

The professional practices of teaching are constructed around the goal of enabling access to a particular kind of social good. But, in our situation, conditions seem to distort, or even prevent, the pursuit of this goal. Apart from many other things that could be mentioned, I think here specifically of the twin factors of lack of resources and numbers of learners.

We see these factors as problems because we understand professional practice not in terms of its definitive goals and principles, but in terms of its particular implementations. When this happens, then professional practice loses its flexibility; it becomes trapped in a socio-historical context that has passed. It is to this problem that I will now direct our attention.

Limited resources and burgeoning numbers of learners

We have all experienced the massive demand for access to the schooling system. At the same time we know that resources for education are limited and, if anything, likely to decline. This sets the trap for professional practice. Most of us have experienced the effects: more learners, crowded classes, 'inadequate' resources, and so on.

Across the world resources for education have declined. Developing countries, especially in sub-Saharan Africa, have spent staggering proportions of their budgets on education, and by now there is widespread skepticism about whether this was a fruitful use of scarce resources. The largest slice (between 75 per cent and 90 per cent) in any education budget is the salaries of teachers.

Given these realities of our situation, what can we do? Apart from contesting whether this *is* the reality, I think we are faced with only three options: firstly, drastically reduce teachers' salaries so that we can employ more teachers; secondly, restrict access to the schooling system so that there are fewer learners to teach; or thirdly, enable teachers to teach more learners.

Politically, the first two options are most unlikely to be possible. In addition, if we did pay teachers less, it is likely – given the consumer orientation of our society – that some of the most talented teachers would simply leave the profession, and its overall quality would suffer. Similarly, given our Apartheid history of limited access to the system and our strong commitment to redress, we can hardly seriously contemplate limiting access to the system. This leaves us with the third option, which is the one I favour. I think it is not only desirable in the light of the political principle of equality of formal access (which is one way of giving body to the ideals of democratic education), but also viable, although not without some quite dramatic adjustment to our understanding of professional practice.

What I am talking about here is a fundamental shift in our entrenched conceptions of professional practice – an adjustment of the conceptual framework in terms of which we think about good teaching. We have a tenacious tendency to lose sight the context-boundedness of particular practices and to base our conception of teaching on them. We need to re-articulate the definitive goals and purposes of the teaching profession and then come to see that particular implementations of those goals and purposes are context-bound.

One key feature of our common concept of teaching is that teaching takes place in a situation where there is one teacher face to face with about 20 learners (or fewer, if possible) for specified periods of time and in particular physical boundaries. We can note the extent to which the very architecture of our school and college buildings reflects this view of what teaching is, and the ways in which we conceptually link the ideas of small numbers and quality. As soon as the number of learners per teacher jumps to, say, 40 or 80, teachers see themselves as in a deficient teaching situation, and many teachers in such situations are overcome by despair and despondency and simply cease to care.

But this particular implementation of the goals and principles of teaching arose in a context in which education was for only limited sectors of the population and where the resources for education, especially the resources to pay teachers, were much more abundantly available. Our problem is that we have tried to take this particular set of practices into a changed context – one characterised by our trying to provide education for the whole population and in which the resources for this project are limited.

What we, as a profession, need to try to do is to discover or invent ways of implementing the goals and principles of the teaching profession in our new context. What this means, in plain language, is that we will have to discover how teachers can effectively teach much larger numbers of learners. This might mean teaching larger classes, but not necessarily, as we might find that the whole tradition of class teaching is fatally tied to the particular conception of the practice of teaching that is inappropriate in our new context.

I might add that were we able to bring about a revolution of this kind, were we able to escape the inherited framework in terms of which we think of professional teaching practices, we might even be able to reach a situation in which the fewer teachers needed in such a system could be more generously and appropriately remunerated for their seminal contribution to the reconstruction of our society.

One key institutional site at which such a revolution would need to be launched, of course, would have to be in those institutions concerned with the professional education of teachers. I shall conclude by drawing out a few implications of the claims I have made for the way we think about Teacher Education.

Some lessons for Teacher Education

Many of our students not only arrive in our programmes, but leave, with deep skepticism about the significance of systematic learning. Given our current situation, a major task of Teacher Education now must be insistently to undermine such skepticism, and show our students how to care about systematic learning, to take it seriously.

We need, therefore, to be much clearer that our central purpose is to initiate our students into the culture of professional teaching. We need to foster in them a commitment to its ideals and show them how to take on board their political responsibilities, as aspirant members of the profession, for *constituting* the sphere of learning. We need to clarify with them the distinctive nature of professional authority and assist them to begin to develop teaching practices that are enabling rather than excluding.

In addition, we need, both in our own practices and in what we tell our students, persistently to undermine some deeply embedded assumptions about the practices of teaching. It is striking to consider the countless ways in which, in our programmes, we assume an individual teacher teaching a small group of learners. Think, for example, of the kind of emphasis we place on individual performance during contact-time, as if that stands at the heart of the practice of teaching. We need to knock contact-time off its pedestal and replace it with something like the idea that teaching is centrally about the organising of systematic learning.

Finally, we need to avoid being overambitious about what can be accomplished through pre-service training. We need to avoid the illusion that we will be able to bring about a revolution in the practices of teaching by sending youthful missionaries into the schools. If we are going to be catalysts in accomplishing the revolution, then we will need to see that what is traditionally called in-service training will have to become a major function of our institutions.

These are some of the thoughts I have about the challenges for Teacher Education as we move into a phase of reconstruction and development.

Notes

1   This essay is an updated version of the original paper published in *Perspectives in Education*, Vol. 17 No. 3, 1999, pp. 149–156, reproduced here with the kind permission of the publisher.

2   Elizabeth de Villiers, *Walking the Tightrope*, Johannesburg: Jonathan Ball Publishers, 1990.

3 *A picture holds us captive*

(Paper presented at Kenton Conference, October 1992)

> 114 ...One thinks that one is tracing the outline of the thing's nature over and over again, and one is merely tracing round the frame through which we look at it.

> 115 A picture held us captive. And we could not get outside it, for it lay in our language and language seemed to repeat it to us inexorably.

> Ludwig Wittgenstein, *Philosophical Investigations*

Pressure for an expansion of higher education

Pressures for an expansion of higher education are typical of sub-Saharan Africa and other parts of the developing world, but they are not confined to such regions. Martin Trow[1] contends that '...pressures for the expansion of post-secondary education are inherent in the development of modern societies'. An increase in the number of students in higher education is a global trend, and in our kind of situation we can add population increase and a skewed demographic profile typical of a developing country, to yield the conclusion that we can expect, if anything, even greater pressure in the years ahead.

Higher education is very expensive. Ever since the salad days of the 60s public funds for higher education have been persistently declining. This tendency struck countries such as the United Kingdom and Australia, and even the United States of America, earlier than it struck us, and the vast 'rationalisation' schemes in those countries are a symptom of that. 'Rationalisation' is now in our midst and it has been with the Committee of University Principals (CUP) university system since about 1987.

The most costly item in any education budget is the salaries of teachers, with estimates for different parts of the system ranging from 75 per cent to 90 per cent of the total budget. Clearly the most effective way to reduce the costs of any education system – including universities – is to reduce the number of teachers it employs. However, more students, limited resources, fewer teachers – this leads to declining teacher-to-student ratios, which, in general, means larger classes. Simple arithmetic tells us this.

Our traditions of protest politics incline us to contest this arithmetic; social facts are never brute, they are constructed in and by our policies, histories, collective self-understandings and aspirations. Large classes, we argue, are more prevalent in historically black than historically white institutions, the evil policies of Apartheid education produced this situation, but it is temporary and will pass into history with the demise of Apartheid and injustice, and the forging of a democratic South Africa in which higher education will be a right, not a privilege. But this is an illusion. We know it and so we should acknowledge that large classes in our higher education system, across the board – with the increasing pressure for redistribution within the system – are here to stay. This situation is not a temporary 'crisis' we face, but the norm of the future.

Our protest traditions are painfully having to confront these brutal facts: we cannot simply remake the social world at will to fit in with our utopian visions and Apartheid is not the source of *all* our problems. Even in the best possible economic scenario, public resources for higher education in South Africa will remain limited, even when a democratic government is in place.

The reasons for this are obvious: along with most of the rest of the world South Africa is in an economic recession, indeed there are some darker visions which use the word 'crisis' and which see the South African economy as on a terminal trajectory. In addition, we have many urgent competing calls on the public purse, from housing, health and other welfare services, and the upgrading of rural and urban environments to pre-primary, primary and secondary schooling. Short of an economic miracle, which, like all miracles, we do not expect, financial resources for higher education are likely, if anything, to decline, while the pressures for access are, no doubt, likely to increase.

Formal and epistemological access in higher education

Given the virtual certainty of limited resources for higher education in the foreseeable future in South Africa, we might try to resist those pressures by further restricting access to higher education, with the political and economic costs of such a policy being weighed and borne by a future government. But would this be desirable? There is a compelling argument that concludes that it would be, which revolves around the slogan that 'more means worse'[2]. I shall get this argument into perspective by way of a consideration of the idea of 'access' to education.

A policy of completely open access to higher education could be a realistic option only in a world in which price was no object. That is not the world in which we live. But let us temporarily ignore this boundary fence and focus on the contours of the field.

Access to education has two dimensions: one is access to the institution[3]; the other is access within the institution to the goods that it distributes. The former is a matter of institutional policy – the issue of how many students the institution formally admits. For convenience we might call this 'formal access'. The latter is the issue of how the institution provides access to the goods it distributes to those it formally admits. Since the main good distributed by educational institutions, especially higher education institutions, is knowledge, we might conveniently call the latter 'epistemological access'. Let us take a little tour around formal access, and then turn our attention to what will become the main sinew of this paper – epistemological access[4].

There are strong arguments in favour of an expansion of formal access to higher education in South Africa. They are well known, but we might just briefly rehearse them here.

A first line of argument (which might be called the argument from equity) will appeal to our democratic commitments. What it will tell us is that higher education is a greatly prized good, and the fair distribution of this good is a necessary feature of a just society. But this good has not been fairly distributed in our society, so justice demands redress; it demands that we dramatically increase access to this good for sectors of our population previously excluded.

This good (higher education) is highly prized not merely because it opens the door to better-paid jobs and a generally more affluent lifestyle for its recipients (which it might fail to achieve in some circumstances), but also because it enhances beneficiaries' understanding of their lives and the cultural, political and moral structures that shape them and, thus, the quality of their lives as human beings, whatever level of affluence they happen to achieve. To describe higher education as a 'good' is to imply that it is an aspect, along with other things we might think of as 'goods' such as health and justice, of our shared understanding of the proper sort of life for human beings.

This line of argument can also appeal to the idea that the maintenance of a democracy depends on the level of education of its citizens, and the greater the proportion of its population for which it provides a higher education, the more that benefit will pervade the whole society. Seeing that this line of argument does not rest its claims on a story about future employment of graduates, it will be unsympathetic to the idea of the 'overproduction' of graduates, and it leads towards the conclusion that we should provide the greatest possible access to higher education.

The second line of argument (which might be called the argument from development) is supposed to appeal to our collective desire for a more affluent future, one which not only avoids the nightmare of spiralling poverty and starvation that stalks many of our neighbours to the north, but provides the basic material conditions for a just and peaceful society and a better quality of life for the whole of our population. This argument typically uses the phrase 'high-level manpower' (we might insist, 'personpower') and talks about how sustainable social and economic development is dependent on our producing sufficient numbers of people with 'high-level' knowledge and skills to sustain a modern economy. Appeal might be made to the results of a UNESCO survey[5] that showed a striking correlation between economic development and the number of university students per 1 000 head of population.

Unlike the first line of argument, this one will not automatically lead to the conclusion that we should expand access to higher education. This second line of argument will incline us to start doing sums to try to calculate, at least roughly, how many higher education places we should provide, perhaps in particular fields. It is also a line of argument that reveals its bias towards a vocational understanding of higher education when it talks about the overproduction of university graduates and the 'sad' spectacle of graduates unable to find jobs 'commensurate' with their qualifications.

However, in general terms, both lines of argument might be used to defend the view that it would be desirable to expand access to higher education. Although these two lines of argument are rivals in respect to their understanding of the nature and purposes of higher education, it might be possible, if we provided less simplistic versions of them, to show that they tend to converge around the idea that independent critical thinking lies at the heart of anything that might properly be called higher education. Higher education develops in its recipients the confidence to have ideas and act on them, and the ability to be intellectually mobile without being slippery. Such abilities and capacities are widely needed by both a democratic society and modern industry, given the ways in which technological revolutions have undermined 19th and early 20th century views of production, economy and society, and are forcing us to think more and more in global rather than local terms. Trow talks of:

> …a growing tendency to call on the intelligence and initiative of larger and larger proportions of the society in the direction and management of more and more complex and rapidly changing social, political and economic organizations.[6]

But arguments like these in favour of increased access to higher education bump their heads against the boundary fence, the problem of scarcity of resources. Here we come to the powerful argument, which concludes that we should limit formal access to higher education – more means worse. Unlike an argument we have already considered, which rests its case on a story about 'unemployed graduates', this argument appeals to the idea of epistemological access.

Where resources are limited, arguments in favour of expanding formal access ignore, or seriously underestimate, the problems of epistemological access. We promise our students higher education by offering them formal access to our higher education institutions, but we renege on our promise by being unable to offer them adequate epistemological access. This is worse than useless; if we formally admit students to higher education when we cannot realistically offer them epistemological access, we not only betray their personal aspirations, but we also undermine some of the central ideals of higher education. In a situation of scarce resources, formal and epistemological access are in direct conflict with each other. The more we satisfy the former the less we can satisfy the latter; we admit large numbers of students into our institutions at the cost of providing them with an inferior form of higher education, or something that can hardly be called 'higher education', and perhaps even any kind of 'education' at all. In a situation of scarce resources, expanding formal access leads to larger classes, but larger classes inevitably lead to inferior 'education'. We cannot really foster independent critical thinking in large classes.

This is a compelling argument. Many of us are driven by it not only in our views about formal access to higher education, but also in our daily practices as teachers in higher education, in our views about the obligations of a teacher in higher education, in our course designs, in our 'strategic planning' exercises, and in our perceptions of the quality and standards of higher education and, for some of us, in our attempts to escape from the responsibilities of teaching. What is the source of this compulsion?

The picture which holds us captive

The source of this compulsion is a particular picture of teaching. For expository purposes we need a name and, with deliberate polemical intent, I shall call it the 'hothouse' picture of teaching. This picture imprisons our professional intelligence and seriously restricts our conception of how we might foster epistemological access. We are intimately familiar with this picture; we dream about it all the time. Here, initially, are a few reminders.

The ideal teaching situation is one in which there is a highly trained academic and no more than about 15 rigorously selected students, with intense and regular face-to-face contact between them over a longish period of time. There is abundant opportunity for a rich and developing dialogue between the academic and the students, during which the students, by active participation in the dialogue, a form of osmosis and a kind of intellectual apprenticeship, become inspired by the particular intellectual vocation of which the academic provides a living embodiment, and initiated into the practices of its rigorous intellectual mobility. The teacher is pictured as an active participant in the intellectual project in question; her research and publications are proof of that. In addition, the teacher has ample time and intellectual and emotional energy to respond with detailed and individual critical encouragement to students' contributions, especially their written work.

Some version of this picture traditionally serves as our paradigm for epistemological access, and shapes our understanding of 'quality' and 'academic standards' in higher education. In this way, it fetters these crucial adjudicatory concepts to an exorbitantly expensive project, one which can be afforded in its ideal form only by some of the richest and most exclusive universities in the world, such as Oxford and Harvard.

Where our understanding of teaching is formed by this picture, we perceive most of the situations in which we actually teach in our higher education institutions as deficient and degenerate, as providing, if anything, only very limited opportunities for epistemological access. In addition, this picture is a potent source of guilt and demoralisation amongst conscientious teachers faced with large classes, and a spur for them to migrate out of teaching into the semi-retirement of 'research' units that have a tendency to characterise themselves as the real heart of universities.

But let us be more charitable about a committed academic teacher in one of our crowded higher education institutions. To the extent that such a teacher's understanding of teaching is driven by the hothouse picture, she is faced with an increasingly suicidal project as the size of her class increases. She will more and more desperately persist with teaching methods appropriate to the hothouse picture in spite of the fact that some of its essential elements and conditions are absent. What drives her along this exhausting and increasingly demoralising path is the idea that the hothouse picture provides the paradigm for how to foster epistemological access and, thus, for what her responsibilities are as a teacher in higher education.

The hothouse picture generates a set of professional responsibilities and obligations which is inhuman if the size of the class jumps from 15 to, say, 150, and is impossible if that figure jumps to 500 or 1 000. That picture projects the idea that the teacher should know each student well enough to be able to track their intellectual development in detail and have a good sense of what is most likely to contribute to that development moment by moment, as it were. Regular and generous face-to-face contact is central to this picture, as is the idea that one of the chief ways of fostering epistemological access is to provide sensitive and illuminating commentary on students' written work.

If these are indeed the professional responsibilities of teachers, then even classes of 30 students pose quite a serious challenge[7], and larger classes will simply defeat the teacher's best efforts and lead either to excruciating paroxysms of professional guilt or cynical despair.

The situation is made even more intolerable if we bloat the teacher's task by enriching the hothouse picture with colourful additions such as 'teaching the whole person' (including 'affect' and 'attitudes' as well as 'cognition'), the potage of mess that comes along with talk about 'process' and the idea of 'continuous evaluation', that what we need to 'evaluate' is not so much outcomes as 'process'. The kind of critical self-reflection which such additions to the teacher's responsibilities encourages, is more likely to induce further despair and guilt than to contribute to an improvement of practice.

Our perception of our actual teaching situations as deficient and degenerate drives us, against the odds, and with the best will in the world, to try to reproduce at least some aspects of the hothouse picture of teaching in less than ideal situations. For example, driven by an obsessive concentration on the small size of the class in the hothouse picture, and losing sight of other equally salient aspects of it, we enthusiastically establish tutorial schemes in which the tutors are not the experienced academic teachers assumed in the hothouse picture, but other students – higher degree students, if we are lucky. There might indeed be virtues in such schemes, but given their over-emphasis on one particular aspect of the hothouse picture, and their dramatic underemphasis on other equally important aspects, perhaps we should be more circumspect about what they might be expected to achieve in respect to epistemological access[8].

I could go on with this description of the ramifying implications of the hothouse picture of teaching in our understanding of epistemological access and its conditions, but perhaps I have done enough to convey its awesome and insidious power. Let me add that in the foregoing there is very little I have had to invent or simply imagine; my examples are drawn from life in one of our higher education institutions.

The concept of teaching

Imagine, now, the case of a person who knows only a single kind of vegetable, say carrots, and who assumes that the word 'vegetable' is the name for that one kind. If we ask this person to go to the storeroom to fetch some vegetables so that we can make a meal, he will come back simply with some bunches of carrots. He will not have brought any of the beans, Brussels sprouts, potatoes, cabbages, leeks, aubergines, gem squashes, onions or courgettes because he will not have seen them as vegetables.

One comment we might make here is that this person, and anyone who depends on his understanding of 'vegetables', is going to suffer from a pretty restricted diet: carrot juice for breakfast, carrot cake and sliced carrot for lunch, and carrot soup, rounded off with grated carrot and glazed carrot, for supper!

Another comment we might make is that this person does not have an adequate concept of 'vegetable'; he thinks that the word is the name for what we can see is simply one kind of vegetable. We can all easily understand the mistake that has been made, perhaps because it is not of much real consequence.

Let us draw a further lesson from this case. We know that 'vegetable' is not the name of one particular kind of vegetable, but sometimes we think that it is the name for all the kinds of vegetables that we know of, that it is a 'collective name'. But this will not do. A catalogue of all the kinds of things we currently count as vegetables is not equivalent to our concept of a vegetable. The concept is a rule by means of which we both classify all those things together *and* consider the inclusion of possible new instances. If the concept of 'vegetable' were simply the name of all the kinds of vegetables we currently know of, then the consideration of potential new instances would not be possible[9].

We know our way around here, we can see the obvious mistake of thinking that the concept of 'vegetable' is simply the name of one particular kind of vegetable, and perhaps we can even see what difference it makes if we see a concept as a rule rather than as a collective name. Yet, in the case of teaching, we plot and plan and act and think as if one particular kind of teaching is the only genuine kind of teaching there can be, and supplies the rule for what can count as a case of teaching. The hothouse picture of teaching captures us in its hypnotic thrall and traps our understanding about teaching and epistemological access in one cramped position. This picture cripples our professional imagination and intelligence when it plays the role of our concept of teaching. This has deep and devastating consequences for how we think about epistemological access.

Here is a possible concept of teaching, one which I do not here have space to defend or even to explain, except cursorily: *Teaching is an activity which embodies the intention that X come to learn Y.* Before I briefly explain one or two of the key elements in this rule, I want to note that my purpose here is to provide merely a glimpse of how our understanding of epistemological access and our professional intelligence and imagination can be unfettered when we escape the hypnotic fascination of the hothouse picture.

This concept of teaching, this rule for our thinking about teaching, talks of an 'embodied' intention. Teaching is not merely fanciful dreaming, it is an activity characterised in terms of its having a realistic chance of achieving its formal object. That formal object is that X come to learn Y. Apart from implying that the teaching activity needs to have a realistic chance of success, the rule is uncommitted as to how the formal object is to be achieved. It is also uncommitted as to how many people might be involved. It is compatible with team teaching and with X being any number of learners without limit. A charismatic figure like, for example, Gandhi or Jesus, might teach thousands, even millions. We have no problem in understanding this or in acknowledging that it is a genuine case of teaching.

Here is an example of unfettering, again drawn from life. A few years ago a colleague and I were responsible for teaching history and philosophy of education to a class that grew from a modest 120 one year, to 200 the next and 300 the next. (At the time of writing, that class had 1 000 students in it.) If we had been held captive by the hothouse picture, we would have been faced with a killer, and we might have sought refuge in some form of tutorial scheme but, guided by the concept of teaching I have mentioned above, we looked for inspiration elsewhere. We looked at distance education, and were impressed by the ways in which, when it is well done, it can provide even better epistemological access than do many residential universities; and it provides that access to large numbers of students simultaneously.

Our analysis of some Open University texts prompted in us the following kinds of thoughts. We noted that a central feature of those texts is the way in which they definitively throw the responsibility for learning on the shoulders of the learners, but they do not do this irresponsibly. Far from abdicating their professional responsibilities as many schemes that emphasise the learners' agency and participation tend to do[10], the teachers who wrote those texts took their professional responsibilities very seriously, more seriously indeed than many teachers who march under the aegis of the hothouse picture. The intelligible structure of those texts, and the thoughtful, lucid, orderly and detailed specification of the tasks to be engaged in by the learners, made most teachers' fulfilment of such professional responsibilities look pretty amateurish and *ad hoc*. My colleague and I drew some lessons from this example of teaching, an example strikingly different from the hothouse picture[11].

We designed our teaching around units, each conceived of as representing one week's worth of student study time. Each unit was a learning package that contained copies of the reading we expected students to do, and an interactive text written by us, which provided an intelligible structure, systematically introduced the problems and issues, led the student through the arguments and material to be covered, and showed them how, and with what purpose, to read the readings. We took seriously into view the importance of active participation in learning. Thus, we tried to help our students to engage with the material by incorporating frequent exercises, questions, and other activities, urging them to form self-study groups and giving suggestions in the learning package itself for what those study groups should do. We regarded as fundamental a question any teacher has to ask in planning any teaching – What will the learners *do*? – and therefore included checklists of tasks in our learning packages.

One very important outome of this experience was that our view of the purpose of contact-time changed dramatically. Because the intelligible structure[12] was expressed in the learning package, we no longer needed to lecture in the traditional sense; instead we used that time in a flexible variety of non-solemn ways: sometimes elaborating on a particular issue in the material, sometimes giving further examples, sometimes working through particular arguments, and sometimes asking students to come with questions that arose for them out of the learning packages. We came to understand that the central purposes of contact-time were to show the ways in which what we were teaching was connected to the current interests of students, to bring the problems and issues vividly and enjoyably to life, and to provide, as it were, a vital example of the forms of intellectual mobility we were trying to foster.

I am not here trying to sell anything, nor do I want to pretend that we had an easy job or solved all the problems, but I do think that we did manage to provide better than average epistemological access to a burgeoning number of students, and we did so without either killing ourselves or betraying our students' aspirations for higher education.

Instead, I am here trying to provide an example of how our professional intelligence and imagination might flourish when we escape from the clutches of the hothouse picture and recapture our sense of the essential intellectual mobility of professional practice. I am trying to urge that we need to concentrate our professional intelligence on how we might offer epistemological access to large numbers of students in higher education, rather than allow ourselves to be captivated by a picture which generates the illusion that the project is hopeless.

Given that large classes are here to stay in our higher education institutions, and if I am right in my central claim that in a situation of scarce resources, we think formal and epistemological access are in direct conflict with each other because our thinking is held captive by the hothouse picture of teaching, then to break the hold of that picture and learn how to teach well in large classes is of the utmost importance for the future of higher education in our country.

Notes

1   Martin Trow, 'Academic standards and mass higher education' in *Higher Education Quarterly*, Vol. 41 No. 3, Summer 1987, p. 289.

2   Such a policy would in any case be self-defeating; fewer students would rapidly lead to fewer academic posts.

3   I say 'institution' but we could also say 'system'.

4   One major purpose of this essay is to imply that our recent obsession with 'policy' issues in education, driven basically by economic and sociological frames of thinking, has seriously diverted our attention away from a consideration of teaching. We need urgently to recapture the link between grand policy and the constitutive point of the whole enterprise.

5   This survey was quoted by Professor Boyson in 'The challenge of numbers', an address to the CUP in January 1990.

6   Martin Trow, 'Academic standards and mass higher education' in *Higher Education Quarterly*, Vol. 41 No. 3, Summer 1987, p. 286.

7   When a group of serious professional academics stubbornly insists, *without being able to provide reasons*, that 30 students is the outer limit for the size of a viable BEd (Hons) class, we know that the hothouse picture is doing its dirty work. Given that picture, we should be filled with admiration for their willingness to take on such a huge task.

8   In popular versions of the hothouse picture a central feature, which tends to be obscured or denied, is the academic quality of the teacher involved; its warm and cosy affective aspects are emphasised to the detriment of its intellectual discipline. When I talk in this way I am adverting not merely to the knowledge in the sense of 'content' which a competent academic has acquired, but to the informed and sensitive perception which she exercises in her academic judgements – which shape not only

her explicit comments, say, on students' written work, but the whole nature of the ongoing discussion. There are severe limitations on the extent to which academic judgement can be expressed in a set of teachable rules – quite apart from the fact that any set of rules needs to be applied in practice, and that itself takes judgement.

There are many ways in which academic work has been mystified, but this is not one of them. Here, as in the case of research, there are no short cuts, no quick training schemes that can substitute for the arduous routes by which academic discipline has traditionally been acquired. We undermine the real value of academic work if we ourselves call simple information-gathering projects, questionnaire surveys, or undergraduate exercises, 'research', or if we convey the impression that after a few quick training sessions a normal third- or fourth-year student in one of our institutions can fill the role of an academic tutor.

Impoverished conceptions of research or academic teaching such as these (frequently driven by a muddled conception of democratising education) threaten to undermine the whole project of higher education. Unless we are very careful, our tutorial schemes run the constant risk of merely recycling intellectual mediocrity, reinforcing undisciplined intellectual habits and widespread misconceptions about the nature of learning and academic work, and betraying our students seeking higher education. Tutorial schemes are frequently said to improve the confidence of both tutors and students, but they might simply reinforce mere self-assertion, which harmonises with the illusion that we can reshape the world at will.

9   This might, of course, not be entirely straightforward and without controversy, because it might, for instance, have consequences for our eating habits, our vegetable markets and other things, but in principle it is quite clear how we proceed. When faced with a new candidate we appeal to analogies between it and already accepted cases, and we do this in terms of the concept we already have. Such analogies are unlikely to appeal to empirical, observable similarities; they are more likely to appeal to similarities between the culinary roles, in the construction of our meals, of traditional vegetables and new candidates. In the ordinary course of events we might not be very clear about exactly why we count something as a vegetable, but this does not mean that we are prepared to count just anything as a vegetable. In problematic cases we might be forced to articulate, in a way not required in the normal course of our lives, what our criteria are for our concept of 'vegetable', and in some cases we might see it as useful or appropriate to extend or refine those criteria in some way, perhaps to accommodate or exclude new candidates.

10 The postmodern dogma that knowledge and power are two sides of a single coin leads to the word 'teaching' becoming a dirty word; it fosters the idea that to be 'progressive'

is to substitute 'facilitation' or 'development' for teaching, and to have a deep distrust of knowledge. It fosters, in short, a degraded concept of teaching (see Note 8).

11 I still think that distance education projects provide an important spur to our critical reflection on our own practices as teachers of large classes in higher education.

12 'Intelligible structure' refers to the underlying conceptual organisation of what we were teaching.

4 The practice of organising systematic learning

(Paper presented at a UNESCO / CIEP Colloquium, Paris, July 1999)[1]

Our inherited conception of basic education

We[2] have inherited a particular conception of basic education. It has its roots in the flourishing of European economies on the backs of their colonial empires during the 19th and 20th centuries, the European Enlightenment, the European religious Reformation and the discourse of human rights, which emerged in Europe and the United States of America during the 18th century. But, in spite of the fundamentally European origins of this conception of basic education, and bitter memories of European imperialism and colonialism, it is embraced across the contemporary world, and is a standard item in the rhetoric of social reformers and political leaders almost everywhere. Our inherited conception of basic education has become universal common sense, an accepted and deep feature of modern life, and a fervent aspiration of millions of marginalised and destitute people across the world.

Our inherited conception of basic education is shaped by ideas such as the following. Basic education is a universal right and it should be provided at public expense for all members of the population, from early childhood to adolescence. It should be provided in institutions, which we call schools, by teachers to groups of about 25 learners. The aim of basic education is to prepare children for what lies ahead of them in their lives, and development, economic prosperity, political justice and the stability of a society are to a significant extent a product of the success of basic education. The curriculum of basic education is, fundamentally, a question of socialising the young into the dominant belief and value systems of their society. This is to be done in terms of a curriculum, which begins by providing the generic decoding skills of literacy and numeracy, and increasingly moves towards more specialised subjects. What those more specialised subjects should be has been a site of constant controversy, with some people arguing that the distinctions between school subjects are 'artificial', others arguing against an 'academic' curriculum which fails to prepare learners for the 'world of work', and yet others arguing that whatever else schooling does it should provide remedies for the economic, social, moral and political ills that plague broader society. But, in spite of such controversies, the curriculum of basic education has remained remarkably stable almost everywhere over the past century.

Our inherited conception of basic education is rooted in a particular epistemology and political theory. That epistemology is a latter-day product of the scientific revolutions of the 17th and 18th centuries which, as the Church of Rome recognised at an early stage, have irretrievably transformed the world in which we live. A central feature of that epistemology is the Baconian idea that knowledge is power, that rational knowledge will enable us to gain control of the natural hazards and forces which, for most of history, have limited and impoverished human lives. This new conception of knowledge repudiated traditional authorities – such as Aristotle – and asserted a vigorous notion of rational autonomy as a capacity inherent in every human being. In a parallel development, traditional political authorities were repudiated to be replaced by the modern forms of democracy founded on the presupposition of the dignity of every person, irrespective of their particular identity, ancestry, wealth or status.

The challenge to reconceptualise the practices of basic education

There have been profound *qualitative* changes in the social and economic world, brought about by revolutionary technological developments, centrally in the spheres of communications and information technology. The certainties of the past have been undermined and the world and the people who live in it have become fluid, mobile and diverse. Traditional boundaries, especially boundaries of time and space, have been rudely disrupted, and the generation of knowledge has become a rout. The world has become a mediated world constructed by instantaneous news, powerful advertising, media images and briefly fashionable catchphrases. National sovereignty is increasingly a shadow of the past and individual identities have become fluid and open to constant revision. Qualitative changes of this order have accelerated during the final decades of the 20th century which, it is said, forces us to think anew about basic education.

These qualitative changes challenge us to reconsider our inherited conception of basic education and define, as far as possible, the new content that basic education in the 21st century should incorporate to generalise the right to education and to enable lifelong learning. This challenge is backed up by two main arguments, which I shall shortly address. However, I shall begin with a few preliminary remarks.

This challenge is not unaware of the extent to which basic education for all has still not been achieved in much of the world, in spite of the enormous efforts of international agencies and national governments. Perhaps part of the message is that a reconceptualisation of basic education might benefit not only those societies in which basic education is already a well-established tradition, but also those that are still trying to achieve basic education for all. Reconceptualising basic education might enable us to see how the right to education could become more attainable for all. I return to this thought in the final paragraph of this essay.

I think we should also note important ways in which the challenge to reconceptualise basic education is carefully circumscribed by the endorsement, indeed reinforcement, of two closely linked and pivotal dimensions of our inherited conception. First, this challenge does not raise questions about the Enlightenment assumption that the capacity to acquire rational knowledge is a universal human capacity. Second, in this challenge, the universal right to education is treated as beyond question; in fact, it is inflated in the claim that the right to education implies not only the right to basic education, but also the right to lifelong learning.

As a matter of logic, talk of 'rights' needs to be partnered by some view about who has the duty to fulfil those rights. If we ignore this logic, 'rights talk' remains vacuous and a potent source of political protest. As noted above, the right to basic education remains an unfulfilled dream for countless people, and this is not everywhere the outcome of lack of goodwill on the part of governments. Depending on the ways in which we conceive of it, if we add the idea of the *right* to lifelong learning (as opposed to the idea that as a matter of fact lifelong learning is becoming the reality in the contemporary world), and think of governments and public funding as being responsible for fulfilling this right, we might be contributing further to the sheer inability, through lack of resources, of poor societies to provide even basic education for their young.

In addition, without wishing in any way to cast doubt on the ideal of education as a fundamental human right, we need to be aware of the ways in which to talk of the *right* to education has a tendency to generate the idea that education can be delivered to learners, like the takeaway food they order over the telephone, and that they are in no significant way responsible for their own education. This thought might be an unwelcome intruder in a discussion of the right to basic education, but I think it has an important role if we stray beyond basic into post-basic and higher education[3].

The 'moving target' and 'no finish line' arguments

The challenge to our inherited conception of basic education rests on two main arguments, linked to each other in an interpretation of the contemporary world. The first argument, which I shall call the 'moving target' argument, is that there are exponential changes in the social, economic and technological world as we move into the 21st century, and that these changes require us to rethink what we mean by basic education which, in its traditional form, is increasingly failing to prepare people for the world in which they will subsequently have to find their way. Basic education can no longer assume relatively stable life forms, or aim at a relatively fixed target.

The second argument, which I shall call the 'no finish line' argument, is that new knowledge is being generated and disseminated at such a pace that we constantly have to update our knowledge. The relatively settled forms of life, including occupational niches, we traditionally take for granted, are being disrupted in such a way that we now have to think in terms of lifelong (or cradle to grave) learning. But thinking in these terms has a wash-back effect on the way we should conceive of basic education. If we take lifelong learning seriously, then our inherited conception of basic education as for the young, and complete in itself, is misleading. We need to reconceive basic education as part of the lifelong learning process as well as its foundation stone.

These two arguments have the following formal shape:

The 'moving target' argument:
1   Basic education should enable the young to become active participants in the social world;
2   But there is an increasing disjunction between our inherited conception of basic education and what the social world has become, and is becoming;
3   Thus we need to reconceptualise basic education.

The 'no finish line' argument:

1   A prominent feature of the contemporary world is dynamic and ongoing change underwritten by the rapid expansion and availability of new knowledge;

2   In this world, lifelong learning has become a necessity;

3   We need, thus, to reconceptualise basic education as a part of, and a launching pad for, lifelong learning.

These two arguments provide the framework for what I shall go on to say, but I want to bring the arguments down to earth by providing a brief account of the state of basic education in present-day South Africa. South Africa is an interesting case because it has a special history in respect to attempts to provide basic education for all, it is not as financially constrained as many other developing countries and – especially since 1994 – there have been strenuous efforts to improve basic education for all.

The condition of basic education in South Africa

South Africa has recently had its second successful democratic election. During the first five years of post-Apartheid government there were, understandably, huge efforts to shuffle off the legacies of centuries of colonialism and its culmination in a half century of legalised segregation. A major dimension of this effort was to try to reconfigure the schooling system, especially in respect to the provision of basic education.

A plethora of new education policies has been produced, driven by the determination to achieve quality basic education for all, to retrieve the 'liberating virtue' of education and to fuel the national economy. A unified system for the administration (including the public funding) of education, to replace the divided systems of the past, has been implemented. A National Qualifications Framework is in the process of being established to try to ensure the equivalence and, thus, the transportability of qualifications across the whole system. A new curriculum for basic education, Curriculum 2005, has been put on the books. Central features of this new curriculum are that it replaces traditional 'subjects' with a smaller number of 'learning areas', and it repudiates 'content' in favour of 'competences'. Many of these policies were constructed on the basis of developments in basic education elsewhere in the world.

These policies are frequently described as highly progressive and at the leading edge of developments in basic education, but it is also frequently lamented that implementation is poor. There is a great deal of debate about the 'gap' between policy and implementation, and how to bridge this gap. Let us think about this.

South Africa suffers from some deeply debilitating social problems that affect basic education. The age profile of the population is typical of a 'developing' society, with more than half of the population below the age of 18. South Africa is a country with one of the highest levels of HIV-positive members of its population. Crime, and especially violent crime, has become an epidemic (more than 100 members of the police force were murdered on duty during the first 5 months of 1999), with some of the highest incidences of rape, murder, child abuse, robbery and car-hijackings in the world. Unemployment is prevalent. In his recent opening address to Parliament the new president said that 30 per cent of the potential workforce are unemployed, but some estimates claim an even higher percentage. In spite of high levels of taxation, the gap between the wealthy and the impoverished is increasing, and many people live in self-constructed shack settlements or rural slums, many with not even basic services such as sewage, a water supply and regular garbage collection. A significant proportion of the adult population lacks even basic print literacy. Such problems which, in their general form, are not unique to South Africa, provide an important background to thinking about basic education.

And when we turn our attention to prevalent conditions in schools in South Africa, the prospects for basic education for all in the near future appear dismal. Many schools, especially those that serve communities disadvantaged by Apartheid, are characterised by endemic disorder. There is poor and irregular attendance of teachers and learners, timetables do not run on a regular basis, many school days are lost to other activities, there is prevalent use of primitive teaching methods and assessment procedures, and there is widespread cynicism about the value of school learning.

A recent project in the Eastern Cape Province – the Centres of Learning Training Project[4] – is based on the view that the first step in trying to overcome what is called 'the breakdown in the culture of learning and teaching', is to pay attention to the leadership, management and administration of schools, and to provide carefully targeted training programmes for those who carry the responsibility for these dimensions of school organisation. The project is based on a theory of organisational development in which organisations can be classified into three broad classes according to what kind of interventions are likely to be effective. Schools were classified as 'rehabilitative', 'developing', and 'excellent' according to their degree of dependence and the current state of their management and administrative systems. But, for our purposes here, the most significant finding is that some 70 per cent of the schools were below the bottom of this scale and were classified as 'dysfunctional' – that is, below the level at which endogenous development might be possible. And, to exacerbate matters, probably something like this percentage is the norm across the whole country. To put these anecdotal considerations into a more systematic framework, I shall refer to the findings of a recent survey of basic education in South Africa.

Getting learning right

The President's Education Initiative Research Project[5] was an attempt by the South African National Department of Education to get a broad picture of the condition of basic education in South Africa during 1997 and 1998. The project included 35 free-standing investigations that covered over 250 schools, 90 per cent of which serve communities disadvantaged by Apartheid. The investigations included a broad range of topics from subject teaching, reading, teaching methods, assessment and large class teaching, to school development. The findings fall into four broad areas and, overall, they paint a bleak picture of the condition of basic education in South Africa. I shall briefly mention some of the findings[6].

One range of findings was that many schools are characterised by a lack of established routines or basic orderliness, and a lack of the threshold capacity to initiate or manage their own development. In many schools timetables and learning spaces are not respected in practice and one study, in which principals were asked to record the number of tuition days lost in the previous year, it was found that, on average, more than 60 per cent of days were lost to a variety of other activities including slow registrations at the start of the year, athletics and music events, meetings (union, district and regional), memorial services, strikes and pay days. In many cases schools seemed reconciled to gross inefficiency, maladministration and endemic chaos.

In respect to pedagogy, curriculum and assessment the findings were similarly depressing. In many cases teachers had a poor conceptual grasp of the subjects they were teaching and knew little more than their learners. In spite of many teachers mouthing the rhetoric of more progressive teaching methods – discovery, building on prior knowledge, working in groups, and so on – their classroom practices directly contradicted this rhetoric. Teachers generally have very low expectations of their learners and this is reflected in assessment practices. The overwhelming majority of questions involved simple data recall, written questions rarely elicited answers longer than a single word, and incorrect answers were frequently not corrected. Books and reading are little in evidence and learners hardly ever write – and when they do, it is generally in the form of single words or short phrases. In general, although teachers said they embrace the broad goals of the new curriculum, few of them have the conceptual resources to put them into practice.

The fiscal crisis, which came to a head during 1996/7, had a profound effect on the proportion of budgets devoted to salaries as opposed to non-salary items such as building maintenance and the provision of stationery and textbooks. The amount spent on the purchase of textbooks dropped from R895 million in 1995/6 to R80 million in 1997/8. In addition to their sheer unavailability, it was found that very few teachers are using textbooks in their classrooms in any systematic way. The researchers suggested that teachers avoid using textbooks because they lack the content knowledge or reading skills to use them, and because they have been influenced by a climate in which textbooks were denigrated as 'pre-packaged material'. In cases where the teachers used other learning material – such as worksheets, newspaper articles, cartoons, and so on – they tended to use them in a haphazard fashion rather than as part of a well-designed learning programme that systematically develops cognitive skills and conceptual knowledge.

Finally, as might be expected in a multilingual society, there were many problems in respect to language. The overwhelming majority of parents and schools, especially in urban areas, opt for English as the language of teaching and learning. One reason for this is the linguistically heterogeneous character of many schools, but another is that English is perceived as a means of gaining access to mainstream national and global society. But there were many teachers whose linguistic competence in spoken English is poor, and whose reading competence is at an elementary level. If we accept that competence in the language of instruction on the part of teachers, but also of learners, is a key requirement for successful learning, then the prospects for achieving the goals of basic education appear to be less than optimistic.

The findings of the President's Education Initiative Research Project, despite its not being a systematic scientific survey from which reliable statistical generalisations can be drawn, point towards some of the very deep difficulties in trying to accomplish the goals of our inherited concept of basic education, even in a society such as South Africa, which is not at the bottom of the scale of impoverished societies and which, in the past, achieved high levels of basic education for a privileged 20 per cent of its population, and which now has a government strongly committed to the ideal of basic education for all. Systemic and institutional malfunction, poor levels of conceptual understanding among teachers – both of the methods and content of teaching – and weak competence in the language of instruction, inhibit the prospects of achieving basic education for all.

The aim of basic education

Let us now turn our attention back to the 'moving target' and 'no finish line' arguments for the conclusion that we need to reconceptualise basic education. I noted previously that the challenge to reconceptualise basic education does not extend to two fundamental elements of our inherited conception: that there is a universal right to education and the accompanying assumption that the capacity to acquire rational knowledge is a universal human capacity. The challenge consists in inviting us, within this framework, to reconceptualise the content and teaching methods of basic education and the forms of Teacher Education that could underwrite such changes.

In order to address this challenge, we need to think about the aim of basic education and about what we mean by professional teaching. In this section I will suggest a characterisation of the former; in the next I shall turn attention to the latter.

One of the characteristics of the world as we stumble into the 21st century is that a possible response to the 'moving target' and 'no finish line' arguments, which might have been available even a few decades ago, is no longer viable. This response is that arguments such as these arise in rich and comfortable societies in which public institutions are well established, and starvation, violence and uncontrolled disease are no longer a serious threat to personal and social survival. Such arguments, it might have been said, are, at best, relevant to such societies. Why, it might have been asked, should those in poorer and less stable societies find such arguments persuasive? Perhaps these arguments are germane to only those societies in which traditional basic education is already to a significant degree an accomplished fact, and perhaps the call to reconceptualise the content and methods of basic education is a way in which rich societies are, yet again, stepping ahead to maintain their dominance.

However, the 'moving target' and 'no finish line' arguments cannot be dismissed in this way. The products, technologies and other artefacts that are aspects of the mutations of the modern world have deeply penetrated the lives and aspirations even of those who live in isolated enclaves and poorer societies, marginalised from the global mainstream. Subtle and powerful marketing techniques, and rapid transport and communication systems – from the bicycle and motor car to trains and aeroplanes, from the printing press and the telephone to radio, the cinema, television and the internet – carry potent messages into the heart of traditional societies. Millions of people, even in remote parts of the world, are being constantly exposed to fashions, products, events, lifestyles and images whose sources are elsewhere and elsewhen. These powerful messages have become a universal currency, inducing unprecedented dissatisfactions and frustrations, fundamentally reshaping images of the desirable across the world. Despite pockets of resistance from some traditional leaders, modernity runs in the capillaries, as well as the arteries, of the contemporary world and the 'moving target' and 'no finish line' arguments have to enter the discourses of basic education everywhere.

But there is an additional reason. Mass schooling of the young is the principal way in which societies have sought to implement the right to basic education for all, and mass schooling is both a product of and a catalyst for modernisation. It is with such considerations in mind that we need to think about the aim of basic education.

The fundamental aim of basic education is to enable access to the modern world. With this as one of the starting points, we can begin to think about the content and teaching methods of basic education, and whether we need to reconceptualise them in the light of the 'moving target' and 'no finish line' arguments.

We can briefly note some of the key characteristics of the modern world, characteristics that have been clichés of social theory since Durkheim and Weber. The modern world is a rationalised world that disrupts traditional communities and forms of life and disrespects cultural, temporal and spatial boundaries. It is a world ruled by clock-time, impartial bureaucratic rules and money economies. Modernity opens the window on diversity and mobility of people, populations and products, and individuals are faced with constant choices about what to have and to be. The relative homogeneity of societies in the past, and the relative stability of their traditions, roles and populations, have been replaced by heterogeneous and unsettled life forms.

Modernity and modernisation are not uncontaminated benefits, either to individuals or to societies. We can note the ways in which modernisation has an impact on the identity of individuals – giving rise, in some cases, to the characteristic psychic illnesses of the modern world[7]. We can note, too, the ways in which modernisation is typically accompanied by a deterioration in natural environments, and in which modernisation has a tendency to distort or suppress cultural differences – leading to the loss of precious traditional languages and life forms. The ecology movements and the demand that education should become more multicultural are symptoms of these effects. Nonetheless, modernisation embodies the promise of a better quality of life for all – and this promise seems indeed to have been largely fulfilled in societies such as Canada, Japan, Western Europe, Singapore and the United States of America.

This provides a sketchy abstract of what I mean by a reference to 'the modern world'. However, despite its universal and universalising dimensions, modernity is exhibited in a variety of forms that rest ultimately on some deep features of the particular cocktail of traditions transformed by the intrusions of modernity. 'The modern world' takes subtly different forms in Sydney and Buenos Aires from that which it takes in Los Angeles, Rome, New York, Paris, Toronto, London, Cairo, Hong Kong, Johannesburg, Montreal or Madrid. In these nodes there are different styles of modernity, but this consideration does not damage the claim that the aim of basic education is to enable access to the modern world, although it does affect the way this aim needs to be interpreted in practice in different historical contexts.

One common feature of modernity, despite its various forms and styles, is that, like any culture, it is relatively opaque to outsiders. As in the case of languages or cities we don't know, or even unfamiliar social situations, those who are not insiders find themselves faced with puzzling obscurities so embedded in the clichés and consciousness of fluent practitioners that it takes special skill to identify or explicate them. In the case of access to the modern world, although, as I have pointed out, there are many products and superficial aspects of modernity that have penetrated the lives of people everywhere, this is not yet *access* to the modern world. Only a shallow or facile contact, as consumers, has been accomplished. The aim of basic education is to enable access to the modern world by teaching learners not merely the vocabulary but also the *grammar* of the modern world. Basic education has the task of developing the capacities to appropriate the forms of modernity and participate in its practices. These thoughts provide us with ways of thinking about the content and teaching methods of basic education at this time.

The 'access' referred to in the claim that the aim of basic education is to enable access to the modern world, is access in respect to the forms of thinking and feeling characteristic of that world. I am not referring to other conditions for access, such as financial and material resources. Satisfying these conditions is indeed important, as poor societies and those who live in them know only too vividly, but it is not the purpose of education to provide them. And this takes us towards a consideration of teaching.

The formal element of teaching

Teaching takes many different forms – there are many different teaching methods depending on such variables as the context, the equipment and facilities available, the age of the learners, what it is that they are being taught, and what the learners already know about the content. The list of teaching methods is not fixed and final, and human ingenuity and technological developments can, and do, extend that list. Many of our current teaching methods are ossified in the assumption of class sizes of about 25 learners, although in poorer societies this is seldom the norm. For financial and other reasons we need to think of teaching methods more suitable for class sizes of, say, 100 or 150 learners. Similarly, much of our teaching in the contemporary world still assumes the 'situation of co-presence' (where the teacher and the learners are together at the same time and place) as the exclusive site of teaching, but modern communication and information technologies – from print to electronic technologies – challenge that assumption, as is revealed in the worldwide burgeoning of distance education at post-basic levels of education systems.

Of course, not all learning results from teaching, as we know only too well. Perhaps one cause of our anxieties is that people, and especially children, learn from many different sources, over many of which we have no control, and that much of that learning in modern or modernising societies pre-empts or perhaps even undermines the learning we try to promote in our formal institutions of teaching.

What characterises professional teaching in all its possible forms is that it is the practice of organising systematic learning. This 'formal element' of teaching provides us with a guideline for thinking about possible innovations and improvements in teaching methods, for thinking imaginatively, but not fancifully, about possible new ways of teaching.

Particularly if we are thinking of professional schoolteachers, and in a country such as South Africa, it is important to emphasise the idea that teaching involves *organising* learning. What is essential to the responsibilities of a professional teacher – so signally lacking in South Africa, if the findings of the President's Education Initiative Research Project are to be believed – is to organise learning in such a way that it leads towards the development of more resonant understanding.

It is in terms of its formal object, which is to foster *systematic learning*, that the practice of professional teaching can be distinguished from the disjointed and fortuitous stream of messages in our information-promiscuous world. The job of teachers is to try to foster that kind of learning which systematically advances the understanding of learners so that they can achieve organising insights into the world as it is. Teaching is to be distinguished from exposure to the atomised stream of information and images that circulate around the webs of the contemporary world. It is an attempt to enable the learners to order the constant flow of impressions and to appreciate and understand at a deeper level the torrent of fleeting images and information that is characteristic of the modern world. Professional teaching aims systematically to develop the conceptual frameworks that render the world less opaque.

New content and teaching methods for basic education?

In our inherited conception, basic education is essentially a matter of socialising the young into the dominant belief and value systems of their society. This is to be achieved in terms of a curriculum that begins by providing the generic decoding skills of literacy and numeracy and, as an extension of those skills, increasingly moves towards more specialised subjects. Are there reasons to think that such a curriculum will no longer serve us well as we move into the 21st century? Do the 'moving target' and 'no finish line' arguments, in particular, persuade us that we need *new* content and teaching methods for basic education? As can be seen from the foregoing sections of this essay, my response to these questions is, fundamentally, conservative. I shall conclude with a few comments about this.

The dominant belief and value systems of societies are increasingly borderless. We can think, for example, of the ways in which the ideas of democracy and rights, which took root in recent centuries in a few societies in Europe and the United States of America, have become seminal ideas across the world. Similarly, we might think of the ways in which convictions about ecology, multiculturalism, and gender and racial equity rapidly become globalised. This is, no doubt, one of the effects of the communications and information revolution, but whatever its causes, it implies that socialising the young into the dominant belief and value systems of (their) society cannot be conceived of, if it ever was, as initiating them into the belief and value systems of restricted societies.

In any case, the generic decoding skills of literacy and numeracy, and the more specialised subjects towards which they lead, themselves serve to subvert the settled certainties of embedded traditions. In addition, literacy, numeracy and the more specialised subjects are ways of enabling access to the modern world by developing the capacity for people to think for themselves.

Perhaps we mislead ourselves by thinking of literacy and numeracy as 'generic decoding skills', as if they were merely useful tools. Developing these capacities profoundly shapes the thoughts and feelings that lie not only in the minds, but also in the hearts, of people's very understanding of the world and the quality of their lives. This is not only a matter of the content of what is read, but of the ways in which written text reconstitutes, constructs and reconstructs experience. For access to the modern world, people need to learn the ways of thinking and feeling of that world, and literacy and numeracy – linked to the idea of 'thinking for themselves' – capture something very central to those ways of thinking and feeling.

The modern world, with its definitive mobility and diversity, requires people constantly to make choices, many of which are unsettling, and basic education has the task of fostering the capacities needed to make such choices reflectively. This is to be achieved not by the increasingly fruitless project of trying to envisage in advance what choices will need to be made, or by imagining that we are going to be able to decide on the content and teaching methods of basic education in terms of a principle of 'relevance' – the 'target' is moving too quickly and unpredictably. On the contrary, it will be achieved, if at all, by enabling learners to acquire the tools for thinking for themselves and learning how to use those tools in unpredictable circumstances. Such tools are concepts and conceptual frameworks, which are the forms of thinking, feeling and acting which structure experience and interpretation[8].

The content and teaching methods of basic education work together to foster a generative kind of learning, in which pivotal concepts are reflected upon in such a way that they continue to shape thoughts, feelings, attitudes and practices while remaining open to revision and modification.

Thus, ideally, the teachers of basic education would themselves be educated men and women – with the disciplined mobility of thinking and feeling which that implies – but in the real world of mass schooling, especially in poorer societies, this has proved to be an unattainable target. Attempts to provide basic education in traditional ways in poorer societies have stretched their human and financial resources to breaking point. This is a good reason to regard textbooks as an indispensable resource for basic education. Well-conceived textbooks can provide context-sensitive and systematic explorations of subject matter within coherent conceptual frameworks. Textbooks are, as it were, teaching in the public realm, open to scrutiny and revision in ways in which conventional teaching in classrooms is not. We can add that although textbooks in printed format are still the most transportable and available form, new electronic and print technologies might yield new kinds of 'textbooks' not yet familiar in our world.

Of course, if we emphasise the use of textbooks as a primary way of promoting the kind of systematic learning that will provide access to the modern world, then teacher training would have to take this into account. Elementarily, it would need to incorporate, in ways that are perhaps uncommon, training in teaching methods that depend on the effective use of textbooks.

The main objections to this view will arise from those who have a view of teaching which emphasises professional integrity and autonomy, and centres around the idea that teaching is a special kind of relationship in which the teacher nurtures the progressive development of each unique learner. My view is that there might be some privileged situations in which such a view of teaching is viable, and has an important role to play, but that if it is mass schooling and basic education for all that we are thinking about, especially in societies in which the snowball effects of traditions of basic education have not been established over generations, it is not viable.

Similarly, driven, perhaps by subjectivist and relativist epistemologies, there is a fashion of emphasising 'process' to the detriment of 'content'. Content tends to be denigrated as simply the sharp edge of the ways in which schooling does its work as an 'ideological state apparatus'. Whatever might be its roles in other contexts – such as, for example, in negotiating conflicts between bitter rivals – in the context of basic education, process without content is vacuous.

The 'moving target' and 'no finish line' arguments lead to the conclusion that we need to reconceptualise basic education. From there it is a short step to thinking that we need *new* content and teaching methods for basic education. My response to these arguments has been that the kind of reconceptualisation of basic education that we need is not a question of thinking of *new* content and teaching methods. We need to revitalise the practices of basic education by taking seriously the Enlightenment ideal that 'rational autonomy' is a capacity inherent in every human being, and re-emphasise this ideal in terms of the view that the capacity to 'think for themselves' is a capacity that can be developed in every human being.

The way to do this is systematically to develop conceptual understanding. This form of understanding is not tied to any particular conception of the social world, so the idea of a disjunction between basic education and the social world is based on an impoverished conception of basic education and the kind of disciplined mobility of thought and feeling that it aims to foster. Similarly, conceptual understanding is itself a 'launching pad' for ongoing learning. The panic that can be induced by the idea of the rapid expansion and availability of new knowledge is based on a false synonymy between 'knowledge' and 'information'.

In the case of both the 'moving target' and 'no finish line' arguments, we can detect symptoms of pervasive instrumentalism in thinking about basic education. The prime virtue of basic education is to have made a good start, not to have arrived at a terminus.

I have one final thought to offer. In thinking about whether we need new content, teaching methods and teacher training for basic education for the new millennium, we are assuming that the systems and institutions of basic education, as we have inherited them, are satisfactory. The same assumption underlies the orthodox hope that schooling systems will be improved by improving teacher training. But perhaps, especially in sympathy for the poorer societies of the world, we need to expand our agenda to include a consideration of whether changes in the social world, and new technologies, might enable us to find new *forms of institutions* in terms of which to try to actualise the right of basic education for all, to pursue more effectively the Socratic ideal of cultivating humanity.

Notes

1   This essay is an updated version of the original paper published in French as 'L'organisation de l'apprentissage systématique' in *Revue Internationale d'Éducation*, No. 25, March 2000.

2   The 'we' in my first sentence is a universal 'we'.

3   See Wally Morrow, 'Entitlement and achievement in education' in *Studies in Philosophy and Education*, Vol. 13 No. 1, pp. 33–47, 1993.

4   The Centres of Learning Training Project, Institute for Development Planning and Research, University of Port Elizabeth, South Africa.

5   N Taylor & P Vinjevold (eds), *Getting Learning Right* (Report of the President's Education Initiative Research Project), Johannesburg: The Joint Education Trust, 1999.

6   I have drawn these details from Nick Taylor, 'Getting learning right', presented at the conference: Teacher Development   Connecting Policy and Practice, 18–20 May 1999.

7   See, for example, Chinua Achebe, *Things Fall Apart*, London: Picador, 1988.

8   I am painfully aware of the major theoretical baggage I am importing into this account, and of the fact that I do nothing here to explicate or justify this baggage but, at the same time, I think that *any* account of the content and teaching methods of basic education presupposes some major theoretical baggage.

.

5 *What is Teacher Education?*

(National Commission on Higher Education, January 1996)

What is Teacher Education?

I propose that for the purposes of developing a policy for Teacher Education in our country at this time we adopt the following definition of Teacher Education:

> *Teacher Education is a kind of education which enables someone to become more competent in the professional practice of organising systematic learning, and nurtures their commitment to do so.*

I shall briefly explicate some of the elements and advantages of this definition.

1 There are countless instances of teaching dispersed through the daily life of any human community, most of them *ad hoc* and unplanned, but professional teaching is a specialised *practice*, especially in modern societies.

   This has more significance than might appear at first glance. A practice is sustained in and by a community of practitioners, and it is not possible for there to be a practice in which there is only a single participant. A practice is an ongoing pattern of human activities which has a history and a tradition, which shape its definitive ideals (those ideals which make it the practice that it is) and give rise to conceptions of excellence within the practice. Practices can, of course, atrophy and lose their vitality; but a living practice is dynamic and changes in response to such things as new technologies, influences from the historical contexts in which it is located, and discoveries about how to pursue its definitive ideals more effectively[1].

2 In addition, once we understand teaching as a *practice*, we can understand why learning how to teach is internally linked to developing a commitment to its ideals; the competence and the commitment are not two separable items. The definitive standards of excellence of any practice and its characteristic competences, are aspects of a unified conceptual scheme that can be understood, or developed, only in relation to each other. Thus, learning how to become more competent at organising systematic learning necessarily involves

coming to understand and care about the standards of achievement in this practice, and becoming committed to its definitive ideals.

3   Any human society, as a *human* society, is a 'learning society'. But those who use this phrase to describe modern societies are trying to do more than utter an empty tautology. Without pausing to spell this out, what they mean is that modern society has been formed by, is dependent on, and thus prizes, a kind of knowledge which persistently opens up new possibilities. In this respect, modern societies can be contrasted with 'traditional' societies, which reproduce fundamentally the same knowledge from generation to generation. But gaining access to the kind of knowledge that characterises modern societies requires *systematic learning*.

Over recent decades, modern societies have become exponentially more 'information rich' and increasingly networked in global systems of instantaneous communication and information exchange. These developments are partly a result of technological developments, but also of the increasing expansion of modern schooling.

Access to much of the information available in modern societies is premised on capacities such as print literacy, which are developed by systematic learning. Teachers cannot compete with electronic and mass media in the business of the transmission of information (although there are many teachers who still see their task in these terms), but such media are seldom in the business of *organising systematic learning*. This is the definitive function of professional teachers.

Thus, the definitive competence of professional teachers is that they know how to organise *systematic learning*. This phrase is intended to distinguish between the activities of a professional teacher and the ongoing, casual and informal teaching and *ad hoc* learning that goes on in any human community. The phrase 'systematic learning' refers not only to learning 'academic' knowledge or traditional 'school knowledge', but also to learning anything that takes some time and is normally assisted by someone who knows. We might think of learning how to swim, or how to repair a motor car, in addition to learning how to read or to do mathematics.

4   One feature of the proposed definition is especially important in our historical context; it broadens the scope of Teacher Education to include

teaching other than primary/secondary school teaching. Kinds of teaching can be distinguished in terms of differences between what is being taught, between learners (age, previous learning, etc.) and between the institutional, technological or other contexts in which it takes place.

An orthodox understanding of Teacher Education is predominantly focused on the pre-service training of primary and secondary school teachers for classroom practice. Such an understanding generates a restricted conception of teaching and marginalises other kinds of teaching – such as the continuing education of (school) teachers (In-service Education of Teachers or INSET) – which are, and are increasingly becoming, a key to our achieving our national aspirations.

The other kinds of teaching I am thinking of here include:
- Pre-primary teaching (educare), which almost has a place in the orthodox understanding of Teacher Education;
- Tertiary teaching, especially in higher education institutions, which is frequently of very poor quality (it is interesting that when we think of how higher education can cope with 'ill-prepared students' we think in terms of Academic 'Development' or 'Support' Programmes before we think of the quality of the teaching in our institutions);
- The teaching of healthcare and other workers;
- The continuing education of already serving teachers (we know that much of the teaching in, for example, primary/secondary schools is of extremely poor quality, and an orthodox understanding of Teacher Education promotes a conceptual and, as a result, an institutional dichotomy between Pre-service Education of Teachers or PRESET, and INSET);
- The teaching of non-tertiary adult learners – Adult Basic Education and Training or ABET (we know that there are very many of our people who either missed the opportunity for schooling or had such poor schooling that they are barely literate or numerate, and at a massive disadvantage in a modernising society);
- The designers of learning resources of various kinds and educational programmes for mass media;
- Teaching in industrial settings (usually called 'training'); and
- Teaching in informal or semi-formal community settings (community development workers).

This list is meant to be illustrative rather than exhaustive. It is meant to illustrate the range included once we define teaching as 'the practice of organising systematic learning', with a view to highlighting the key role of competent and committed teachers (generously understood) if – as a society – we are serious about overcoming the legacies of our past, achieving a more just distribution of capacities in our society, and collectively appropriating the benefits of the modern world.

5   One advantage of conceiving of teaching as the organising of systematic learning is that it helps to release us from the limiting and atrophying grip of the idea that teaching is essentially a kind of face-to-face live performance in classrooms; it throws much more emphasis on such competences as the design of programmes of systematic learning and the discovery of how to provide productive feedback to learners. We can better understand why the traditional dichotomy between 'contact' (or anachronistically 'residential') and 'distance' teaching is breaking down, and why, although it remains important for some kinds of teaching, skilled individual public performance is not the key competence to be developed in Teacher Education.

The professional development of teachers

The professional development of teachers is urgently needed in South Africa. The professional development of teachers includes, but is not exhausted by, Teacher Education.

6   The decay of schooling in our country is only one prominent symptom of a more widespread breakdown in the cultures of teaching and learning. This breakdown has serious consequences for the whole future development of our country, especially if we take account of our national aspirations to redress the imbalances of the past and become part of the modern world. It is common cause that we need a renaissance of the cultures of teaching and learning.

Effecting such a renaissance is going to involve a range of measures – from improving the governance, administration and management of institutions, to establishing accountability systems and other kinds of incentives for professional teachers, to putting in place support systems for teacher development. However, such mainly structural measures are only a *means* to the improvement of the practice of teaching. Professional teachers are the key agents of such an improvement, and many need professional development in order to enable them to do so effectively.

But the professional development of teachers is not synonymous with Teacher Education and it would be an error to understand the professional development of teachers exclusively in terms of Teacher Education. In points 7 and 8 below I shall briefly mention some of the other kinds of issues involved.

7   We should be concerned about the increasing de-professionalisation of teaching. There are many teachers, especially schoolteachers, who have a self-understanding of themselves as exploited workers. This has had the effect of their being dissatisfied about their status and remuneration in a way which disconnects these things from their professional competence and their commitment to the ideals of service that characterise teaching as a profession. While there are some teachers for whom this is not true, we have to acknowledge that there are many teachers, both in and outside of the schooling system, whose professional competence and commitment leaves much to be desired.

In response to this deterioration there are calls for 'teacher accountability', but such accountability is typically conceived of as accountability to the immediate school community. There are two problems in conceiving of it in these terms. One is that it applies mainly to schoolteachers (and perhaps teachers in other formal institutions of learning, such as colleges and universities), but another is that it assumes that local lay communities are in a good position to judge the quality and effectiveness of teaching. The former is a problem if we accept a definition of teaching which is not restricted to school teaching. The latter impoverishes the idea of 'service to the community' and has a tendency to undermine the distinctive kind of service which a profession provides. Teaching is not a commodity in relation to which immediate 'customer satisfaction' is the only criterion of quality. The quality of teaching might sometimes become evident to its beneficiaries only years after the event.

Nonetheless, accountability of professional teachers is important, especially in our context and if we acknowledge that our future development is significantly dependent on moving towards becoming a 'learning society'.

But for accountability to have this kind of promise we need to professionalise teaching. And we need to understand that the accountability of professional teachers needs to be accountability to the teaching profession[2].

Although we can understand the roots of this situation in the divisions of the past, and the ways in which teachers have conceived of themselves as employees, that we do not have a national unified professional body of teachers in our country at present is a cause for some concern[3]. Perhaps consideration needs to be given to the registration, perhaps even the licensing, of professional teachers, together with sanctions for teachers who do not maintain and improve their professional competence, or who fall down on their professional responsibilities. Sanctions are required not as the normal motive for competent and committed teachers, but as a guarantee that teachers who are competent and committed will not be sacrificed to those who are not[4].

8   But, at the same time, we need to avoid too individualised a conception of the professional development of teachers. The practice of teaching is typically located in institutions and organisations, which provide it with a home but which can hinder and distort it. To urge individual teachers to 'develop', without taking account of the enabling or inhibiting effects of the organisational contexts within which they work, might be merely to increase their levels of guilt and frustration without improving the practice of teaching.

It is in this regard that we can understand the value of the idea of 'whole school development'. Improvements in the practices of teaching depend on both the efforts of individual teachers and the creation and maintenance of organisational environments that encourage professional development and enable the practice of teaching to flourish.

9   Teacher Education has an important contribution to make to the professional development of teachers, but it is not equivalent to, nor a substitute for, it. Professional development is generated within the profession itself and the institutions and organisations formally dedicated to teaching; Teacher Education is a deliberate intervention into the ongoing process of professional development. We need to avoid being overambitious about the kind of contribution Teacher Education can make to the professional development of teachers. Much depends on the kinds of factors indicated in the previous paragraphs.

One of the traditional aspirations of Teacher Education is that the initial training of new teachers can reform the schooling system. But the experience of at least a century of formal Teacher Education has proved this aspiration to have little substance. We need a suitably moderate view about what Teacher Education (even understood as embracing both initial and continuing education) can, at best, accomplish, in respect to both the professional development of teachers and the regeneration of the cultures of teaching and learning.

Teacher Education as a form of professional education

Teacher Education should be understood as a form of professional education. Professional education is a kind of career education that straddles the commonly assumed boundary between vocational and academic education, and includes an ethical dimension. Professional education develops the professional knowledge of the learner.

10 The goal of any educational programme is to prepare the learner to become more competent in some or other practice (or practices). We might distinguish between different 'kinds' of education in terms of distinctions between the practices for which that education is preparing the learner. The purpose of professional education is to develop the learners' competence in a professional practice, and a proper understanding of, and commitment to, its ideal of service. Thus Teacher Education is the development of the learners' competence in, and commitment to, the practice of professional teaching.

11 Recently in the United Kingdom[5] a broad distinction has been made between two kinds of higher education: one the traditional academic (or disciplinary) education and the other a work-oriented education that is designed to prepare learners for a future occupation. The former is said to have the goal of developing academic competences, and the latter to have the goal of developing occupational competences.

The first point to make about this is that competences can be understood only in relation to practices. Although there are clearly some competences that might run across practices (we might think of reading – but there are problems even in this case), and this is what underlies the idea of transferable skills, if, in general, we disconnect competences from practices, we run the risk of reifying competences and thus depriving them of their significance and sense.

A second point, and this is one that is important if we are to come to understand professional education, is that the distinction between 'academic competences' and 'occupational competences' is operating at an extremely abstract level. Are we to assume that there is some kind of unitary practice which might be called 'academic practice' and some overarching kind of practice to be called 'occupational practice'? Even a brief reflection on this matter shows this to be a silly assumption to make. Within each of these 'categories' there is a wide diversity of practices that are constituted by webs of criss-crossing and overlapping competences. And this leads into a third point.

While we can make a distinction between academic and occupational competences at an abstract level, it is an error to use this distinction as the basis for a distinction between two competing, and perhaps incompatible, kinds of higher education. For many occupations in the modern world (and this is clearly the case in respect to those occupations which are called professions) some kinds of academic competences are required. If this were not the case, then it is difficult to know what the rationale is for some kinds of occupational education to be located in higher education.

12 At the same time, it is important not to collapse the distinction between academic and professional education. The goals of these two kinds of education are different from each other. The goals of academic education are to develop the capacities of objective enquiry and judgement; the goals of professional education are to enable the learner to participate more successfully in a particular professional practice. This difference is also reflected in the sources of the discipline involved in academic or professional work. The source of the discipline of academic practices is internal to the particular academic discipline(s) involved; the source of the discipline of professional practices is their specific ideals of service and the practical contingencies of the situations and contexts in which those ideals are pursued.

This distinction is expressed in common-sense views such as the following: a highly competent academic researcher in, say, the field of medicine, might not be a good surgeon or general (medical) practitioner; an excellent legal academic might not be a good practical attorney; a superb historical scholar might be an inferior teacher of history; and a good, even outstanding, researcher in a field such as physics or chemistry might, nonetheless, be a mediocre or even poor teacher of physics or chemistry.

13 Professional education is, indeed, a kind of 'career education' but we need to take account of what distinguishes it from other kinds of career education. In general terms there are two distinguishing features. One has to do with the theoretical nature of professional practice, the other with the ethical dimensions of a profession.

One of the marks of a professional practice is that it is constituted in terms of theoretical concepts. A professional practice is shaped and guided by the theory that informs it, and by the concepts, beliefs and principles of those who participate in it. In this sense, a professional practice is 'cognitive' and socially constructed and maintained, in a much stronger sense than in the case of other practices such as, for example, driving a bus or playing tennis. The quality of a professional practice is, thus, much more crucially dependent on the quality of the thought of its practitioners than is the case in other practices.

I have already claimed that competence and commitment are not two separable elements of professional practice, but we need to add a stronger ethical dimension to this claim. Competence in a professional practice is conceptually linked to commitment to the standards of achievement in the practice, but those standards need to be framed by an ideal of service. A competent surgeon can as skilfully murder the patient on the operating table as she can remove the cancerous growth; a competent civil engineer can as easily design a bridge that can withstand a force-nine gale as he can design one that will collapse under the impact of a stiff breeze.

Professional competence, even with the commitment to the relevant standards that it includes is, in this sense, ambivalent. For the protection of the clients, patients, learners or other recipients of professional services, and the quality of life in society, one also needs those who acquire professional competences to understand the effects and consequences of their professional interventions, and to commit themselves to ideals of service. The Hippocratic oath is a traditional attempt to underwrite the latter kind of commitment.

The kind of ethical commitment developed by professional education is unlikely to be fostered by sermons and other exhortations; it is more likely to be absorbed from the implicit attitudes of the providers of that education, and the ethos that characterises the institutions/organisations in which it takes place. Whatever might be said to be their shortcomings in other respects, at their best Colleges of Education are characterised by their potential strength in maintaining an appropriate professional ethos. One of the major shortcomings of many of the current Colleges of Education in South Africa is that they lack a professional ethos of this kind.

It is these two features of professional education – that it is preparation for participation in a 'theoretical' practice and the kind of ethical commitment it involves – that distinguish it from other kinds of career education. Teacher Education should not be understood as merely preparation for an occupation.

Professional education should develop the professional knowledge of the learner. But is professional knowledge a distinctive type of knowledge? In the following section I will argue that it is.

Professional knowledge

Professional knowledge is practical knowledge harnessed to an ethical ideal. It is a qualitatively distinct kind of knowledge, different from academic and technical knowledge, although it draws on both.

14 A key to understanding the distinctive nature of professional knowledge is to understand the relationship between theory and practice. One reason for the constant controversy at this site is that there is disagreement not only about the kind of relationship involved here, but also about the nature of theory and the nature of practice. Consequently, in a sense there is no reliable anchor in the dispute.

The common understanding is that theory and practice are *externally* related to each other; that is, either can be grasped and cultivated independently of the other, and that whatever relationships there are between them are contingent. This way of thinking goes along with the common idea that practice might be improved by the *application* of theory to it – I will take up this view in point 15. Here I want to raise the question of what is implied about theory and practice, if we think of them as externally related.

Theory is understood in terms of 'theories' – that is, as intellectual, discursive and codified 'texts' which, if they are not written down, might be – rather than as the activity of theorising. Theory is thought of as universal, in the sense that its truth is not dependent on its location in time and place, and as explanatory, in the sense that the theory will offer scientific (i.e. deductive-nomological) explanations for what happens. Such an understanding of theory is dominant in our world, and is indeed appropriate in some fields, broadly those in which human intentions are not a significant variable, but it is misleading if we are thinking about a field such as teaching or Teacher Education. The 'laws' of teaching not only attempt to explain it, but to explain *and* guide it.

In addition, the common view impoverishes our understanding of practice; it drains it of conceptual and intellectual substance and encourages us to think of it as of less value and importance than theory. It cannot take into view the necessarily theoretical nature of professional practice. The whole thrust of this essay has been opposed to this view of practice. It has been argued that – certainly in a case such as teaching – practice is theory-laden; it is suffused with theory, and cannot be understood independently of the theorising (understandings and concepts) that makes it the practice that it is.

The opposing view can be expressed in the claim that in the case of a professional practice, theory and practice are *internally* related to each other. By this I mean that neither can be adequately pursued, understood, learned or appreciated independently of the other.

But we can now add a further dimension to this claim. Practices can be conceived of as falling along a continuum according to the degree to which they are theory-dependent and, on this continuum, professional practices are towards the end which is more theory-dependent.

15 For reasons such as the foregoing, we can now see why it is inappropriate to think of the theoretical dimensions of professional knowledge as theory to be *applied* to practice. To think in this way would be to misunderstand the kind of theory and theorising that are part of professional knowledge; it would also be to misunderstand the nature of professional practice.

One way of bringing out this point clearly is to say that professional knowledge is not a kind of technical knowledge such as the knowledge one needs to fix the plumbing or put out a fire on an oil rig. Technical knowledge is instrumental; it is a set of techniques for practical problem solving. Technical knowledge can be made more rigorous and effective by the incorporation of scientific theory and explanation.

But, even if some aspects of professional practice make use of technical knowledge, professional practice always involves more. Professional practice involves what has been called 'situational appreciation' (that is, a professionally appropriate perception of what is salient in particular situations), 'judgement-in-context' (professional judgements that take informed account of the details of particular situations) and 'knowledge-in-practice' (as opposed to knowledge of practice)[6].

There have been frequent unsuccessful attempts to try to develop a 'science' of teaching, but if we understand professional practice adequately we will understand why such attempts are, in principle, doomed to failure. There are no 'universal laws of teaching' that might replace professional judgement with the application of algorithms or that could reduce professional practice to pre-specified routines. There are some aspects of teaching that are indeed routinisable (machines might enable learners to learn some of what teachers now spend their time teaching them), but this can never exhaust what is involved. There are logical reasons why the practice of teaching cannot be reduced to a mechanical process and professional judgement cannot be certain. Were a science of teaching possible, Teacher Education would be a much more straightforward matter.

Professional judgement is intrinsic to professional practice and professional knowledge. Professional judgement cannot be 'scientific', but it is, nonetheless, rational. Although the success of the organising of systematic learning can never be guaranteed, this does not imply that it is merely accidental.

Professional Teacher Education should develop the professional knowledge of the learner. This involves improving the rationality and reliability of the professional judgement of the learner.

16 In the National Commission on Higher Education (NCHE) there has recently been vigorous and fruitful debate about the distinction between two 'kinds of knowledge' said to be relevant to higher education. These are

called 'mode 1' and 'mode 2'. Mode 1 knowledge is traditional disciplinary knowledge; mode 2 is problem solving in the context of application, and the knowledge involved is transdisciplinary. For our purposes here, we might ask whether professional knowledge is mode 1 or mode 2 knowledge.

We might at first think that professional knowledge is a kind of mode 2 knowledge; it can be construed as a kind of problem solving in the context of application and also as transdisciplinary. However, there might also be grounds for construing professional knowledge as mode 1 knowledge[7]. 'Education' might be seen as a 'discipline' alongside traditional disciplines such as mathematics or history. But we run into problems on both these construals. Mode 2 knowledge has little to do with constituting or maintaining practices, and mode 1 severs the necessary link between professional knowledge and professional practice.

The distinction between mode 1 and mode 2 knowledge does not have conceptual space for professional knowledge. And if we try to characterise the kind of knowledge involved in higher education exclusively in terms of mode 1 or mode 2, then professional education has no place in higher education.

This suggests shortcomings in that theory. The theory is not so much a theory about 'kinds of knowledge' as about the social organisation of the 'knowledge production'. Although we can accept a close relationship between epistemology and social theory, they cannot be conflated. One cannot draw epistemological conclusions from social arguments.

In addition, this theory encourages us to think about higher education essentially in terms of 'knowledge production' (otherwise known as 'research'), with teaching as an optional extra. But this is a restricted view of higher education and it marginalises professional education, including Teacher Education.

Perhaps 'action research' is an attempt to align professional education with such an interpretation of higher education. But one can seriously doubt whether 'action research' is a kind of 'research' at all, rather than an attempt to retain a sense of the dynamism and flexibility of a living practice and the ways in which the improvement of practice is likely to arise from more adequate reflection-in-practice.

17 In Teacher Education there is a strong tendency to pay insufficient attention to *what* is to be taught, to construe teaching and learning as generic activities, with scant reference to the *content* of what is being taught or learned. In our situation, an underemphasis on the content of teaching is a prevalent and serious problem in schools and other institutions, but also in fields such as adult education[8]. In the case of any teaching, the teacher must know the content being taught. Content knowledge is a necessary precondition for any teaching.

But in considering the distinctive nature of professional knowledge, we have to recognise that the teacher needs an additional kind of knowledge and understanding of the content. We might again think of examples such as that of the brilliant biochemist who is a poor teacher of biochemistry. The teacher needs to be able to dis-embed her knowledge of what is to be taught (the content), and this is an important dimension of teachers' professional knowledge[9].

A teacher needs to understand the content in such a way that she can enable access to it. The practice of teaching, understood as the practice of organising systematic learning, requires a special kind of knowledge of the content, one which we might describe in terms such as the grammar or syntax of what is to be taught. This special kind of content knowledge is an important theoretical dimension of the practice of professional teaching.

Programmes of Teacher Education

The constitutive goal of professional Teacher Education programmes is improved competence in the professional practice of teaching (and this is what should underpin programme design, accreditation [approval] and assessment).

18 In order to design a programme of Teacher Education, one needs an analysis of professional practice which distinguishes between different elements or components of that practice. It is on the basis of an analysis of this kind that the standard distinction between 'subject knowledge', 'methodology' and 'theory' is drawn.

It has recently become fashionable to analyse the practice of teaching into 'competences' and to design Teacher Education programmes with a view to developing these competences. I shall argue that this is a sensible approach to adopt, provided we avoid a behaviouristic interpretation that leads to a technical and mechanistic understanding of the practice of teaching. The various competences into which we analyse the practice should not be isolated from each other and need to be understood in the light of the principle of unity that holds together our concept of teaching. In addition, the assessment of competences requires interpretation, not mere observation.

There are advantages we might gain from thinking of Teacher Education programmes in terms of competences. One major advantage is that it definitively shifts our view away from thinking in terms of propositional knowledge to thinking in terms of practical knowledge, which is eminently appropriate to Teacher Education. The acid test of the success of a Teacher Education programme, or course, is improved competence in practice.

In addition, provided we had a well-founded analysis of the competences of professional practice, competences, or sets of cognate competences, could provide the basis for thinking of Teacher Education programmes in terms of credit-bearing modular courses. This would open up programmes in fruitful ways.

Teacher Education is typically premised on the idea of producing a 'complete' teacher, with the full range of competences of an expert professional schoolteacher. This idea, which has its roots in a holistic conception of professional practice, is inappropriate in the case of initial Teacher Education which, at best, can provide only a good (or bad) start, and is a hindrance if we want to think more broadly and flexibly about Teacher Education in our historical context. Different teachers have different strengths and weaknesses. But this is not a cause for regret; various teachers can make distinctive kinds of contributions to the cooperative practice of organising systematic learning. A more explicit recognition of a division of labour in teaching might provide an important clue to how to address some of our main current problems (think of the problem of rising learner–teacher ratios) and Teacher Education programmes could be designed with this in mind.

In the realm of continuing Teacher Education (for *all* teachers, not only schoolteachers) we can think flexibly in terms of courses targeted to the development of particular competences. As needs change, courses could be modified or new courses developed.

The broadening of the conception of teaching recommended earlier in this essay requires us to think imaginatively about what kinds of courses might be appropriate for different kinds of teachers, and modular course design, based on a reliable analysis of 'competences', is likely to open up the possibilities of doing so.

Finally, greater degrees of cooperation between various providers of Teacher Education, and cross-institutional mobility, will be encouraged in a system of credit-bearing modular courses.

19 In the light of the arguments put forward in this essay, we might briefly speculate on four fundamental categories of competence that need to be taken into account in Teacher Education programmes.

   (a) The first would be to develop a strong and properly grounded conception of teaching and an effective grasp of the definitive ideals of the professional practice of organising systematic learning. This would involve some understanding of the history and traditions of this practice, and the ways in which it has been pursued in other places and times. But it would also involve coming to understand the ethical ideals that frame the practice and provide the moral, political and social justification for its support in society.

     Amongst other things, developing this competence would involve distinguishing between the accidental features of the practice, which are the product of the technologies available at particular times and places as well as the conditions and contexts within which it has been pursued, and the definitive features of the practice.

     We might comment that this category of competence is of particular importance in our context because of the deep and widespread prevalence of misunderstandings of the justificatory aim of the practice of teaching and the nature of systematic learning.

   (b) The second would be the kind of second-order knowledge of content needed in order for it to be possible to teach it. The teacher needs to know how to make the content accessible to the learners she is teaching, and this requires an articulated conceptual understanding of the content. I have discussed this matter in point 17 above, and here I shall add two additional comments.

Straightforward content knowledge is a necessary condition for teaching it, in spite of the fact that it is not sufficient. I have already mentioned, but it is certainly worth re-emphasising, that in our context a prevalent deficiency in teaching (not only school teaching) is the lack of an adequate understanding of the content being taught. It is also worth re-emphasising that the professional knowledge of the teacher, in this regard, *presupposes* standard content knowledge. A teacher of mathematics, for instance, must have an adequate understanding of mathematics to provide the platform for the kind of understanding of mathematics she needs in order to be able to teach it. In our context, there are good grounds in some cases for emphasising the straightforward teaching of content in Teacher Education courses, and this is likely to be especially important in thinking of continuing Teacher Education.

The standard phrase 'subject knowledge' applies to only a restricted range of kinds of teaching, those typically associated with primary/secondary/tertiary schooling. But any teaching – be it teaching someone how to repair a motor car, or how to grow vegetables on a small piece of ground – has some content, and the point made here thus applies to any kind of teaching.

(c) Knowledge of the social, organisational and institutional contexts, and other conditions of the practice of teaching, is the third kind of competence. What I have in mind here is an adequate pragmatic understanding of the ways in which structural factors both enable and place limits on the possible implementations of the practice of teaching.

(d) A fourth competence, which is the principle competence of a professional teacher, is competence in organising systematic learning. It should be clear that this competence has a logical status different from the previous three; it presupposes and draws on them. Professional judgement has a decisive role to play here, as here considerations about what it is possible for the particular learners in question to learn, and expertise in inventing ways of enabling them to learn the relevant content, are paramount. The issue of 'course design' is crucial.

20 Programmes of professional Teacher Education are defined by their practical goal – to improve competence in the practice of teaching. But much Teacher Education is driven by a shallow conception of practice, and we should vigorously oppose tendencies to de-theorise teaching. The professional practice of teaching is necessarily theoretical (in an appropriate understanding of 'theoretical'), and Teacher Education programmes need to be designed, accredited and evaluated with this in view.

The increasing tendency to move towards 'school-based' Teacher Education, to understand it as a kind of apprenticeship, needs to be handled with great care and some skepticism, especially in our historical context. This tendency is based on a theory of learning by modelling an expert practitioner, but expert practitioners are in short supply in our context. And, in any case, the success of such an approach depends not only on the *quality* but also the qualities of the models available, especially the depth and rigour of the kind of understanding of the practice of teaching indicated in point 19(a).

'School-based' Teacher Education has the virtue of emphasising the *practical* goal of professional education, but it runs the risk of being enormously conservative. In our context, we need an overall dramatic improvement in the practice of teaching and, provided we understand what kind of theorising we need, good theory is, potentially, one of the most effective catalysts of change and innovation.

The academic study of education

Professional and academic programmes are commonly confused in education, and we should distinguish clearly between them. The goal of academic programmes in education is improved competence in the practice of educational research.

21 There is a widespread tendency to fail to distinguish between professional and academic programmes in the field of education. But this is detrimental to both kinds of programmes.

The goals of these two kinds of programmes are different. Professional programmes set out to develop competences in the practice of teaching; academic programmes set out to develop competences in a different practice – that of the rigorous study of education. There might, indeed, be overlaps between the two constellations of competences and their characteristic excellences, but they are not synonymous. The distinction made here between professional and academic programmes does not depend on 'education' being a unified mode 1 academic discipline, although I think there are grounds for such a view.

Perhaps a failure to distinguish adequately between the two kinds of programmes lies in a confusion between the aims and the effects of programmes of systematic learning. The aims of a programme provide the principles for course (or programme) design, the evaluation of a course and the assessment of learner progress. But a programme might have effects that lie outside of its aims. Thus, although it is not the aim of a programme of the academic study of education to enable a person to be more successful in the practice of professional teaching, this might be one of its effects. However, we would not judge such an academic course to be a failure if it did not lead to improvement in the practice of professional teaching.

Perhaps it is worth adding that I am here referring not to the academic study of content – I have already discussed the role of this kind of study in professional education – but to the academic study of education. And this kind of academic study – including the kind of research to which it is dedicated – has importance and significance in its own right. If it were found that it made little contribution to the professional education of teachers, this would not be a ground for rationalising it out of existence.

In some conventions there is a distinction between degrees and diplomas, with the former (more) firmly linked to academic competences and the latter (more) firmly linked to professional competences; a diploma is not a 'lesser' kind of degree, but something qualitatively different.

I think that this convention has much to recommend it, and I do not think that it is a good idea to see Bachelor of Education (BEd[10]) and Master of Education (MEd) degrees as 'further professional education'. Such degrees are not a kind of INSET, as seems to be assumed by the discussion in the Committee on Teacher Education Policy (COTEP) document of July 1995[11], and in the statistical tables provided in the National Teacher Education Audit[12]. In these terms the phrase 'an all-graduate profession' refers to the academic level at which teachers of school subjects are qualified in their content knowledge, rather than to re-labelling professional qualifications as degrees.

22 This line of argument leads in the direction of support for the view that the remuneration of teachers should be tied to their professional qualifications (keeping in mind that qualifications in the content to be taught are a prerequisite for professional education) rather than their qualifications in the academic study of education. A better academic, even one whose field of study is education, is not necessarily a better teacher.

Conclusion

By way of a summarising conclusion to this essay, I shall gather together its central claims.

Teacher Education is a kind of education that enables someone to become more competent in the professional practice of organising systematic learning, and nurtures their commitment to do so.

The professional development of teachers is urgently needed in South Africa. The professional development of teachers includes, but is not exhausted by, Teacher Education.

Teacher Education should be understood as a form of professional education. Professional education is a kind of career education that straddles the commonly assumed boundary between vocational and academic education, and includes an ethical dimension. Professional education develops the professional knowledge of the learner.

Professional knowledge is practical knowledge harnessed to an ethical ideal. It is a qualitatively distinct kind of knowledge, different from academic and technical knowledge, although it draws on both.

The constitutive goal of professional Teacher Education programmes is improved competence in the professional practice of teaching, and this is what should underpin programme design, accreditation (approval) and assessment.

Professional and academic programmes are commonly confused in education, and we should distinguish clearly between them. The goal of academic programmes in education is improved competence in the practice of educational research.

Notes

1 This account of practice is drawn from Alasdair MacIntyre, *After Virtue*, London: Duckworth, 1981.

2 Wally Morrow, 'Accountability and the idea of a profession' (1980) in *Chains of Thought*, Johannesburg: Southern Book Publishers, 1989.

3 This shortcoming has subsequently been redressed. The South African Council for Educators (SACE) was established by an Act of Parliament in 2000. See Government Gazette #21431, 2 August 2000.

4 HLA Hart, *The Concept of Law*, Oxford: Oxford University Press, 1961: ' "Sanctions" are required not as the normal motive for obedience, but as the *guarantee* that those who would voluntarily obey shall not be sacrificed to those who would not...what reason demands is *voluntary* cooperation within a *coercive* system.' As quoted in H Sockett, 'Towards a professional code of teaching' in P Gordon (ed.), *Is Teaching a Profession?* London: Heinemann, 1985, p. 37.

5 Ronald Barnett, *The Limits of Competence*, Bristol: SRHE and the Open University Press, 1994.

6 See, for example, Donald Schon, *The Reflective Practitioner: How Professionals Think in Action*, Novato, CA.:, Arena, 1991; and Shirley Pendlebury, 'Luck, knowledge and excellence in teaching', unpublished DEd thesis, UWC, 1991.

7 J Muller, 'Knowledge and higher education', pp. 15–16, NCHE Taskgroup 2, November 1995. In this paper Muller seems to understand professional knowledge as a kind of mode 1 knowledge: 'There may well also be strategies of *resistance* to mode 2. We should expect to find various strategies for shoring up or insulating the centrality of mode 1 in the face of burgeoning mode 2. Medical faculties have for years practised a form of *defensive incorporation* with respect to demands for community health, creating an adjunct category of "barefoot professionals" alongside the orthodox mode 1 professional.

8 See Crispin Hemson, 'In defence of content', unpublished paper presented at the Kenton Conference 1995, for a discussion of the way in which adult education courses tend to underplay the issue of content.

9 Eric Hoyle & Peter John, *Professional Knowledge and Professional Practice*, London: Cassell, 1995 (p. 65) refer to Lee Shulman (1987) 'Knowledge and teaching: foundations of the new reform' in *Harvard Education Review* 57, as follows: 'Shulman's discussion suggests that expertise in teaching requires knowledge not only of the substantive and syntactic knowledge of the subject, but also an integrated and conceptual understanding of the domain itself. Thus pedagogical content knowledge is unique to teachers and forms a central part of their professional knowledge.'

10 Subsequently renamed BEd (Hons).

11 Committee on Teacher Education Policy, Norms and Standards and Governance Structures for Teacher Education, Pretoria, July 1995.

12 Jane Hofmeyr & Graham Hall, *The National Teacher Education Audit: Synthesis Report*, Pretoria: National Department of Education, 1995.

6 *What is teachers' work?*

(Paper presented at Kenton Conference, October 2005)[1]

Teaching is impossible.

> Lee S Shulman, *The Wisdom of Practice*

The job of teachers is to teach

But Shulman tells us that teaching is impossible. If this is true then we have a bizarre situation. Most of us here (and thousands of others) have devoted our lives to an impossible activity, and many of us have spent years of our lives on the (impossible) task of trying to teach others how to engage in an impossible activity!

Surely Shulman can't mean what he says? After all, he himself had the reputation of having been a teacher of some note and, surely, this included teaching? Perhaps his statement that teaching is impossible is merely a polemical device to emphasise something else?

Of course this is the explanation. Here is the quotation in context:

> Teaching is impossible. If we simply add together all
> that is expected of a typical teacher and take note of the
> circumstances in which those activities are to be carried
> out, the sum makes greater demands than any individual
> can possibly fulfil.[2]

What we need to notice here is Shulman's easy conceptual slide from the word 'teaching' to the word 'teacher'. His first sentence says that *teaching* is impossible, but the next sentence refers to all that is expected of a typical *teacher*, and the circumstances in which teachers work. So he really must mean that given current (USA 1983) expectations of teachers and the circumstances in which they work, it is not possible for them to teach. But perhaps this is a parochial comment about teachers' work in the USA in 1983? Perhaps the situation is different in other places and at other times?

In the dark ages (South Africa 1962), when I first began my career as a teacher, I was soon so overwhelmed by the work that I ceased to have any life outside of teaching. My training had somehow conveyed to me a conception of teaching that proved to be impossible in practice, and a source of constant professional guilt. I had gained the idea that good teaching involved being responsive to each of the individual pupils for whom I was responsible – to get to know their quirks and uniquenesses and to gear my teaching to those. In particular, I had been taught that a key element of successful English teaching was for each pupil to write at least one piece each week, and for me, as their teacher, to comment in writing on their individual efforts so as to provide sensitive, formative feedback to each budding author. Had I been responsible for, say, 15 pupils, I suppose these tasks would have been feasible, and I might even have had a few hours left over for a personal life of some kind. But I was teaching 7 classes, with an average of 35 pupils in each – a total of some 245 pupils. Even to learn all their names was a major task – never mind being responsive to all their individual uniquenesses and providing well-targeted feedback to each of 245 written pieces each week.

And then, in preparing this essay, I came across a website[3] about a National Agreement in the UK, signed by employers, government and unions in January 2003, called 'Raising Standards and Tracking Workload'. This Agreement was an 'acknowledgement' that schools have to deal with a number of issues, amongst which were:
- Workload is the major reason cited by teachers for leaving the profession;
- Over 30 per cent of a teacher's working week prior to the National Agreement was spent on non-teaching activities;
- Teachers generally had a poor work/life balance.

At the heart of this Agreement is a concerted attempt to 'free teachers to teach' by transferring to support staff all administrative and other tasks not intrinsically related to teaching. 'Cutting unnecessary burdens on teachers is essential to ensuring a valued and motivated teaching profession.'

These are three examples, at 20-year intervals, in vastly different places, of a widespread problem: conscientious teachers are constantly chronically overloaded. But what causes this problem, and why does it remain stubbornly unresolved?

Let's go back to the beginning. The job of teachers is to teach. This seems obviously true and quite straightforward. It is probably true, although it is not at all straightforward.

When Shulman tells us that teaching is impossible, he is thinking of teaching as necessarily embedded in the accidents and contingencies of 'expectations' and 'circumstances' (context). In my early days as a teacher, I was overwhelmed by my work because of a disjunction between the conception of teaching with which I was working and the number of pupils in relation to whom I was attempting to embody that conception. And the UK project of 'Raising Standards and Tracking Workload' assumes that we are quite clear about which activities are 'non-teaching activities', and about which burdens are 'unnecessary burdens on teachers'. The ringing cry that we need to 'free teachers to teach' has considerable appeal – but it all depends on what we mean by 'to teach'.

Our problem is that we are here embrangled at the intersection between a concept of what it is to teach and the institutional and other contextual realities of the situations in which those whose professional task is to teach try to carry out this activity; or the intersection between the idea of teaching and the roles and responsibilities we ascribe to those employed as 'teachers', and the conditions in which they are expected to carry out these roles and responsibilities. And it is difficult, as the example of Shulman's slide from 'teaching' to 'teacher' shows, to disentangle these two strands in our thinking. And it is especially difficult if we are skeptical about theory or abstract concepts, and are taken with the practical idea that learnerships provide the royal road to learning how to teach.

Teaching in South Africa

It is sometimes claimed that in post-1994 South Africa we have developed a bold and imaginative (a 'magnificent') set of education policies, admired across the world, but that our problem is lack of implementation. Why do we have this problem? Who is to blame?

Well, in the first place we have some educational institutions (at all levels of the system) that remain stuck in Apartheid traditions and have not yet embraced 'transformation'. Thus, for example, they persist in implementing exclusionary admission policies and non-democratic modes of management and organisation.

But, in the second place, we have thousands of deficient schoolteachers, teachers who do not have the competences, or perhaps the willingness, to implement our policies capably. Educational change depends on what teachers do and think[4], but we have a huge problem when such a high proportion of our teachers have not yet accomplished the 'paradigm shift' they need to if they are going to be competent implementers of our fine policies.

It is not that we have not made considerable efforts to overcome these problems. We have, for instance, prioritised the issue of educational management. We have offered many workshops for education managers and literally thousands of 'educators' are signed up for advanced certificates, honours degrees and even master's degrees[5] in the field of educational management. Indeed, in some cases the offering of education management programmes has proved to be a lifeline for Faculties of Education in the face of declining numbers of recruits for initial Teacher Education programmes.

And in respect to teachers, we have devoted massive human and financial resources to overcoming their deficiencies. We have concentrated on training, or retraining, maths–science–technology teachers, and poured a king's ransom into this field. Over the past years, we have released teachers from their normal duties for a week at a time to attend workshops focusing on accomplishing the needed 'paradigm shift'[6] and training them in the implementation of the Revised National Curriculum Statement. But, although we can claim some successes[7], we don't seem to be moving very fast[8], and while we persist in intoning the inspiring slogan 'The Right to Quality Education for All', we are faced with the haunting thought that the quality of schooling for, perhaps, 80 per cent of our population might actually have deteriorated over the past decade.

Education transformation in South Africa

Let us take a quick tour through some elements of education transformation in South Africa. At the bottom stands Outcomes-Based Education (OBE), originally marketed as *the* (only) alternative to Apartheid education[9]. At the root of OBE is the entirely sensible idea that the way to assess the success of any teaching is in terms of its 'outcomes' for learners. What matters at the end of the day is what the learners learn. But this sensible idea is suffocatingly wrapped in a range of other matters which, piled on top of each other, take the workload of teachers towards impossibility.

We say, for example, that teaching needs to be freed from the dominance of textbooks. Teachers themselves need to design learning programmes sensitive to their learners and responsive to their contexts, and develop appropriate resources and other learner support material, in order to achieve the nationally mandated learning outcomes. It is, after all, 'obvious' that there can be different 'learning pathways' to the same outcomes, and teachers need to map out suitable pathways for their own learners. 'Process' is all-important, and the old-fashioned emphasis on 'content' is merely a hangover from pre-OBE paradigms, especially Apartheid education.

As further suffocating wrapping on the work of teachers there is then the nightmare of 'continuous assessment' – known as CASS by the *cognoscenti*. The idea is that teachers need continuously to track the progress of their learners, in order to provide them with constant 'formative feedback' – that is, feedback that will enable each learner to understand how to improve their progress towards the pre-specified learning outcomes. CASS is often considered as a supplement to formal examinations, reflected in the use of 'year marks' in computing the final grade for a course. In some cases, CASS is understood as a more reliable form of assessment of learner achievements than high-stakes 'summative examinations', and it is felt that it should replace these hazardous examinations. There are, of course, hazards in the case of CASS as well. Frequently, 'continuous assessment' turns out to be little more than an unbroken stream of tests, projects and exercises that merely spread the misery. Learners are constantly under the burden of knowing that everything they do will be 'assessed' and might have consequences for their eventual 'success'. And teachers tend to be driven to such frenzy about assessment and portfolios[10] that they have little time to teach. But these hazards, we say to ourselves, are likely to be the product of teachers not understanding the true purpose of CASS; with more workshops and training we can overcome them.

And then there is 'learner-centred education', another half-truth. Of course, any effective teaching needs to take account of the learners for whom it is intended. But what does 'take account of the learners' encompass? On the one hand, we know that it is useless to try to teach quadratic equations to learners who do not yet have a grasp of the number system or to teach computer literacy to a learner who thinks that a laptop is a kind of dance. But it is also true that teaching becomes, if not useless, then at least less likely to succeed, if the learner is suffering from the trauma of having recently lost a parent to

AIDS, or whose friend has been abducted on the way to school, or who comes from a household so destitute that they are lucky to get something to eat more than twice a week. This list could go on. The question is, does learner-centred education imply that teaching includes taking account of the detailed conditions and circumstances of the personal lives of learners? And what happens if a teacher has not one learner[11], but a couple of hundred?

And then we need to think about the conditions in which a high proportion of schoolteachers in South Africa try to teach. The HIV prevalence rates, the Poverty Index, the levels of adult illiteracy and widespread unemployment, the lack of functioning and maintained school buildings and equipment, the failure of the delivery of stationery and books, the breakdown of school feeding schemes, the increasing linguistic and other diversities of learners, never mind the levels of gang-related activities, are not merely statistical abstractions to be included in annual reports of government departments. They are indicators of harsh and inescapable realities faced by many schoolteachers on a daily basis. The miracle is that any teaching takes place at all.

The Norms and Standards for Educators *and the inflated role of teachers*

The *Norms and Standards for Educators*[12] remains the ruling policy for Teacher Education and the recognition of qualifications for the purposes of employment in education. But it entangles the two strands of our thinking – a conception of teaching, and the roles of those employed as teachers – and, partly due to that, inflates the work of teachers beyond the capacity of all but the exceptionally talented and obsessively committed. Let's examine the evidence.

The *Norms and Standards* announces that it will use the word 'educator' to refer to the full range of employees in the education system:

> The term *educator* in this policy statement applies to all those persons who teach or educate other persons or who provide professional educational services at any public school, further education and training institution or departmental office. The term includes educators in the classroom, heads of departments, deputy-principals, principals, education development officers, district and regional managers and systems managers. (p. 9)

We are already in trouble. The homogenising of these different roles in the education system – from teachers to district managers – occludes the central role of teaching[13] in any education. The phrase 'educators in the classroom' – which presumably refers to teachers – assumes that teaching takes place only 'inside classrooms'. And more corrupting than these troubles is the use of the word 'educator' for the diverse employees of the Department of Education[14]. One trouble here is that this move completely smudges the word 'education', disperses its moral aura and deprives us of our chief justification for committing a significant percentage of our public resources to schooling.

Thinking now of teaching, consider the way in which the *Norms and Standards* has generated a conception of teaching, articulated in terms of 'roles', which has seeped into the whole education system:

> The policy describes the *roles*, their associated set of *applied competences* (norms) and *qualifications* (standards) for the development of educators. It also establishes key strategic objectives for the development of learning programmes, qualifications and standards for educators. These norms and standards provide a basis for providers to develop programmes and qualifications that will be recognised by the Department of Education for purposes of employment. (p. 9)

Seven roles are specified:

1   Learning mediator
2   Interpreter and designer of learning programmes and materials
3   Leader, administrator and manager
4   Scholar, researcher and lifelong learner
5   Community, citizenship and pastoral role
6   Assessor
7   Learning area / subject / discipline / phase specialist. (pp. 13–14)

These roles are 'meant to serve as a *description* of what it means to be a competent educator'[15] (p. 13). The roles are further explained in 'a manner appropriate for an initial teaching qualification', first in a brief description on pages 13–14, and then in considerable detail on pages 15–22, in terms of three interconnected kinds (p. 10) of *Applied competence – Practical, Foundational, and Reflexive.*

But this description of what it means to be a competent educator is lethally ambiguous. It is attempting to do at least two logically distinct things at the same time: to specify the requirements of an employee of the Department of Education – something like a high-level 'job description' – and to provide a formal definition of teaching (educating). These two different things are run together as if there is no significant difference between them. Earlier in this essay I noted Shulman's easy conceptual slide from the word 'teaching' to the word 'teacher'; here we have a related problem.

Let us provide ourselves with a little bit of technical terminology to help us to articulate the problem. We can distinguish between the *material* and the *formal* elements of a concept. The material elements refer to the ways in which an object or action may vary without ceasing to be an object or action of a particular kind; the formal element is the reason we provide for saying that it is an object or action of a particular kind. Without the formal element we would not know how to specify the material elements; a list of the material elements presupposes the formal element[16].

Kovesi introduces this distinction in relation to those pieces of furniture we call 'tables'. The material elements of tables are 'any characteristics in which the object may vary without ceasing to be a table'. Thus, the materials out of which we construct tables, their shape and whether they have three legs or four are the material elements of tables. By contrast, the formal element of tables provides us with 'an answer to the question of why we call a large variety of objects "tables" and refuse the word to other objects'.[17]

Using this terminology we can now say that the description of 'what it means to be a competent educator', which is central to the *Norms and Standards*, fails to distinguish between the formal element of teaching and its material elements, a failure that carries enormous consequences[18]. What the *Norms and Standards* in effect does, is to provide a list of some of the possible material elements of teaching (in terms of the seven roles and their elaboration) and present it as a formal definition of teaching. This is one reason that description comes across as utopian.

A formal definition of teaching (one which specifies its formal element) is not context-specific; material elements are necessarily rooted in specific contexts. But the *Norms and Standards* description of what it means to be a competent educator is context-blind, and this is one reason it leads to the overload of teachers.

The seven roles outlined in the *Norms and Standards* ignore the reality of the conditions in which the majority of teachers in South Africa work and, in this way, inflate the conception of their workload. For a conscientious teacher, this characterisation of their work is likely to be a source of acute professional guilt as they struggle to cope on a daily basis; 'it makes greater demands than any individual can possibly fulfil'. Similarly, it ignores the manifest differences between the institutional contexts in which teachers work. The work of a teacher in an efficiently organised and functioning school[19] is very different from the work of a teacher in a dysfunctional or barely functioning school. The seven roles seem to be assumed to be the roles of each individual teacher, and there is no suggestion that there might be a division of labour in an institutional setting that allocates these different roles to different individuals.

Careful readers of the *Norms and Standards* might now point out that it contains another set of distinctions, which show that it acknowledges the difference between a concept of teaching and the job descriptions of departmental employees. In the initial characterisation of Role 4 we find that 'The educator will achieve ongoing personal, academic, occupational and professional growth...' (p. 13), and in Role 7 we find a reference to 'professional or occupational practice' (p. 14). Subsequently, in the section on the Qualifications Framework (p. 23ff) we find that 'Although the BEd (Honours) must include some specialisation and focus on research, the nature of these will vary depending on whether an academic, professional or occupational focus is chosen.' In addition, this section points out that the purpose of the Postgraduate Diploma in Education is 'to accredit advanced and specialised occupational, academic and professional study' (p. 25). But these 'distinctions' remain at a rhetorical level; they are not reflected in the seven roles, nor used elsewhere in the *Norms and Standards*. They do not provide a conceptual framework for the discussion and, if anything, they further reinforce the idea that there is no significant distinction between the idea of teaching and the job descriptions of employees of the Departments of Education.

To clarify what is at stake here, consider the difference between the two questions: 'What is waitrons'[20] work?' and 'What is (medical) doctors' work?'

There is little mileage in trying to provide an abstract answer to the question: 'What is waitrons' work?' We have to ask: 'Which waitrons? Where?' In different situations the job descriptions of waitrons is likely to be vastly different. In one restaurant or hotel, waitrons might be required to set the tables; in another, they might be required to bring the food to the tables; in a third, they might be required to open the wine bottles, but not bring the ice bucket, etc. The question 'What is waitrons' work?' cannot be answered in 'general' terms; we would need to consider the various job descriptions of waitrons in various contexts.

By contrast, we can very well provide an abstract (context-blind) answer to the question: 'What is (medical) doctors' work?' We have a conception[21] of doctors' work (we have some sense of a formal element here) that is not embedded in particular contexts. The work of doctors is to do what they can, in the light of their knowledge of medicine, to contribute to the health and flourishing of those who are ill, injured or diseased. Unless a doctor is doing this, in whatever circumstance she finds herself, she is not doing (medical) doctors' work. We can of course add that in specific contexts – say in a hospital – there might very well be other work that doctors will need to do depending, for instance, on the availability of nursing staff and perhaps even equipment.

What we now have to determine is whether the question 'What is teachers' work?' is logically more like 'What is waitrons' work?' or 'What is (medical) doctors' work?' Despite its being context-insensitive, and doffing the cap to 'academic, professional and occupational practices', the *Norms and Standards* treats teachers' work as logically more akin to waitrons' work than to (medical) doctors' work. The baby has been thrown out with the bath water; Departments of Education, as the employers of teachers, can define teachers' work according to their requirements as employers[22] and, by a stroke of luck, have a ready answer to the failures of policy implementation.

A National Framework for Teacher Education *and the practice of teaching*

In the opening section of this essay, I mentioned the widespread problem of conscientious teachers being constantly and chronically overloaded and then posed the question of why this problem remains stubbornly unresolved. One main claim in this essay is that a failure to recognise the distinction between formal and material elements of the concept of teaching provides at least part of the answer. In our Teacher Education programmes and elsewhere we repeatedly define the work of teachers in terms of its material elements and, because we think we are providing a formal definition, we ignore the restraints of the contexts within which teachers are expected to teach.

The report of the Ministerial Committee on Teacher Education, called *A National Framework for Teacher Education in South Africa*, 16 June 2005[23], was an attempt to overcome this problem. In the very first recommendation there is an articulation of the formal element of teaching:

Recommendation A1

Retrieve the word 'teaching', understand it as the practice of organising systematic learning, and relocate it at the heart of how we think about, plan and organise the education system.

There are a number of points to make here. One is that there were those in the Department of Education who objected to the words 'retrieve' and 'relocate'. It was said that these words unjustly imply that the department had lost sight of teaching and did not prioritise it in their planning or recognise that it is the core function of any schooling or education. But we do not need to pause at this dispute, as there are more important issues to bring to light.

Teaching is characterised as a practice. This carries some weight. To call something a 'practice' is to locate it in a history and a tradition; practices are not invented by individuals, and anyone who engages in a practice must acknowledge that the standards of success and excellence are neither subjective nor imposed by those with institutional and systemic power. They are interpersonal standards agreed by those in the community of practice.

Furthermore, teaching is characterised as 'the practice of organising systematic learning'[24]. The word 'organising' does not imply anything specific about how or in which setting this organising is to be done; it is conceptually tied neither to classrooms nor to class sizes nor to any particular teaching methods. It might, for example, include preparing learning material, but it might not; it might include live performance in front of a group of learners, but it might not; it might include using a textbook, but it might not; it might include continuous assessment, but it might not; it might include using the telephone or email, but it might not, etc. The word 'organising' leaves unspecified these material elements – and it is thus, clearly, part of the formal element of the practice of teaching.

Along the same lines, to say that teaching is 'the practice of organising systematic learning' leaves entirely unspecified whether it is individuals or teams that engage in this practice. Individual teachers can teach, but so can teams of teachers making various contributions to a shared goal. And this, again, shows that what we have in view here is the formal element of teaching as opposed to a specification of its material elements.

Teaching is not impossible, but it needs to be differently pursued in different circumstances. But we make it impossible if we 'define' it in terms of its material elements while ignoring the actual conditions in which teaching is expected to take place.

The second recommendation brings teachers into view:

Recommendation A2

Accept that professional teachers are the essential resource of the education system, and configure our programmes of Teacher Education (IPET and CPTD)[25] and support systems to reinforce the professional competences and commitments of teachers.

The key factor to notice here is that 'teaching' and 'teachers' are located in separate recommendations – there is no easy conceptual slide from teaching to teachers. Teaching is a practice, and professional teachers are those 'with the educated competences and abiding commitments to engage successfully'[26] in this practice. An adequate answer to the question 'What is teachers' work?' must necessarily include a reference to teaching, but in particular contexts it might include other aspects as well.

The reason for this is that, unlike the work of waitrons, the work of teachers must be within the boundaries of the formal element of the concept of teaching. Unless someone is doing something that exhibits some characteristic or characteristics of what is involved in 'organising systematic learning', they are not doing teachers' work, but something else – perhaps the work of clerks, administrators, police officers, counsellors, welfare agents, social workers, gardeners or sports coaches.

The functions of schools and teachers' work

Part of the reason for the heavy workload of teachers revolves around the functions of schools in our society. We can say that the constitutive functions of schools are, broadly, to provide both teaching and caregiving for the young[27]. There are some views of teaching that do not clearly distinguish between these two functions, but we need to insist that, although there is a sense in which the two functions are related to each other, they are not the same. 'Organising systematic learning' might, in some ways, involve seeing to the preconditions of learning, but we can rapidly run beyond the boundary of the formal element of the practice of teaching.

The traditional model of schools assumes that the young live in secure family settings. Such settings were assumed to include literate (middle-class) members, and to provide reliable shelter, nutrition, clothing, emotional support, cognitive stimulation, monitoring of health status, protection from violence, and so on. In such an ideal situation, the 'caregiving' functions of schools can be secondary relative to their 'teaching' functions; the need for caregiving is likely to be limited to relatively rare cases. And, partly for this reason, it could be assumed that 'teachers' would, by and large[28], take on the caregiving functions of schools in addition to teaching.

But in our context, the caregiving functions of schools need to be dramatically expanded. The reasons for this are obvious to most of us. They include the disruptions of community safety nets as urbanisation proceeds apace; the increasing rarity of two-parent nuclear families with two or three offspring; the increasing proportion of orphans and vulnerable children in our schools; the high levels of adult illiteracy; the increasing immiseration of the already poor; the high levels of unemployment; the disastrous impacts of the HIV/AIDS pandemic; and the increasing levels of violence and lack of safety in the streets. In many instances, it is already the case that teachers are so overwhelmed by these caregiving functions that they have precious little time and energy to devote to teaching.

The question for us as a society is whether, if we understand schools as welfare institutions for the young, we expect teachers to be responsible for this function in addition to teaching. Is part of our answer to the question 'What is teachers' work?' that it includes caregiving for the young[29]?

If we cast our mind back briefly to the UK National Agreement – 'Raising Standards and Tracking Workload' – we will notice that at the heart of that project is 'freeing teachers to teach', and their main issue is to free teachers of 'administrative and other tasks not intrinsically related to teaching'. While in our context we need to agree that we should develop strategies to reduce the administrative tasks of teachers, perhaps, as in the UK, by employing competent administrative clerks to do this work, this is only the tip of the iceberg of the current workload of a great number of our teachers. Our context forces on them a range of labour-intensive and energy-consuming responsibilities not 'intrinsically related to teaching'. Given the cost of educating and employing teachers, perhaps we need to consider whether it might be not only cost-saving, but more effective on both counts as well, to employ in schools people whose job will be to be responsible for the caregiving functions of schools.

Learning to teach

Any Teacher Education programme[30] is based on two presuppositions, linked to each other: (i) an answer to the question 'What is teachers' work?' and (ii) a particular idea of the schools or other institutions in which the students will seek employment.

We can again go back to the beginning. The job of teachers is to teach. And this implies that the principal task of Teacher Education programmes is to teach their students how to teach. But we are now in a position to see that this involves developing an understanding of both the formal and the material elements of teaching; both a constitutive conception of teaching and a set of suggestions for how it might be embodied in a range of contexts and conditions. A Teacher Education programme that fails to devote sufficient attention to both of these elements is to that extent deficient.

The Departments of Education themselves (reinforced by the *Norms and Standards*), and indeed even many higher education institutions that provide Teacher Education, have a strong tendency to argue that the only justifiable answer to the question 'What is teachers' work?' lies in faithfully preparing teachers for the roles they will be required to undertake in schools, especially the implementation of the Revised National Curriculum Statement. The fashionable idea that learnerships are the royal road to learning how to teach appears to be based on the same answer to the question. But this, as we can now clearly see, is to understand teaching in terms of its material elements. And this is a trap. If my class is too big, or the stationery has not been delivered, or there are no desks for the learners, then teaching is 'impossible' and I might as well stay away from school or sit in the sun with my fellow teachers and complain about the corruptions and inefficiency of the education department.

Programmes of Teacher Education typically assume a relatively stable schooling system with relatively predictable roles for teachers in that system. Thus, they train teachers for specific phases of the school system or specific learning areas, while ignoring the fact that once they get a job in a school they are likely to have to teach in whichever phase or learning area the school has a gap. In addition, the school curriculum – even the Revised National Curriculum Statement – is a transitory organisation of knowledge that can change quite unpredictably. So, unless we think of our Teacher Education programmes as providing teachers with a deeper understanding of some field of knowledge – deeper than the current school curriculum – we are setting them up for frustration and failure in their professional careers.

A principal shortcoming of most Teacher Education programmes[31] is that they fail to reflect a distinction between the formal and the material elements of teaching. They thus tend to define teaching in terms of a favoured set of teaching methods that presuppose particular facilities, conditions and resources. If students remain mired at this level, the level of the material elements of teaching, they are unable to develop their capacity as professional agents. And, unless the students come to an effective practical understanding of the formal element of teaching, a non-context-bound conception of teaching, they are unlikely to be able to develop the flexible competences that will enable them to teach no matter how unpromising the contexts and conditions may seem. The key question that those learning how to teach need to learn how to answer is: How can I organise systematic learning in *this* context and *these* conditions?

If we continue to muddle the formal and the material elements of teaching, we will continue to produce teachers who will be faced with a suicidal workload and who will lack the professional autonomy and flexibility that is, and will increasingly be, required in the rough and volatile world in which we try to achieve the ideal of providing quality education for all.

Notes

1 An updated version of the original, this essay has been submitted to the publishers of *Journal of Education* (University of KwaZulu-Natal), who acknowledge its publication in this volume.

2 Lee S Shulman (1983), 'Autonomy and obligation – the remote control of teaching' in *The Wisdom of Practice: Essays on Teaching, Learning, and Learning to Teach*, San Francisco: Jossey-Bass, 2004, p. 151.

3 <www.teachernet.gov.uk/remodelling>. The quotations that follow are from the Agreement.

4 MG Fullan, *The New Meaning of Educational Change*, London: Cassell, 1991, p. 117.

5 We must keep at bay the thought that a reason for the popularity of such programmes amongst teachers is that they aspire to find a career path that will provide a route out of teaching and into 'management'. (We all want to be 'managers'.)

6 A 'paradigm shift' in a week!

7 See DoE (2005b), *An Assessment of 10 Years of Education and Training in South Africa*, available at <http://education.pwv.gov.za>.

8 Because we should be deeply ashamed of them, we need to bury in a little endnote the devastating results of the Third International Mathematics and Science Study (TIMSS) studies and the depressing indications of the Grade 3 and 6 systemic studies.

9 See Essay 7.

10 In recent times 'portfolios' of learners' work, put together over a period of time, have become a fashionable form of assessment.

11 JJ Rousseau can be regarded as the inspiration for 250 years of thinking about 'child-centred education' – at least in the western world. *Emile* is premised on the idea that there will be a 'tutor' for each pupil (a 1:1 pupil–teacher ratio!), and he adds, for good measure, that: 'A tutor is not bound to his charge by the ties of nature as the father is, and so is entitled to choose his pupil...' (As quoted in W Boyd, *Emile for Today*, London: Heinemann, 1956, p. 20).

12 See DoE 2000.

13 'Teaching is and has always been at the centre of all education and educational reform.' Shulman (1992) 'Research on teaching' in *The Wisdom of Practice*, San Francisco: Jossey-Bass, 2004, p. 364.

14 I once argued (at Wits during the 1970s) that the Transvaal Education Department should, for the sake of conceptual clarity, be called the Transvaal Department for the Administration of Schooling – it was doubtful whether it had anything to do with *education*.

15   I am struggling to try to imagine how these roles apply in the case of district managers and others who work in departmental offices. Learning mediators? Designers of learning programmes? Researchers? But perhaps I have a weak imagination.

16   We can note that the UK National Agreement 'Raising Standards and Tracking Workload' simply *assumes* that we know what the formal element of teaching is.

17   Julius Kovesi, *Moral Notions*, London: Routledge & Kegan Paul, 1967, p. 4.

18   Consequences for the workload of teachers, and the status of teachers as members of a profession.

19   One, for example, that has a timetable on the first day of school, in which the absenteeism of teachers is rare, in which there are school 'traditions' that ensure a modicum of orderliness, and the work of teachers is supported by an efficient administrative system.

20   I assume that the reader will know that for gender-sensitive reasons the word 'waitron' has replaced the gendered words 'waitress' and 'waiter'.

21   This conception is *not* a generalisation from observation.

22   For pragmatic reasons they had better take account of what the teacher unions say.

23   See DoE 2005a. Available at <http://education.pwv.gov.za>. The quotations that follow are from the Framework.

24   The point of the phrase 'systematic learning' is to emphasise that the practice of teaching is not the business of transmitting bits of information – that is a task that is amply fulfilled by the technological accompaniments of the 'information explosion'. It is absurd for teachers to conceive of themselves as in competition with mass media. The practice of teaching is a practice that centres around the design of learning programmes that foster the gradual development of competences that cannot be learned in an instant.

25   Initial Professional Education of Teachers and Continuing Professional Teacher Development.

26   See DoE 2005a, p. 6.

27   We might add that other functions of schools are as symbols of access to the modern world and, in some cases, may be the only stable institutions in disrupted and destitute communities. But my story would become excessively complicated if I tried to include these additional functions.

28   There were, typically, other employees in the school who could take on some of the caregiving functions. Sometimes there were school 'nurses' and in many cases (as still happens in many schools and universities to this day) people employed, for example, as secretaries, who provided a sympathetic ear for students in difficulties.

29 We can notice how we have come around again to one of the dimensions of 'learner-centred education' – but this time perhaps we should drop the 'education'.

30 Learning to teach, like learning to read, has no finish line. Learning to teach involves an initial phase, usually but misleadingly called 'pre-service Teacher Education', but it also involves ongoing professional development, usually but again misleadingly called 'in-service training'. 'Teacher Education' encompasses both.

31 This was a central shortcoming of the programme to which I was subjected many moons ago, and is a feature of almost all of the Teacher Education programmes with which I have had some contact.

7 *Scripture and practices*

(Paper presented at a Western Cape Education Department conference, December 1999)[1]

Scripture

Outcomes-Based Education (OBE) was launched in South Africa as *the* alternative to Apartheid Education. At the centre of the rhetorical frame stood a simple dichotomy: Apartheid Education bad – OBE good. Of course, we all know what Apartheid Education is, so we need no impartial analysis or investigation of the concrete realities in the schools established under the Apartheid regime. In advance of any such investigation we know that it is evil, and a bad form of education. We then ascribe to Apartheid Education whatever we think are the characteristics of bad education: non-transparent governance structures, teacher-centred teaching, authoritarianism, rote learning, an obsession with content, lack of integration between education and training, rigid divisions, punitive formal examinations designed to yield high levels of failure, and so on. Given the rhetorical frame, OBE, as a 'paradigm shift', must then represent the contraries of all these bad and evil things.

We are in dangerous territory here, a territory characterised by political correctness, sacred texts and suspicion about critical or independent thinking. Anyone, even if his name happens to be Professor Jansen, who shows an inclination to be skeptical about OBE, thereby shows that they are in favour of retaining Apartheid Education. What possible motive could anyone have for raising doubts about OBE except that they have benefited from Apartheid Education and, thus, have a strong interest in perpetuating it? If we are opposed to Apartheid Education, then we must be in favour of OBE. We might be a bit unsure about what OBE is, but we must find ways to 'make it work' because it is the path we have chosen to 'transform' education in South Africa; it is our New Scripture[2].

As cracks begin to be revealed[3], we need to redouble our efforts; we need to understand that such a fundamental transformation, like a conversion to a new faith, is something that will take patience and persistent collective effort to accomplish. Our discourse must serve to reinforce the purity of our faith, and we cannot afford to have skeptical voices in our midst. If our spirits begin to flag, we need, at whatever cost, to import evangelists and foreign missionaries to re-inspire us, to reveal the true faith. Those of us who do not have the charisma to be evangelists, or the inclination to be missionaries, need to adopt the humbler role of advocates.

Nationally, we have decided on what path to take, we have been through all the appropriate consultations with the relevant stakeholders and overseas experts, and our job is now to implement the democratic will of the people. Commitment to the national effort requires that we should all now promote OBE. Those of us who work in ivory towers need to understand that we are not legislators but interpreters, and loyalty to the nation requires that we devote our intellectual energies to providing workable interpretations of OBE. And those of us who work in educational administration must take on board the responsibility to implement OBE effectively, to 'make it work'. The idea that OBE might not have been a viable path to take in transforming education, that perhaps it cannot be 'made to work' because there is something wrong with it, is a form of dangerous heresy, a symptom of arrogance and lack of faith and, without any need to investigate it, we should, in the national interest, repudiate this idea.

As a member of a triply threatened species, I shall here switch on some conceptual hazard lights about OBE, to which, if we take seriously the profound longer-term consequences of the matters we are discussing, we need to pay attention.

Transparency

Transparency is one of the key principles of our new democracy – we want the sources of power to be manifest. One of the dreams of OBE harmonises neatly with this principle. Once we have agreed on 'outcomes', education will become transparent, not only to teachers and learners but to the public at large. The hidden sources of power and mystification which traditionally characterise education – and took virulent forms under Apartheid – will be dispelled. We will all know what we are doing, and the enterprise of education will be open to egalitarian public scrutiny and assessment.

But this dream is based on the shallow and one-dimensional view that all knowledge stands at one level above unmediated experience, and can be made explicit. Whatever we might think of transparency in the realm of political power, we need to investigate its viability in the realm of education. We can briefly begin to explore this issue by thinking about the practices of teaching and learning in relation to knowledge.

During my early days as a schoolteacher in Johannesburg, we were assailed by the 'objectives movement'. The basic idea was very simple: unless as a teacher you can spell out your objectives in advance, and in language which is cleared of the mystifying 'mentalistic vocabulary' of such words as 'understanding' and 'appreciating', you really do not know what you are doing. This was a strong challenge based on some plausible ideas.

It was, and is, quite clear that many teachers in formal institutions of learning are quite muddled and confused in their practice. To say to them that they need to achieve a much sharper focus on their main task can make a contribution to their clarifying their practice. The question 'What are you trying to teach?' is certainly a way to encourage teachers to think clearly about what they are trying to achieve and this is, at least, a good first step towards helping them to make their practice more effective. Similarly, to say that teachers should be encouraged to think more clearly about how they describe what it is they are trying to achieve, and to think about this in view of how they are going to find out to what extent they have achieved it, has the potential, at least, to prompt teachers to clarify their practices. But as soon as it is claimed that you cannot be teaching rationally unless you can specify your objectives in detail in advance, and in the appropriate 'objective' language, then one's hackles begin to rise. There are three linked themes in this mystifying story that can disturb a teacher and disrupt her practice.

In the first place, once we try to meet these requirements, we find that we land up with lists of detailed 'objectives', horrible little bits of 'behaviour' which, far from clarifying what we think we are doing, serve to corrupt it. We put all the trees in neat lines, but we can no longer see the wood. In the second place, the wholesale revision of our language that we are invited to undertake – the elimination of such key words as 'knowing', 'appreciating', 'thinking', 'valuing' and 'understanding' – distorts and thus undermines our understanding of what we think we are doing. In the third place, the suggestion that rational teaching necessarily requires that one can say, in detail and in advance, what one's objectives are, is based on a one-sided and impoverished view of what it is to be rational.

Bloom's 'Taxonomy of educational objectives', with its detailed classification and categorisation of different kinds and levels of 'knowledge', was an attempt to rescue the objectives movement from mystification and impoverishment. But it is founded on the very same theory of knowledge, the same empiricist epistemology.

There are well-known and powerful objections to this epistemology. This is neither the occasion nor the place to enter into a full-scale argument, but we can note the following. Although we can analyse any complex activity, such as playing tennis, teaching, or doing mathematics, into its separable elements, competent engagement in the activity is not merely the sum of these atomised elements. We might say that playing tennis involves being able to hit overhead smashes and backhand drives, being able to volley at the net and serve from the baseline, but to play tennis is to bring such elements together in a fluent overall performance. The knowledge of a good tennis player, or successful mathematician, goes beyond the reach of the project of spelling it out in explicit detail. And the same is true of the knowledge of a good teacher. Although we can specify some of the elements of the practice of teaching, it is not possible to make the practice entirely explicit. Too much depends on such things as appropriate commitments and an educated perception of the specificities of learners, situation and context. In this sphere, total transparency is an illusion. As in the cases of tennis-playing and doing mathematics, in this case as well, good or successful practice escapes our attempts to give a complete and detailed description of what it involves.

In the second place, it is not true, as the epistemology in question assumes, that the meaning of words and language is to be understood on the model of naming an independent reality – that all meaningful uses of language eventually correspond item by item with 'facts in the world'. There are multiple problems with this assumption[4]. Language is a complex web of meanings. Some words and statements can be cashed in terms of correspondence with observable objects and events in the world, but this is a relatively small and unrepresentative set, and not a foundation for meaning. Within a language, the meanings of particular words and phrases are held in place by a web of relationships between them and their embeddedness in non-linguistic practices. Coming to learn a language involves gradually coming to find one's way in this complex web of meanings, and in the context of the non-linguistic practices in which they play a role. Language is not transparent, and we don't learn a language by abstracting from our experience, nor from merely learning lists of words.

In the third place, the view of rationality that challenges the rationality of the teacher, if she cannot specify her objectives in detail in advance and in the appropriate 'objective' language, is an aspect of the baleful influence of a particular view of science that dominates our world. In this view, the only kind of rationality worthy of that name is 'scientific rationality', and scientific rationality is the only source of objectivity. The dream of a science of teaching has a long pedigree and the reasons for the failure of this dream have nothing to do with lack of centuries of intelligent human effort to implement it. The dream is, in principle, unattainable[5].

Let's now think about learners and learning. One of the claims sometimes made on behalf of OBE is that it is a form of learner-centred education. We might note how this view slots in neatly with some of the inflated things we say about learners' rights and the misleading things we say about the salience of providing learners with choices about what to learn. Is it possible for learners to understand in advance what it is they are going to learn?

In the case of some atypical kinds of learning this might indeed be possible. I am thinking here of a mature learner who sets out to learn, say, how to drive a motor car or do embroidery. The crucial feature of these examples, which sets them apart from most of what we are trying to enable learners to learn in our formal institutions of learning, is that the activities of driving motor cars or doing embroidery are visible; they can be understood by one of us from seeing other people drive motor cars or do embroidery. But, in the case of other kinds of learning, it makes no sense to say that the learner can understand in advance what it is they set out to learn. The kind of example I have in mind here is of a learner setting out to learn how to read or do elementary arithmetic, or any other sophisticated practice, such as how to play the violin, tennis, chess or cricket, or how to read literature, to write coherently, to do mathematics, or to think in a scientific way. The only language in which we can specify what it is to learn such practices is *internal* to the practices themselves.

I cannot in non-aesthetic language describe what it is I am trying to achieve in teaching someone how to read literature or appreciate music; neither can I in nonmathematical language describe what I am trying to teach in teaching someone mathematics. From outside these practices it is not possible to understand what these practices are, or even what their value might be. By definition, the learner is outside of the practice or, at best, is a novice in respect to the practice. Thus, it is not possible for the learner to understand in advance what it is she will learn when she learns to become a participant in the practice. The idea that we can make learning transparent to learners by being clear about learning objectives is an illusion. Either those objectives will not properly describe what it is we are trying to achieve, or the learner will not be able to understand them.

OBE, of course, usually vigorously denies that it is a fellow-traveller with the 'objectives movement', and most of its evangelists and advocates dismiss the suggestion that it is a form of behaviourism. But the dream of transparency in education takes it inexorably in this direction. Certainly education – and indeed most training – would be much simpler if all knowledge was transparently available. There would be no problem about epistemological access, and perhaps there would not be any need for formal institutions of learning at all; we could all simply open our eyes and ears and acquire whatever knowledge we wanted, perhaps with a little help from our friendly facilitators.

The triumph of instrumental reason

Let's think about the 'integration' of education and training – sometimes regarded as one of the shining virtues of OBE. Those who want to announce their commitment to the faith now talk self-righteously of 'OBET' and 'ABET'.

We inherit, and not merely from Apartheid incidentally, a system of 'educational' institutions loosely constructed around a distinction between training and education. On one side we have technical colleges and technikons[6], which are said to be in the business of 'vocational education'; on the other, we have mainstream primary and secondary schools and universities, which have sometimes been said to be in the business of 'academic education'. We might have questions about what 'business studies' and 'metalwork' are doing in ordinary schools, and what 'medical' or 'engineering' education are doing in universities, but this does little to blur our perception of a sharp distinction between the two kinds of institutions.

We also, of course, inherit a swathe of other institutions, which are rather too tricky to classify according to this simple classification scheme. On which side of the tracks do we put special schools and police or agricultural colleges? And what do we say about institutions traditionally devoted to 'preparing' school teachers and nurses? Not too far in the past we quite unembarrassedly referred to these as 'training colleges', but more recently this has been resisted. We now talk of colleges of education and nursing colleges, although these institutions are currently in the process of losing their independent identity as they merge into our brave new ecumenical and universally accessible 'higher education' system.

But without trying to sort out the classification of these latter institutions, we can note that the main division between these two types of institutions has, or had, the following characteristics. The qualifications structure of these two types of institutions was separated, which created and reinforced a lack of 'horizontal mobility', with lifelong consequences for those who started on the wrong side of the tracks. These two types of institutions have sharply unequal social status, with those learners who 'can't make it' in ordinary schools or universities either being shuffled off to technical colleges and technikons or choosing these institutions as, quite clearly, a second option. A matriculation certificate or university degree has traditionally been regarded as more worthwhile than a technical certificate or technikon diploma, in spite of the fact that their value has sometimes been doubted on the ground that there are some people with matric certificates or university degrees who have found it difficult to get a job. Of course, the assumption is that those with technical college and technikon qualifications do, standardly, get a job, although I cannot recall ever having seen statistics to underwrite this assumption.

The debate about this issue is laced with considerable political passion. One of the sources of this passion has its roots in the way Marxist theorists sometimes distinguish between 'manual' and 'mental' labour – between 'hand work' and 'head work'. They then proceed to make an argument along the following lines. It is unjust for 'manual workers' – who are the primary producers in any society – to be paid less and to have lower status than 'mental workers' who, if not merely parasites, do little more than to reinforce the dominant ideology that keeps the whole iniquitous system in place. Sometimes, paradoxically from a Marxist point of view, the supposed historical examples of Western Germany and Japan are thrown into the pot. In these societies, it is said, 'technical' and 'academic' education are 'integrated' – and just look how economically successful they have been!

One of the central purposes of the National Qualifications Framework is to generate a single qualifications ladder that will undermine the traditional 'rigid' division between the two kinds of institutions and their characteristic qualifications; and OBE is the main tool to accomplish this 'integration'. The 'outcomes' of OBE will provide the common currency for 'horizontal mobility' and for working out the exchange rates between different qualifications, and the doors of 'higher learning' will be opened to all.

On this occasion I do not want to contest this thrust towards undercutting the division between the two kinds of institutions and their characteristic qualifications which, in any case, in the realm of higher education, has already been significantly eroded. But I would like to focus our attention on the underlying conceptual distinction – that expressed in the contrast between the ordinary English words 'training' and 'education'.

The basic point is that training is always *for* or *as* something. It is unintelligible to claim to be training someone without being able to say for or as what one is training them; we must be training them for a particular task in a factory, for secretarial work, for a particular role in our company's business, or as a waitron, a pilot, a fitter and turner, a hairdresser or a heavy vehicle driver. There is a strong conceptual link between training and outcomes. The only way to design a training programme is to specify its outcomes clearly and in advance, and then to construct the learning programme so as to achieve those outcomes. We could make no sense of an eclectic training programme that has as its envisaged outcome that those who follow the programme might turn out as either pilots or waitrons or heavy vehicle drivers or hairdressers. The concept of training is rooted in an entirely instrumental outlook. Training is the means taken towards a clearly circumscribed end, and it is possible to evaluate training programmes in terms of the extent to which they do indeed regularly achieve their claimed outcomes.

It is true that many of us have a deep-rooted bias against training, seeing it as limited, and perhaps simply as a way of teaching people to be obedient carriers-out of other people's projects and purposes. We train circus animals and sheepdogs, as well as workers for little bits of a production process. But if we allow ourselves to suspend this bias briefly, we can see that some of the most efficient teaching we ever experienced was at the hands of those who were good at training.

An example from my own experience is of learning how to touch-type in the days before PCs were even dreamed of. We worked on keyboards with blank keys. After a little bit of rote learning of 'QWERTY' and 'ASDFG', and a little bit of practice using one finger at a time, then two and three fingers simultaneously, on the correct keys, we had to practise copying given texts which, although they became progressively longer, had to be copied in a standard number of minutes. At regular intervals, although not 'continuously', we had to do 'tests' that the teacher then marked 'diagnostically' and, on this basis, gave each member of the class an individually-targeted series of exercises. 'The little finger on your right hand is still lazy.'

Over a period of only six weeks, this pattern was repeated at more and more advanced levels, and most of us were pleasantly surprised by our rapid progress. Our progress depended to some extent, of course, on how conscientiously we did our prescribed exercises, and there might have been those in the class who flattered their self-esteem with the thought that this was the main cause of their success. But a closer look reveals that we were in the grip of a superbly designed training programme, and in the hands of a teacher who knew how to implement it systematically and with the appropriate encouragement in times of despondency. No one showed any inclination to ask whether it was worthwhile to learn to type – that was the given end – and the standards we were trying to achieve were manifest and precisely measurable – the number of words per minute at which we could copy a previously unseen bit of text. The evidence was plain, and no one felt inclined to accuse our teacher of subjectivism or to feel insulted by being required to do yet another series of exercises to develop the skill of the still lazy little finger on our right hand. At the end of the programme no one failed, although admission to the more advanced programme did require a minimum of 40 words a minute. We were each issued with a certificate which confirmed the level we had reached; some received certificates that confirmed that they had reached 10 or 20 words a minute, others, the stars of the class, reached the heights of 40 or 50 words a minute.

This is an example of good training; the efficient use of effective means to reach an unambiguous and clearly circumscribed end. The force of the example is that the 'outcome' – what we were being trained for – was a measurable skill, and a most useful skill we might add, the exercise of which did not require reflection or autonomous judgement. We were never offered a choice about which fingers to use to strike which keys, or whether to use our thumbs to strike the space bar; nor were we invited to reflect about these matters. Indeed, real success consisted in being able to produce typed text without any explicit thought about which of our 10 fingers were striking which keys.

But as soon as we think of more complicated examples, critical reflection and a capacity to consider alternatives come to the fore. We certainly want our aeroplane pilots, dentists and surgeons to be well trained in their characteristic skills, but we want something in addition. We want them to exercise their skills with reliable judgement and a well-grounded understanding of the consequences of what they are doing. We want them to be flexibly intelligent in the exercise of their skills and to know how to cope in non-routine or emergency cases. The description of the outcomes of a good learning programme for dentists will indeed include some obviously manual skills, but it will also include some knowledge of human anatomy and physiology, with a particular focus on the human mouth and its physiological neighbours.

But beyond this we get into even trickier territory. The skills and broader systemic knowledge we want in our dentists and civil engineers need to be supplemented by non-technical skills such as a practical understanding about how to communicate with, and relate to, other people, awareness of local customs and etiquette, and an operational understanding of moral principles, especially as they play themselves out in their field of professional expertise.

There is, now, a question about whether this further range of capacities, seen as 'outcomes', can be understood as resulting from a programme of training, or whether there are some other kinds of teaching involved. We might even be tempted to let the word 'education' slip into the way we think about this.

But before we raise some doubts about the ubiquity of 'training' we might consider the suggestion that whatever these other outcomes are, it must be possible to spell them out, and to spell them out in a non-mystifying mode. In thinking about the training of dentists, managers, architects, shop stewards and lawyers, we might think of developing the capacity to 'identify and solve problems in a way which shows that responsible decisions using critical and creative thinking have been made'[7]. Such an outcome might seem generous enough to include those kinds of capacities I referred to as 'trickier territory', although its gains in generosity entail losses in clarity. And if we use this as one of our envisaged outcomes in designing our training courses for medical doctors, TV presenters, financial directors and landscape gardeners then, in principle, even if we are getting into even more mushy regions, it must be possible to design relevant training programmes which systematically develop these capacities.

So far, perhaps, so good. But if we now broaden our focus beyond the project of training for specific professional or occupational practices and think about, say, the enterprise of compulsory public schooling for the young, what might we say about its envisaged outcomes? Taking our cue from one of our evangelists, we might now think that, whatever else schooling is for, it should prepare people for 'life roles'[8]. So now, when someone asks what schooling is for, we can say that it is a 'training for life roles' – and we might add that this will also, obviously, include training for 'earning a living'.

But the marshes seem to be getting soggier, and we might begin to get the feeling that our path has led us into sinking sand. What do we mean by 'life roles', and how can we understand what might count as training somebody for 'life roles'? These questions can bring about even stronger sinking feelings in a world which, we are told from all sides, is characterised increasingly by rapid and unpredictable change. But perhaps these anxieties are misplaced. We have, after all, already decided on the 12 'Critical Outcomes' that provide us with the answers to these questions. These Critical Outcomes are presented as the anchor of the whole OBE system and, surely, they give us something to hold on to. When we look at the Critical Outcomes, we see such things as: 'work effectively with others as a member of a team, group, organisation or community' and 'be culturally and aesthetically sensitive across a range of contexts'.

Having identified our outcomes, we can now set about developing learning programmes to achieve them. Or can we? There are a few problems with this project. One problem is that the Critical Outcomes are not clearly circumscribed and are far from transparent. Instead, they are at a high level of abstraction and there are many different ways of interpreting them in the practice of designing learning programmes to achieve them. This might be presented as one of their virtues – they open up freedom for teachers to exercise their professional judgement. But, unless they imply *some* boundaries to what could count as fulfilling them, they cannot have any guiding function; they are no advance on simply saying 'Do whatever you want to', or 'Do what you think is best'.

We might think of a contrast between the murky situation we find ourselves in here and my example of learning how to touch-type, or even of the more complex examples of training people as veterinarians, floor managers or packaging designers. In all these cases, we can construct models of successful performance in the relevant practices, and can then, by analysis, try to work out how to train people for such successful performances. It is a little more difficult to start trying to construct a model of 'successful fulfilment of life roles', and here even the 12 Critical Outcomes run into the same kind of difficulty. For example, what does it actually imply at the practical level of programme design and delivery when we say that learners need to learn how to 'use science and technology effectively and critically, showing responsibility towards the environment and the health of others'?

Well, what we do is to designate 8 'Learning Areas', and then articulate the 'Specific Outcomes' of each – 66 in all (although I must say that in some of the lists I have seen there are 67). Some examples of Specific Outcomes are: 'select and evaluate products and systems', 'critically analyse economic and financial data to make decisions', 'measure with competence and confidence in a variety of contexts', 'demonstrate a knowledge and understanding of the relationship between science and culture', and so on. What is going on here is that we try to prescribe the limits to the range of appropriate interpretations of the Critical Outcomes by making the atomising move to try to get 'closer to reality', although it is a moot point whether we are indeed 'closer to reality'.

I don't want to claim that it is not possible to implement this recipe – there are linguistically fluent teachers who can redescribe what they would in any case have done so that it appears, at least, to satisfy the designated 'Critical' and 'Specific' outcomes, and there are other teachers who conscientiously design 'learning programmes' along the designated lines. But I do want to switch on a conceptual hazard light.

I previously commented that the concept of training is rooted in an entirely instrumental outlook; that training is the means taken towards a clearly circumscribed end. This is a valuable and important concept, but as soon as we try to stretch its range to include everything that we are trying to teach in our ordinary schools we run into troubles. The only plausible way of talking about what general 'outcomes' we expect of our schooling system is to say something vacuous about 'life roles' or 'earning a living' and, perhaps if our consciences are particularly delicate, we add on something about 'life skills', 'values' and 'citizenship'.

Our problem is that we are trying to force education into an ill-fitting conceptual harness. Without thinking about it, we embrace an instrumental outlook, and then we think that unless schooling is a means to some pre-specified 'outcomes', it must be useless. This looks like a classical example of the triumph of instrumental reason. One can gain the impression that the vaunted 'integration' of education and training so central to OBE is not so much an 'integration' as the reduction of education to training. Without actual evidence, training is implicitly regarded as 'practical' and 'useful' while, in contrast, education is regarded as 'impractical' and 'useless'. So, as we lurch myopically towards a thoroughly instrumental understanding of education, we congratulate ourselves on having taken a giant leap forward in our transformation of education.

An instrumental outlook might be seen as quite benign, if not neutral. However, it gives a particular cast to the way we think about education. It has a particular slope and, as the vacuous attempts to lay down the outcomes of schooling show, it is a slippery slope down which it is fatally easy to slide, and to lose our deeper sense of what we were fighting for in the long years of struggle against Apartheid.

Perhaps the most appropriate way to interpret the story about 'life roles' and the 12 Critical Outcomes, is as being located in the centuries-long debates about the aims of education. Seen in this light, they hardly make a significant contribution; they reveal a shocking ignorance of the tradition in which they are located, and a shallow understanding of the history of education, or even the history of mass schooling.

I shall conclude this section by reminding you that the issues at stake here have been at the heart of debates about education at least since Plato wrote *The Republic*. Plato seems to have held the view that only some people in a society had the capacity to lay down the broad direction of the republic – and those people, 'the guardians', needed education; the remainder simply needed to be trained to implement decisions taken by those at the higher level. This is hardly a path we should be willing to follow in our recently accomplished democracy, but OBE, with its tendency to collapse education into training, takes us in that direction.

RS Peters[9] was picking up on this tradition of debate when he wrote about these matters. He argued against the view that the value of education is to be judged in terms of something which lies outside of it – such as the needs of the captains of industry, the whims of current political leaders or the demands of the labour movement. In discussing debates about the 'aims of education' he expressed the view that aims of education are not goals which can be reached, as we are driven to think if we are thinking in an instrumental mode, but are 'regulative ideals' – ideals that regulate and guide our educative practices. To be educated, he said, is not to have arrived at a destination but to travel with a different view. In resisting the reduction of education to training he said that we should ask not what education is *for* but what it *is*. Perhaps gnomic slogans like this, rudely lifted out of the contexts of their original arguments, can't help us to design a school curriculum, but they at least point to the deeper conceptual frameworks in which we try to think about these things. They can also warn us that a thoroughly instrumental outlook on what we are trying to do in schools might undermine why we think schooling is valuable in the first place.

I think that OBE is embedded in an instrumental mode of thinking and, if I am right about this, then it risks being a path that will take us into bogs and sinking sands: it risks impoverishing our understanding of education and undermining our sense of why we think that it is so valuable that we are prepared to allocate more than 20 per cent of our national Budget to try to make it available to all our people.

Inputs and outcomes

One of the central claims of OBE is that although 'outcomes' – specifying what learners (we no longer have 'pupils' or 'students') should know and be able to do – will be officially prescribed, teachers will be free to decide how to accomplish those outcomes. There will be no prescription of learning programmes and teachers will freely construct interesting, locally-sensitive and imaginative learning programmes to reach those prescribed outcomes. In this section, I shall argue that this 'freedom' is an illusion and that, in our context, given the mainstream legacy of schoolteacher preparation in our country, a deeply misleading illusion.

In a paper[10] entitled 'Outcomes-based education has different forms', Cliff Malcolm raises the question of what the 'common ground' is of the various models of OBE. He claims that one key feature of all models of OBE is that they 'break the nexus' between 'inputs' and 'outcomes', and he regards this as a chief way of distinguishing between OBE and the 'objectives movement'. In his view, 'breaking the nexus' between 'inputs' and 'outcomes' is 'contrary to the tradition of behavioural objectives' (p. 80). Subsequently, he says that, 'The basic distinction between inputs and outcomes, with schools responsible for designing inputs to suit nationally defined outcomes, is at the heart of Curriculum 2005' (p. 102).

In the next section, I will return to a consideration of the relationship between OBE and behaviourism. In this section, I want to consider the claim that OBE 'breaks the nexus' between inputs and outcomes, and I shall begin with two preliminary comments about the use of the word 'inputs' in the context of talking about the practices of teaching and learning.

The natural home of talk about inputs and outputs is in relation to a manufacturing process, where the inputs might be such things as raw materials and human labour, and the outputs are the products produced. Potentially, we can do a cost-benefit analysis of the various inputs in order to assess their efficiency in producing the product and, in these terms, we could compare the efficiency of various production processes in producing the products. We know what we are taking about here, and we also know that we are in a field where human ingenuity constantly yields new and innovative inputs such as new procedures, new materials, and so on.

By metaphorical extension, we can then expand the application of this model to other fields such as electronic or financial systems, for example, or agricultural or ecological systems. However, conceptual strains begin to felt when we extend the application of this model into other realms of endeavour, such as doing mathematics, playing music or singing in a choir, writing novels, designing advertisements, or teaching and learning. Driven by the 'input–output model', we might here find ourselves trying to fit such things as human efforts and aspirations, imagination and interest into the 'input' pigeonhole, and begin to get the strong impression that something has gone wrong. Again, without trying to argue to the bottom of this impression, we can note that the source of the feeling that something has 'gone wrong' is that we are putting pressure on our conception of intentional human agency, our conception of human beings as being not merely the victims of blind forces, but themselves, at least potentially, as one of the originating sources of what happens in the world. We might think how differently our thoughts would be shaped if we thought of learning in terms not of an 'input–output' model, but in terms of tasks and achievements.

We can now, in defence of Malcolm, note that he talks not of 'inputs and outputs' but of 'inputs and *outcomes*', and perhaps that might be thought to make a difference. Perhaps, too, his use of the word 'inputs' to refer to whatever goes on in the processes of teaching and learning might have been a mere rhetorical accident, with nothing like the dramatic significance I have ascribed to it in the previous paragraph. But if we consider the gloss he provides of 'inputs', other problems arise, which takes me to my second preliminary comment.

Malcolm tells us that 'Inputs are the experiences from which children learn; outcomes are the results of learning' (p. 80). This does have dramatic significance; it commits us to a particular epistemology – our old friend, empiricism. According to empiricism, all knowledge and learning are based on 'experience'. Again, we are at a point at which a full-scale argument against this view, and there is a long tradition of argument here, is not appropriate in the context of this essay. Perhaps we can simply note that the various sources of learning include, for instance, other people, living in a family or a community, what we read or see on TV or hear on the radio, well-designed teaching programmes and wise, skilful and sympathetic but purposive teachers and, most basically, trying to do things we cannot yet do. Now, as soon as we try to simplify this situation by saying that all of these sources of learning can be reduced to experience – a move which seems both innocent and illuminating – we run into major conceptual problems. We normally conceive of 'experience' as passive (my experiences happen to me), private (only I can have my experiences) and subjective (only I know what my experiences are). But all three of these dimensions turn out to be incompatible with what we understand by learning.

Unlike, for instance, digesting, learning is not a passive, subjective or private process; nor is it a simple 'product' of our experiences. A learner is not an 'input–output system'; she is an intentional agent, and learning is more like an activity than something that simply happens to the learner. Learning sometimes happens by sheer chance but, more usually, it is a matter of focused effort on the part of the learner that has ineliminable interpersonal dimensions. To the extent that the slogan 'All Learning is From Experiences' makes us ignore these dimensions, it undermines what we know about learning and serves to warp our understanding of the tasks and commitments of both teachers and learners.

To learn how to touch-type is not a private mission. Success consists in reaching interpersonal standards and, in a sense, the 'experiences' of the learner drop out of the picture as irrelevant. Say we discovered that the star of the class, the one who achieved the highest number of words a minute, had the experience of the keyboard as her lover whom she was stroking, we would, sensibly, say that we were not, at least not in respect to thinking about her learning, interested in this fantasy. Similarly, in other cases of learning, a learner in the learning area of Mathematical Literacy, Mathematics and Mathematical Sciences learning how to 'analyse natural forms, cultural products and processes of representations of shape, space and time' can hardly depend on her own untutored experiences to guide her efforts. Her own experiences might guide her efforts wide of the prescribed outcome. The same applies to a learner in the learning area of Arts and Culture trying to learn how to 'demonstrate an ability to access creative arts and cultural processes to develop self-esteem and promote healing'. She needs informed teaching, not simply the instruction to get in touch with her own feelings. And success here is to be assessed not in terms of what the learner experienced during the process, nor in terms of her positive feelings of confidence and self-satisfaction about what she thinks she has accomplished, nor in terms of an enhancement of her own self-esteem. Success is not subjective; it is to have reached interpersonally-agreed standards, and the learner's feelings about the matter could be completely disconnected from those standards.

Let's now turn our attention to the idea – which is near the heart of the claims of OBE – that once 'outcomes' are specified, teachers have the freedom to design learning programmes to accomplish them. The first thing we notice is that this has a tendency to imply that learning is entirely mysterious – as though we have no idea at all about how someone learns how to be a good opening bowler, a competent pianist, an expert waitron, a superior swimmer, a rapid and accurate solver of mathematical problems, a neat and imaginative embroiderer, an accurate and reliable bookkeeper, or even an ordinarily competent driver of motor cars or rider of bicycles.

In all these cases, it cannot be true that the 'process' of learning is mysterious and unrelated to what it is that is learned. If someone told us that they had taught someone how to be a good opening bowler by showing them how to bake biscuits, that they had taught someone how to be a competent pianist by the unusual method of preventing them from even touching a piano, or how to be an expert waitron by the novel method of teaching them how to walk on their hands, we would be, at the very least, highly skeptical. We know that these stories sound like nonsense because we know there is a connection between the content and method of learning and what it is that is learned. It is not a mere accident that if we want to teach someone how to play the piano, we need to get them to practise playing the piano. Nor is it entirely arbitrary that if we want to teach someone how to solve mathematical problems, then we find or invent *mathematical* exercises for them to do, exercises which, if our programme is well designed, will begin with simple examples that the learner can now do fairly easily and with little effort, and we will take them systematically through more and more sophisticated exercises that draw closer and closer to the ideal of their being able to solve mathematical problems.

Thus, the process of learning is related to that which is being learned and the freedom of teachers in relation to prescribed outcomes is constrained by this consideration. It is misleading to imply that OBE 'breaks the nexus' between inputs and outcomes, if this is taken to mean that OBE provides teachers with unrestrained freedom. There are limits to what kinds of learning programmes could conceivably lead to a prescribed outcome. One of the characteristics of OBE, a characteristic which is sometimes presented as one of its virtues, is that it refuses to prescribe the content or methods of teaching, claiming that this is up to teachers to decide. Indeed, in some of the rhetoric, it is said that Apartheid Education prescribed 'content' and, by virtuous contrast, OBE does not. In some more extreme versions of the rhetoric, it is common for OBE to be contrasted with 'content teaching'.

But this itself is another form of nonsense. There can be no such thing as any teaching or learning without content, something that is being taught or learned. There is, of course, a lot more we need to say about what we mean by content. It is clearly the case that the learning of bits of information – sometimes called facts – is increasingly only a tiny part of what we want learners in school to learn. If this is what is meant by content, then it is clear that an obsession with content is poor education. But content can and does refer much more centrally to skills, capacities and dispositions, and the practices in which we are trying to enable learners to become practitioners. Furthermore, it is only in analytical mode that we can distinguish between content and methods; in practice they are intertwined. It is the content of learning that relates the process of learning (the input?) to its outcomes. There is a strong conceptual connection between the content of learning and the outcomes of learning and, if the 'freedom of the teacher' is understood to imply that this conceptual connection can be ignored, then we are in the realm of fantasy.

Of course, that there is a conceptual connection between the content and the outcomes of learning implies neither that there is only one learning path to the attainment of those outcomes, nor that the choice of learning path is a matter of subjective judgement or mere personal opinion. Different teachers, all good teachers, might use different actual exercises, or deploy them in different sequences, depending on such situation-specific factors as the interests of the learners or the levels of understanding they have already reached or local contexts. But professional choices and decisions of this kind are not subjective. Instead, they express a conceptual understanding of what the teacher is trying to enable the learners to learn.

Nor does the conceptual connection between the content and outcomes of learning imply that the actual examples or exercises used need to be identical in all cases. If, for example, the arithmetic teacher is trying to teach learners how to add and subtract positive whole numbers, it really doesn't matter whether they are asked to work with apples or cows. The content in such a case is the rules for addition and subtraction, not the substance of the examples used. The situation is similar in teaching the scruples and intellectual disciplines of participating in the practice of doing history. These are capacities which can be developed in relation to examples of the history of the revolution in the USA or France, or the Napoleonic wars, or the invasion of the interior of southern Africa or the liberation struggle in South Africa, or even the history of our local community. What is being taught, the content, is the scruples and intellectual disciplines of doing history – not the particular examples in relation to which these capacities are exercised.

We can draw one obvious lesson from this point. If the content and the outcomes of learning are conceptually related to each other, then the wise choice of content will depend not only on the teacher's sensitive understanding of the local context, but also on her conceptual understanding of what she is trying to teach. And if any teacher's conceptual understanding is shallow or inadequate, they will be in no position freely to design learning programmes to attain the prescribed outcomes. Taking account of the deep legacy of the quality of teacher preparation under Apartheid, we have many schoolteachers who need assistance in the design of learning programmes. One way in which we might do this is to provide well-designed textbooks and other learning materials. The practical success of such a strategy would depend, amongst other things, on overcoming two illusions fostered by OBE, or some of the heated rhetoric in which OBE is promoted: the illusion that given the prescribed outcomes teachers have unencumbered freedom in the design of learning programmes, and the illusion that OBE is opposed to 'content' in education.

Outer and inner

There is one last conceptual hazard light I want to switch on in this essay that signals a very deep problem in the way we understand what we are up to in education. One way of expressing this problem is to say that it has to do with the ways we understand learning in relation to objectivity and subjectivity. In respect to OBE, we are here faced with a major interpretive fault line which, if we don't attend to it, can rapidly become, if not merely a source of muddle, then a major conflict between rival interpretations of OBE. It hardly needs mentioning that the rival interpretations are not merely part of an intellectual game, but can lead to contradictory teaching and learning practices that can subvert our project of overcoming the principal faultline in the educational system we inherit.

Cliff Malcolm, in the article previously referred to, provides us with a lucid starting point. Under the bold sub-heading 'What is meant by learning?', he sketches out two forms of OBE, one which he links with Bill Spady and the USA, the other which he refers to as 'The Australian view'. I am not here interested in the scholarly questions of whether Malcolm in this passage contradicts his previous claim that OBE 'is contrary to the tradition of behavioural objectives' (p. 80), nor in whether he provides us with a fair interpretation of Spady's view or an accurate glimpse of what the Australians think. What I am interested in is the ways in which the concepts of objectivity and subjectivity are used in this passage, and the links that are made between those concepts and what is supposed to be 'inside' or 'outside' of the learner. What is revealed in the following passage is a conceptual dilemma which we all share – I am not here interested in merely criticising Malcolm's view. To provide a richer flavour of the way the argument goes I will quote quite a long passage[11]:

What is meant by learning?

Spady sits ultimately in a behaviourist position. Outcomes must be demonstrations or performances, not thoughts, understandings, beliefs, attitudes, mental processes; not grades, numbers, averages. He distinguishes between psychological models of learning (what happens inside a student's head), and sociological models ('ability to translate mental processing into forms and kinds of action that occur in real social settings' (Spady, 1994)). Outcomes must be of the sociological kind. The behaviour is the learning and thing assessed. What happens in the mind helps learning but the outcome is the behaviour. Verbs such as understanding, knowing, appreciating have no place in Spady's OBE (Spady, 1994). He makes his case from the need to have assessment criteria public. He also needs to circumvent criticism that OBE is trying to mould students' thoughts, beliefs and values. Accordingly, he presents learning as objectively defined and coming from outside. (It is interesting that in the USA planned modification of behaviour is generally acceptable, but planned changes in beliefs and values are not.)

The Australian view of learning is much closer to a constructivist one. Learning takes place in the mind and expresses itself in many ways, of which performance is one. What happens in the mind entails a complex of cultural, social and personal factors – world view, perception, imagination, values, purposes, social interactions, cultural expectations. The curriculum is therefore subjective, not only in the way it is experienced, but in what is learned.

Because learning takes place in the mind, assessment is achieved by inference, not measurement. Performances are not the measure of learning, but clues about what and how students think. The 'public' and 'justifiable' requirements of assessment are met by teachers' being able to point to convincing evidence for their judgements. Their evidence might be test answers, submitted assignments, performances, drawings, students' claims and introspective reports. In this approach, performance is an indicator of learning, not the learning itself. Behaviours in the Australian model are called pointers, not outcomes.

So, on the Spadian (objectivist) side, we have a rejection of 'psychological models of learning' that are interested in 'what happens inside a student's head', and a commitment to a 'sociological model' that understands learning as 'ability to translate mental processing into forms and kinds of action that occur in real social settings'. The positive claims on this side are that 'the behaviour *is* the learning', and that learning is 'objectively defined' and comes 'from outside' (outside of the student's head?). Assessment criteria are public and, in principle at least, we can 'measure' the degree to which outcomes have been attained.

On the Australian (subjectivist) side, we find that 'learning takes place in the mind' and that, therefore, both the curriculum and 'what is learned' are subjective. Learning is 'constructivist'[12] (coming from inside the student's head?) and 'performance is an indicator of learning, not the learning itself'. In relation to assessment, we can no longer talk of 'measurement' with its implications of 'objectivity'; we need now to talk of 'inferences' from performance, of 'clues' about 'what and how students think' including, for instance, 'students' claims and introspective reports'. In this view, 'performance is an indicator of learning, not the learning itself' (obviously, because 'learning takes place in the mind'). If asked to justify their 'judgements', teachers must be able to 'point to convincing evidence'.

We find ourselves here embrangled in a conceptually horrible thorn bush, and we are offered only two possible ways out, neither of which gives us much comfort. What can we possibly answer to such questions as: (i) Is learning the behaviour or is it something that 'takes place in the mind'? (ii) Is learning 'something that happens inside a student's head' or is it an 'ability to translate mental processing into forms and kinds of action that occur in real social settings'? (iii) Is 'performance' an 'indicator of learning' or is it 'the learning itself'? (iv) Does 'what happens in the mind' merely 'help' learning or *is* it learning? (v) Does learning 'come from outside' or is it 'constructed' 'in the mind'? (vi) Is what is learned 'objective' or is it 'subjective'? (vii) Is the curriculum 'objective' or is it 'subjective'? (viii) Is assessment a kind of 'objective measurement' or is it a kind of subjective inference from the clues of performance to what and how students think? (ix) Are 'outcomes' 'demonstrations or performances' or are they merely 'pointers' to some unobservable happenings hidden in learners' minds? (x) Are 'assessment criteria' public or are they personal?

If we are thinking clearly, the answer to all of these questions is 'none of the above'. As in the case of the question, 'Are you still beating your wife?' the appropriate response is not to try to answer the questions, but to reject them on the ground that they arise from an assumption that is unacceptable. To try to answer any of these questions merely reinforces the conceptual framework that generates them.

The two rival interpretations, and the ten questions, force us into conceptual dead ends. Of course learning is not something that 'takes place in the mind', but that does not mean that it *must* be 'the behaviour'. Of course learning is not 'something that happens inside a student's head', but that does not mean that it *must* be 'an ability to translate mental processing into forms and kinds of actions that occur in real social settings'. Of course assessment in education is not 'objective' (if we mean by 'objective' something similar to measuring the length of the table), but that does not mean that it *must* be 'subjective'. And so on. As practising, or ex-practising, teachers we know these things, but we are inclined to forget them when we move into theorising gear.

The two rival interpretations of OBE, and the ten questions, arise out of a conceptual framework founded on an exclusive dichotomy between what is 'inside' and what is 'outside' an individual person's mind, harnessed to an exclusive dichotomy between subjectivity and objectivity in the field of educational assessment. The rival interpretations are merely a local dispute within this conceptual framework and what we need to think about is the framework itself, not about how to answer the unanswerable questions that it generates.

Again we are faced here with an issue which has been at the centre of debates in philosophy since the time of Descartes, and emerged in a crude form in the disputes between behaviourism and humanistic psychology in the USA during the 1960s and 1970s. It is unlikely that we can definitively solve the problem in this context, but I will make a few comments that might perhaps gesture towards a different way of thinking about these things[13], a pointer to how to escape the horrible thorn bush and avoid the conceptual traps set for us by Malcolm's rival interpretations of OBE.

One way to do this is to shift the centre of gravity[14] in the way we think about education: about teaching and learning, the curriculum of common schooling and the assessment of learning achievements. We need to get the concept of practices to displace the exclusive dichotomy between what is inside and what is outside the mind, and the corresponding dichotomy between subjectivity and objectivity in assessment. All I can do here is to provide a fleeting glimpse of this different way of thinking about these things.

Practices are the shared activities that constitute our human lives. Reading is a practice, but so is playing soccer, doing beadwork, writing literature, making clay pots, curing illnesses or injuries, doing mathematics, playing cricket, writing history, teaching and learning. In all cases, to learn a practice is to become a participant, or a more competent participant, in the practice. All practices are indeed 'invented' by human beings; they didn't simply drop from the sky, nor are they aspects of the natural world in which we live. But this does not imply that we could simply invent new practices at will, or change them to suit our fancy. Practices have histories, not merely pasts, and within those histories there are some practitioners who are regarded as having achieved excellence in the practice, and even some who – through their excellence – revealed new ways of participating in the practice.

The curriculum for common schooling is made up from a selection of practices that we, collectively, if we are in a democratic society, regard as particularly important for the young of our society to learn. To learn a practice is to become a participant in that practice. This does not imply merely 'learning to behave in the appropriate way', but nor does it imply 'having the right thoughts in one's head'. This dichotomy doesn't fit the way we actually understand how someone learns to become a participant in a practice. We can make no sense of the question of *where* learning takes place, 'in the head' or 'in the behaviour'.

It would be bizarre to describe learning how to participate in a practice as 'learning how to *translate mental processing* into forms and kinds of action that occur in social settings', and we are not interested in the question of 'what comes from inside' or 'what comes from outside' the learner. What we are interested in is the extent to which the learner is trying to participate in the practice, and the extent to which he can now engage satisfactorily in the practice. These are not things we can measure with the degree of precision we expect from measuring the weight of a brick or the size of a window. The teacher of any practice makes judgements about the extent to which the learners are now competent in the practice and about how to enable them to become more competent. Such judgements are not 'inferences' to something which is essentially hidden, nor are they 'subjective'. They are assessments of what can actually be observed by any person who *understands the practice* and, especially, the standards of achievement and excellence which serve partly to define the practice. It is an absurdity to think that such standards are 'barriers to learning'; they are an indispensable part of what the learner is trying to learn. Furthermore, the constitutive standards of a practice are not 'attainable outcomes'; they serve to guide and shape the practice, which remains a constantly open project. And such standards are shared in the community of practitioners, both past and present; they were not 'invented' by any individual, but emerged gradually within the tradition of the practice.

Practices are sustained or corrupted to a considerable degree by the ways in which participants and significant others interpret, think about and discuss them. But those interpretations, thoughts and discussions do not float freely above the 'reality' of the practice. Instead, they are part of that reality, and for this reason they can serve either to enable the practice to flourish, or to undermine it by depriving it of its sense and identity. Practices can and do change, they have histories, but it is rare for such changes to be brought about by legislation, as the history of revolutions demonstrates. Sometimes changes are developments or improvements, but sometimes they are deteriorations.

If we are interested, as we must be, in improving education in South Africa, and have to be committed to OBE, then it would be wise for us to avoid interpreting it in such a way that it might undermine the practices of education. The choice between the two alternative ways of interpreting OBE offered by Malcolm serves to perpetuate a conceptual problem that has haunted education for a long time. OBE might be used as a lever to shift the centre of gravity in the way we think about education, but then it might be sensible to stop talking about 'outcomes' or 'pointers' and to talk, instead, about practices and achievements in those practices. Whether this could still be presented as OBE is a question that we can leave to those politicians whose main purpose is to hang on to their power.

Conclusion

The project of transforming an education system is the project of changing the vast webs of practices which constitute it. Given the size and complexity of the system, it is most unlikely that it can be transformed by the wholesale attempt to replace all current practices with new practices. If this is the purpose of OBE, it is bound to fail, and no new legislation or punitive regulations can rescue it. But if it is the project of trying to improve current practices by introducing a more illuminating way of talking and thinking about them, then it would be well for OBE to be interpreted in a way that avoids the conceptual hazards I have suggested in this essay. And one way to do that would be to locate the concept of practice at the heart of how we think about teaching, learning and schooling.

Of course, given the prevalence of the practice of 'scriptural' reading in South Africa, this will be no easy task to accomplish, but it might be worth at least giving it a try instead of continuing to stumble blindly along a path that seems to be leading either to nowhere or to disaster. I have tried to switch on some conceptual hazard lights. To say that this will, at best, appeal to only a certain sector of our population is hardly a way of contributing responsibly to the development of education in our country. The point about conceptual difficulties is that if we ignore them, they will come back further along the path to haunt us.

Notes

1   This essay is a slightly edited version of the original paper, which was published in the conference proceedings, Nelleke Bak (ed.), *Making OBE Work?* Cape Town: Western Cape Education Department, February 2000; and was later published in *Perspectives in Education,* Vol. 19 No. 1, 2000, pp. 87–106, reprinted here with permission.

2   In a paper written as far back as 1986, I first tried to come to terms with this mode of reading. See Wally Morrow, 'To gather the living flower: Some problems about critical thinking and education' in *Chains of Thought,* Johannesburg: Southern Book Publishers, 1989.

3   For a depressing report on the current state of education in South Africa, see Nick Taylor & Penny Vinjevold (eds), *Getting Learning Right,* Johannesburg: The Joint Education Trust, 1999.

4 For a devastating attack on this view of language see Noam Chomsky, 'Review of BF Skinner's *Linguistic Behavior*' in *Language*, Vol. 35 No. 1, pp. 26–58.

5 See Shirley Pendlebury, 'Luck, knowledge and excellence in teaching', unpublished DEd thesis, UWC, 1991, for an excellent elaboration of why this dream is unattainable.

6 Since this essay was written, technikons have been renamed Universities of Technology.

7 This is one of the critical cross-field outcomes specified in the architecture of Outcomes-Based Education.

8 It is quite difficult to understand what the advance is in talking of 'life roles' rather than 'adulthood', which is deeply embedded in the thoughts of countless teachers in South Africa who went through the mill of Fundamental Pedagogics, and which continues to construct their conception of education. Why do we have such short memories?

9 RS Peters, 'Education as initiation' in RD Archambault (ed.), *Philosophical Analysis and Education*, London: Routledge & Kegan Paul, 1965; and RS Peters, *Ethics and Education*, London: Routledge & Kegan Paul, 1966.

10 Cliff Malcolm, 'Outcomes-based education has different forms' in Jonathan Jansen & Pam Christie (eds), *Changing Curriculum: Studies on Outcomes-based Education in South Africa*, Cape Town: Juta, 1999.

11 Cliff Malcolm, in Jansen & Christie (eds), *Changing Curriculum*, p. 91.

12 Given a straight choice between these two interpretations, most South African teachers will, partly because of the perceived success of protest and interest group politics in our recent history, be drawn to a 'subjectivist' rather than an 'objectivist' interpretation of learning and curriculum. For a chilling glimpse of the effects of 'constructivism' on the way teachers conceive of their tasks in South Africa, see Taylor & Vinjevold (eds), *Getting Learning Right*.

13 For a different attempt to come to grips with the same problem, see Roger Deacon & Ben Parker, 'Positively mystical: An interpretation of South Africa's Outcomes-based National Qualifications Framework' in Jansen & Christie (eds), *Changing Curriculum*, Cape Town: Juta, 1999.

14 What I am recommending here is an epistemological change – a rejection of an empiricist epistemology – and it is no easy matter, either individually or collectively, to accomplish such a change.

8 *Aims of education in South Africa*

(First published in 1990)[1]

Aims of education under Apartheid

Apartheid is a classic case of social engineering; of shaping the social world according to a blueprint. Apartheid is legislated racial domination, but its defenders have avoided the vocabulary of 'race'. Their self-understandings revolve around the concept of a 'population group'. This concept has become deeply embedded in the ramified and tightly knit web of regulations, practices, institutions and relationships which constitute the asymmetrical structures of power of Apartheid society.

Social engineering, if it is to have any chance of success, must work with material provided by history. In South Africa, as in other colonised societies, the colonists distinguished themselves sharply from the indigenous population. As in other parts of the British Empire, the indigenous population were called 'natives', and were perceived as deficient or inferior in all important respects, especially in respect of 'civilisation' and 'culture'.

The military conquest of the 'natives' in South Africa was more or less complete by about 1879, but for the previous two centuries people of colour – the indigenous population, those who had been imported as slaves and those of 'mixed' parentage – had been perceived and treated as different from those who claimed to be 'European'. One aspect of this is that the colonial authorities persistently saw schooling for the colonised as needing to be different from schooling for the colonisers. Whether or not black people should be 'educated' (i.e. provided with schooling) at all was contested right up into the 1930s. A 1936 government report, known as *The Welsh Report,* notes the following:

> From the evidence before the Committee it seems clear that
> there still exists opposition to the education of the Native on the
> grounds that (a) it makes him lazy and unfit for manual work;
> (b) it makes him 'cheeky' and *less* docile as a servant; and (c) it

estranges him from his own people and often leads him to despise his own culture.[2] (RT: 232)

The *Welsh Report* provides an argument for the traditional assumption that schooling for black people should have different aims from schooling for white people. The problem is posed in terms of the following two alternatives:

> Are we to Europeanise him as quickly as possible so that he can take his place in our pattern of Western civilization with as little trouble as possible? Or are we to prepare him to 'develop along his own lines'? (RT: 233)

and it opts for the latter, on the following grounds:

> ...the two social orders for which education is preparing White and Black are not identical and will for a long time to come remain essentially different...The education of the White child prepares him for a life in a dominant society and the education of the Black child for a subordinate society. (RT: 233)

and that:

> It is no use shutting our eyes to the fact and ostrichlike positing aims for Native education which the very circumstances of South Africa make impossible to realize, merely because these aims are laudable and we should like them to apply to the Black people as well. (RT: 233)

The Committee did not consider the possibility that schooling systems with different aims might be one source, maybe a crucial source, of different 'social orders', rather than a given 'fact' that 'realistic' aims for schooling should take into view. The Committee felt that '...it will not be quite honest to avoid stating clearly *that a full liberal philosophy is not at present applicable to Native education*' (RT: 234, emphasis in the original).

Historically, the ground had been well prepared for Apartheid. Soon after coming to power in 1948, the National Party, which still rules South Africa more than four decades later, set up a commission to make plans for 'education for Natives as an independent race' (RT: 244). The 1951 report of the commission, known as *The Eiselen Report*, provided the theoretical foundation (the rationalisation) for Bantu Education. The *Eiselen Report* emphasised the cultural coherence and integrity of the different 'peoples' (later to become 'population groups') of South Africa, and the way in which the schooling provided should be in harmony with the other social institutions of these different 'peoples' and should aim to prepare people to serve their 'own' communities:

> We turn now to the question of why it should be *Bantu Education.* A number of witnesses laid it down as axiomatic that education was one and indivisible; others maintained that all education to be efficient should be expressed in terms of the needs of a particular people, situated in a particular environment, at a particular stage in their development. (RT: 251)

The *Eiselen Report* also picks up the idea that the aims of schooling should be 'realistic' in terms of the social and economic opportunities 'available' to those who attend them:

> Attention, however, must be drawn to the fact that much of what is taught and learnt in Bantu schools is never applied in practice, because the economic incentives which should operate when children leave school are either absent or of such a nature as to undo the work of the schools. The reform of these economic conditions cannot be the function of an Education Department, but the success of the work of the schools is dependent upon the existence of social and economic opportunities for absorbing the products of the schools. (RT: 245)

An overall educational policy which embodied traditional 'white' sentiments such as these, and which is one of the keystones of the Apartheid blueprint, was legislated into existence by the passing of three seminal Acts of Parliament: the *Bantu Education Act* in 1953, the *Coloured Persons Education Act* in 1963, and the *Indian Education Act* in 1964.

The 37 million people who live in South Africa[3], with an age distribution typical of a society in a phase of accelerated population growth, are still officially divided into four 'population groups': 'Africans' (about 75% – of whom some 45% are under the age of 15), 'Whites' (13%), 'Coloureds' (9%) and 'Indians' (3%). The *Population Registration* Act of 1950 ensures that every person is appropriately classified. Apart from a few 'mixed' private schools, there are separate schools for the four population groups; it is illegal for a person to attend a state school designated for a population group other than that to which she has officially been assigned, or for a school to admit as a student someone from the 'wrong' population group.

Along almost any dimension of comparison, there have been, and are, glaring inequities among the four schooling systems in South Africa. This applies to teacher qualifications, teacher–student ratios, per capita funding, buildings, equipment, facilities, books, stationery, and so on, and also to results measured in terms of the proportions and levels of certificates awarded. Along all these dimensions, 'White' schools are far better off than any of the others, and 'Indian' and 'Coloured' schools are better off than those for 'Africans'. Schooling is compulsory for 'Whites', 'Indians' and 'Coloureds' but not for 'Africans'.

'White' schooling is recognisably normal to anyone familiar with schooling in industrialised societies. On the surface, extraordinarily in such a politically volatile society, it is apolitical and academic progress is smooth and regular. In sharp contrast, schooling for black people in South Africa, and especially that for 'Africans', is a 'site of struggle', a political cauldron in a chronic state of crisis; it is chancy and sporadic, subject to frequent disruptions and other kinds of breakdown, and usually in radical disarray. A high proportion of students are first-generation students, dropouts are likely to be leaving school permanently, and the security forces (police and military) keep 'black' schools under close surveillance and, in many cases, are a constant physical presence. Students and teachers are frequently detained – often without being charged – and threatened, restricted and harassed in other ways. And 'black' students, usually at a very young age, come to realise the political roots of their situation.

These four separate schooling systems transmit deep and insidious messages, wrapped in the naturalistic disguise in which they play an organising role in the construction of the common-sense understandings of the vast majority of South Africans. These messages are complementary for the four population groups; they consolidate and reify the concept of a 'population group', and deeply penetrate individuals' self-understandings, their personal relationships and their perceptions of where they 'belong' in this hierarchical scheme of things, as well as their understanding of what the central lines of political cleavage are in this society.

Successful social engineering, particularly that kind that is widely regarded as unjust, needs to hide its mechanisms from public view. One way in which this can be done is to appeal to a plausible theoretical story. In the case of Apartheid, this story is constructed on the theme of 'cultural' (and moral) relativism. That different population groups have different, and incompatible, 'cultures' is a convenient myth that occludes the thought that the artificial separation of population groups might itself spawn separate 'cultures'. This myth underpins the theory of education, called Fundamental Pedagogics, which the overwhelming majority of education students in South Africa are taught.

Two key aspects of this theory are its distinction between 'scientific' and 'post-scientific' work in education, and the claim that 'adulthood' is the overarching aim of education. 'Scientific' work provides the formal framework for any 'proper' education; 'post-scientific' work is the filling appropriate for people who hold different 'life- and world-views'. The framework is presented as 'objective', 'neutral', and 'universal'; the filling as relative to different 'cultural groups'. 'Adulthood' must be interpreted appropriately in the light of the divergent and incompatible founding traditions and convictions of those who hold various 'life- and world-views'. Thus, education must be an 'own affair', and the aims of education must, for plausible theoretical reasons, be different for the different population groups.

One of the appalling things about Apartheid is how successful it has been in those respects relevant to education. Apartheid has always depended on brutal repressive methods, and in more recent years, especially since the declaration of the State of Emergency in mid-1985, such methods have increasingly been used in an effort to control the situation. Nevertheless, the understanding of the vast majority of South Africans has been constructed along the lines of population groups, and schooling policy is, and has been, one major instrument in the production of this result.

During the past decade, under severe pressure, the government has pursued a policy of 'reform': a political strategy designed to maintain and perpetuate the established order while abandoning or modifying regulations that have become widely regarded as unjust and unacceptable. Some classical Apartheid legislation has been abandoned or modified, and Apartheid is no longer what it was in its heyday. Nevertheless, what has not been abandoned or modified are the pivotal concept of a 'population group' and the maintenance of the policy of separate schools for the four population groups. These aspects of the blueprint, crucial to maintaining the current relations of domination, are still in place.

According to official spokespersons the future nightmare for South Africa would be 'group domination', with a consequent loss of 'group identity'. The irony of this description seems to have escaped the party rhetoricians. Over a long period of time, South Africa has been dominated by one population group, which has powerfully exploited and oppressed the other groups. South Africa lives a nightmare from which it is trying to awaken.

On discussing the aims of education in South Africa

There is, of course, a sense in which a discussion of the aims of education might be entirely ahistorical – an analytical or academic exercise that might be engaged in, in any historical situation. However, a significant discussion of the aims of education – that is, a discussion which could have some purchase on schooling policy and educational practice – presupposes the satisfaction of particular historical preconditions. In South Africa at the present time[4] a significant discussion of the aims of education is not possible because the historical preconditions for such a discussion do not exist. A main argument in what follows is that a shared moral discourse has not been able to develop in South Africa, and that without a shared moral discourse it is not possible to have a significant discussion of the aims of education.

We can begin by noting that Apartheid is a form of oppression that has disempowered its victims. By persistently treating them as objects of policy, by refusing to *see* them as wholly and rightfully human, as beings who have moral titles and standing, Apartheid has dehumanised its victims; their dignity and self-esteem as persons, and their intellectual and moral confidence and autonomy, have been damagingly undermined.

At the same time, as the long history of resistance in South Africa shows, the victims of Apartheid are not powerless. Those struggling against Apartheid have engaged, not without effect, in direct, often physically dangerous and increasingly violent, confrontation with the repressive apparatuses of the Apartheid state. And any black student leader or activist will know that the student movement, especially since 1976, has brought significant pressure to bear on the authorities and, at least arguably, has forced from them some policy changes and other concessions. Paradoxically, in a country in which increasing numbers of people see themselves as politically impotent, black students in South Africa, or at least their leaders, see themselves as significant political actors.

The conjunction of these two contrary effects of Apartheid has given rise to a political perspective that is unsympathetic towards a discussion of the aims of education. I shall try briefly to explain what I mean. The only form of power available to those who struggle against Apartheid might be dubbed 'negative power'. In some situations, and South Africa provides a classic example, the use of negative power requires virtues such as courage, ingenuity and commitment; those who use such power in South Africa are faced not merely with inconvenience, discomfort and reprisal, but with the retributive violence of the aggressive agencies of the established order.

Nevertheless, it is a corrupting form of power that generates the belief that difficulties and problems can instantly be solved by the assertion of an opposing will[5]. The political effectiveness of such power depends centrally on the maintenance of unity amongst those who use it, an uncritical commitment to the goals of the struggle and a belief that all difficulties and problems have their source in the malice of the oppressors. This form of power gives rise to a suspicion of intellectual virtues or a nuanced moral stance, which can be seen as harbouring the seeds of division, factionalism and doubt. Such suspicion reflects and reinforces the disempowering effects of official policy.

A vigorous rejection of the labels 'deficient' or 'inferior' has been accompanied by a willingness to accept the label 'deprived', but this is itself corrupting. It tends to induce a new form of dependency – of intellectual and moral heteronomy – to undermine a sense of responsibility, and to provide a universal excuse for any shortcomings or failures. In education, it fosters the stance that academic work requires no serious effort and, to the extent that it seems difficult, this is simply because it has artificially been 'made difficult' by those who, consciously or not, are trying to prevent others from attaining the privileges of the 'educated'.

These tendencies culminate in a general suspicion of intellectuals and intellectual work. Intellectuals are products of the status quo (by virtue of their training in Apartheid institutions), and it is a short step from this to the view that intellectual work, of which a discussion of the aims of education is one form, in general merely serves the interests of the current asymmetrical structures of power. One can add to this that for the vast majority of black people in South Africa, the experience of schooling is likely to have consolidated the conviction that the intellectual virtues, which schools and universities are supposed to foster, are more likely to be artificial and mystificatory barriers to, rather than instruments of, liberation.

In addition to these effects, which are aspects of a political perspective unsympathetic to a discussion of the aims of education, Apartheid as a form of social engineering has undermined the ground for a significant discussion of the aims of education in another profound way. The dominance of a social engineering model of schooling fosters moral relativism and a technicist stance that drains policy decisions of their moral dimension. Aims of education come to be conceived of as merely the schooling policy of those who hold the political whip hand; merely an aspect of their social blueprint.

Once the aims of education are conceived in this way, any discussion of the aims of education is pointless unless those engaged in that discussion can see themselves as having a reasonable chance of actually controlling the schooling system. Thus, the issue of the control of the schooling system comes to be seen as having priority over any consideration of the aims of education; strategic thinking comes to occupy the whole field. The primary task is to attain control over the schooling system; until this task has been successfully accomplished, a discussion of the aims of education is merely academic, disconnected from the real historical process with no power to affect its course. The example of 'People's Education' can illuminate this way of thinking.

From 1984, and reaching crisis proportions by the end of 1985, black schooling increasingly broke down. With the example of the successes of 1976 as an inspiring model, there had been widespread protests at black schools, which also involved extended school boycotts and stayaways. The situation had been exacerbated by the official reaction of closing down schools at which there was 'trouble' or 'agitation'. By the end of 1985, schooling had effectively ceased altogether for a significant proportion of black students.

A problem was that the combined effects of boycotts and school closures led to the dispersal of students, especially those who were politically more active, so that they no longer had a place (i.e. the schools) at which to organise collective action. Increasingly their power as a force for change was dissipated.

The slogan of that time – 'Liberation Before Education' – had, paradoxically, deprived students of the very site of struggle on which they could fight the battle for liberation.

Concerned community leaders organised a series of meetings which gave rise to the NECC – National Education Crisis Committee – and the emergence of People's Education, under the slogan 'People's Education for People's Power'. Faced with the prospect that black schooling might collapse entirely, and holding the political conviction (which, in retrospect, was correct) that the Apartheid regime was not on the point of demise, the NECC persuaded students to return to school in exchange for an agreement that a set of demands would be put to the authorities. Students did return to school, although the extent to which the demands were met was doubtful.

The issue of the control of schooling was still at the top of the agenda but, as can be seen from the slogan 'People's Education for People's Power', some attempt was made to open up space for the discussion of the aims of education. Underlying this slogan is the hope that education has a role to play in the liberation struggle; that there can be an alternative to Apartheid Education, an alternative which will empower people and contribute to the destruction of Apartheid. However, for various reasons, People's Education remained at the level of a political rallying cry; it has not developed into a theory of education.

People's Education was seen as a threat by the authorities, who banned the NECC and engaged in a systematic campaign to eliminate People's Education as a focus for opposition. The organisations of People's Education were broken apart, its leaders and spokespersons restricted and detained, and school principals and teachers suspected of being sympathetic to the ideals of People's Education were replaced, demoted or transferred. One effect of these destructive measures has been to reinforce the conviction that the question of who holds executive power over schooling takes priority over questions about the aims of education.

Attempts to articulate the ideals of People's Education, or to develop its practices, have been hampered by the heavy-handed, coercive and repressive actions of the authorities. In addition, they have also been distorted by competing political groupings contesting the authority to speak for People's Education. I think there is still agreement that People's Education might be seen as an aspect of the reconstruction of South Africa along non-racial democratic lines, but this is, at best, only an optimistic starting point for an articulation of the aims of education for a future South Africa.

A basic problem is the lack of a shared moral discourse in terms of which a significant discussion of the aims of education might take place. Let us try to get to grips with this directly. One reason why a shared moral discourse has not developed in South Africa lies in something I have already noted: the moral relativism that underpins Apartheid and Apartheid Education. Where moral relativism holds sway, a critical consideration of public moral issues is undermined, and a discussion of the aims of education becomes merely an assertion of incommensurable convictions. Another reason is that this country has a history of 'moral' language being used as an instrument of betrayal. The political rhetoric in terms of which Apartheid has been defended is laced with moral concepts, albeit frequently with a strong dimension of paternalism. As a result, moral language has tended to be drained of significance, to lose its force in public discussion.

To these reasons we can now add another. Many of those opposed to Apartheid have come to conceive of the struggle against Apartheid as a titanic conflict between the forces of Good and Evil. Evil is identified with Apartheid and all its works, and the overriding moral virtue is to be opposed to Apartheid. To be opposed to Apartheid is to be Good. The manifest justness of the cause guarantees the moral purity of those who act in its name; the righteousness of the cause leads to self-righteousness amongst those who support it. Morality comes to be seen as spontaneous amongst the oppressed. Moral purity is refined in the crucible of struggle. To criticise those on the side of Good is to demonstrate that one is on the side of Evil. The spontaneous moral intuitions of the oppressed will lead them, given the chance, impeccably to do the right thing, in the schooling system as elsewhere. Any question about what the 'right thing' might be is construed as prevarication on the issue of the justness of the cause. While it is understandable, this stance and the simple and uncritical moral theory on which it is founded provides infertile ground for the discussion of the aims of education.

There are urgent theoretical projects in education in South Africa at present, but the establishment of a shared moral discourse is not amongst them – such a project is not *theoretical*. One theoretical project must be the rigorous critique and deconstruction of the forms of understanding that shape and maintain the institutions, relationships and practices that constitute Apartheid Education. Unless this project is undertaken, the effects of Apartheid Education will stretch forward into the future and hamper attempts to reconstruct South African society as a non-racial democratic polity. Such a critique must, at least, imply some positive alternative. But, as I have argued, I do not think that this means that we can now set about discussing the aims of education in South Africa with any expectation that it will have any significant impact on what happens in the schooling system in South Africa now or in the future.

The liberation movement and People's Education contain the seeds of a shared moral discourse. But this nascent discourse has been so fragmented by the repressive reactions of the South African authorities, and so distorted by the culture of negative power that it cannot, at least not yet, provide the ground for a significant discussion of the aims of education. To this it might be responded that one reason for discussing the aims of education might precisely be to help to foster a shared moral discourse. I am, hesitantly, prepared to concede this, but I would want to add that whether or not this might occur would depend on the acknowledged political authority of those engaging in such a discussion, and on who might be paying any attention to it in a climate of radical political conflict.

I think my central claim is that there might be a possibility that a discussion of the aims of education in South Africa could be used as a stalking horse to encourage the development of a shared moral discourse, which is a necessary condition for a significant discussion of the aims of education in South Africa. The knotted complexities of this claim are a symptom of the predicaments in South Africa at present.

Notes

1   This essay was originally published as 'Aims of Education in South Africa' in the *International Review of Education* 36(2): 171 181, 1990. It is reproduced here with the kind permission of Springer Science and Business Media.

2   B Rose & R Tunmer (eds), *Documents in South African Education*, Johannesburg: AD Donker, 1974. All the quotations I provide in the text are from documents republished in this book, which is a rich source of documents related to education in South Africa. I have referenced the quotations I use with the abbreviation RT followed by a page number.

3   This demographic information is derived from statistics provided in SAIRR, *Race Relations Survey* 1987/8, Johannesburg: South African Institute of Race Relations, 1988. These annual surveys are an invaluable source for unpropagandised information about South Africa.

4   The 'present time' refers to 1989, when this essay was written.

5   See Colin Bundy, ' "Action, comrades, action!": The politics of youth-student resistance in the Western Cape, 1985', in W James & M Simons (eds), *The Angry Divide*, Cape Town: David Philip, 1989. Bundy talks of 'immediatism' as a characteristic of the politics of that time: 'This mode of activist politics could also nurture a political perspective that one might dub "immediatism": an impatient anticipation of imminent victory, unrealistic assessment of progress made, and underestimation of the extent of state power. This is not surprising: when political baptism comprised a heady mix of exhilaration, raw courage and group solidarity, expectations could easily outrun actuality' (p. 21).

Teacher Education, pluralism and the ugly lines of segregation in South Africa

(First published in 1996)[1]

In South Africa public debate about multiculturalism and multicultural education has not been very prominent. This might be thought to be an anomaly. South Africa is, after all, a 'plural society' with a vengeance, a 'rainbow people'[2] in the process of escaping the dark clouds of its history. South Africa comprises a breathtaking diversity of more or less recently imported cultures, almost a complete range of racial groups, 11 official languages and very high discrepancies between rich and poor. How might we explain the apparent anomaly that in this diverse society multiculturalism has not (yet, perhaps) become a major issue for debate? Here is a possible explanation.

Apartheid and the politics of difference

Almost a century ago a religious, linguistic and cultural minority group, the Boers, with little economic power, at the 'far end' of Africa, fought a second bitter war against what was still at that time the major imperial power. They lost the war and then, as the victors began to 'reconstruct' the country along 'civilised lines', were faced with the prospect of losing what was most precious and sacred to them, their cultural identity. They were being marginalised in what they saw as their 'own' country, and their very survival as a distinct cultural group was under threat. Struggle on the cultural plane was not new to them, and they took up that struggle again, in a condition of considerable poverty. For example, to prevent their children from being homogenised into the alien culture provided in the state schools, they tried to establish their own community schools, employing teachers who shared their religious convictions. They adopted what we might now call a politics of difference, demanding recognition of, and respect for, their cultural distinctness.

The settlement of 1910 was classically colonial, providing only restricted rights and representation to the majority of the population, and recognising only two 'official languages' – Dutch and English. But the language spoken by the minority, who had fought the war 10 years previously, was not Dutch, but a version of Dutch that had been modified by isolation and dynamic interaction with other languages. This spoken language was sometimes demeaningly referred to as 'Kitchen Dutch', but the people themselves called it 'Afrikaans' and called themselves 'Afrikaners'. In 1926, Afrikaans replaced Dutch as one of the 'official' languages of the country.

But this victory, important as it was, was only a symptom of a much deeper struggle, the struggle for cultural security and permanent cultural survival. The Great Depression of the early 1930s rubbed salt into the wounds, and the decade of the 30s was a period of intense cultural and political mobilisation, not uninfluenced, we might comment, by the rising tide of racialism and nationalism in Germany. Some of the greatest Afrikaner sons[3], who had been prominent in the political life of the country, and even influential on the international stage, came to be seen as having betrayed the struggle by becoming co-opted into the alien culture.

Against the tide of political expectations, the party of the Afrikaners (the National Party) won the general election of 1948, and had rapidly to put a government together. Within a few years the policy of Apartheid was being systematically implemented. In 1953, the first of the Acts definitively to segregate the schooling system was passed, the notorious *Bantu Education Act*. Bantu Education was, at least in the rhetoric with which it was introduced, intended to establish a 'culturally sensitive' form of schooling for those classified as 'African', and subsequent Acts established similarly culturally targeted schooling for the distinct cultural groupings that were to be formally recognised in both the intimate and the public life of the society. Amongst other things, schools for whites, some of which were previously 'dual' or 'parallel' medium (Afrikaans and English), now became single medium. Other parts of the education system, especially teacher training colleges and universities, were also segregated along the perceived lines of cultural differentiation, with language as a key marker. Teacher Education, a decisive site of cultural generation, was conceived of as monocultural, the only morally justifiable way to give proper recognition and respect to 'obvious' cultural differences.

Intellectual defenders of Apartheid denied that its intention was to dominate[4]. They understood it as the alternative to an assimilationist policy of blandly ignoring cultural differences in the public sphere and, thereby, subtly undermining their chances of survival. Apartheid was defended as a formal, culturally neutral framework within which the cultures of the major sectors of the society would be accorded political recognition, and each would have the opportunity to flourish and develop according to its own distinct and cherished traditions and deeply held convictions, undistorted by a hegemonic culture.

Such a stance is quite understandable once we grant the premise that the deepest source of one's identity is one's culture, vulnerable in a world of hegemonic cultures, and deserving of, and even needing, recognition and respect from others. Refusing such respect can inflict grievous damage on those who are denied it (as Afrikaners had themselves experienced) and is itself a form of oppression.

And what could be a locus of more crucial cultural significance in these respects than schools, and the teachers who teach in them. Schools stand at a major intersection between the intimate and the public spheres; schoolteachers are public officials in the business of contributing to the development of the intimate self-interpretations of learners. The segregated systems of schooling and Teacher Education, which were a key dimension of Apartheid, can, or so it was claimed by its defenders, be seen as a serious attempt to give respectful and equal recognition to the distinctive cultural aspirations of the major different cultural groups that constituted the society.

The politics of equal dignity

But Apartheid was seen as an evil both by the world at large and by those who suffered its ruthless implementation, supported by others who, if they did not directly suffer, thought they understood that suffering. The intellectuals who had defended Apartheid were seen as deceiving apologists for a manifestly and insufferably unjust policy. The intellectual defence of Apartheid, in terms of not only protecting cultural identity, but also providing social and political space and even encouragement for its continued survival and development, was seen as merely epiphenomenal, or as an ideological mask for a vicious system of racial and economic oppression and exploitation.

Apartheid came to be seen by both its local and international critics as an affront to human dignity, the very institutionalisation of inequality, and the virulent tail end of colonialism. A key weapon of colonialism was the imposition on the colonised of an image of their culture dreamed up by the colonisers, an image constructed around the presumption of inferiority. The colonised tend to internalise this image and develop a crippling form of self-hatred that deeply undermines their capacity to oppose their subordination; they become complicit agents of their own oppression[5]. And their embranglement is even more insidious if it is obscured by the rhetoric of cultural respect, as it was by Apartheid.

One response to Apartheid was the brief flourishing of a local Black Consciousness Movement, with Biko[6] as its boldest and most effective spokesperson. Its emphasis was on undermining the images of inferiority projected by the dominating powers and replacing these images with a self-confidence founded in deeper traditions. In effect, it proposed that a way out of oppression is for the oppressed themselves to recover respect for their own culture, to use the politics of difference against the dominant powers. Its thrust was on finding a cure for the psychological damage wreaked by colonialism and Apartheid, and perhaps there are traces of this same thrust in some contemporary calls for white teachers to be removed from their teaching posts in black township schools. After all, whatever their good intentions, whites can never really comprehend black culture.

Although, to my knowledge, the local Black Consciousness Movement did not express itself on the issue of Teacher Education, it has fairly clear implications for what an appropriate kind of Teacher Education would be; it would be one in which prospective teachers would need to come to see the restoration of the self-esteem of the oppressed as their guiding professional ideal. Such a view is in harmony with some of the thinking of Paulo Freire[7]; it would recommend that teachers should understand that a definitive feature of their responsibility as teachers is to restore to the oppressed a sense of their own historical agency. This would be to line up Teacher Education with the politics of difference.

But mainstream opposition and resistance to Apartheid had the politics of equal dignity as its guiding thread. This kind of politics is based on a demand for the recognition of universal human needs and capacities, and it is inhospitable to the claims of a politics of difference. The politics of equal dignity is 'difference blind', as is succinctly expressed in what became a key demand of the resistance movement in education in the late 1980s, for a single education department to replace the 17 or so education departments then in existence. This can be read more as a cry for equality of recognition than as an administrative recommendation. It is also expressed in the non-racial stance of the ANC government, and the development of a Bill of Rights that will underpin the equality of all citizens.

A black American scholar, writing not about South Africa but about manifestations of racism in many USA colleges and universities in the late 1980s, expresses the same line of thinking:

> (The) elevation of difference undermines the communal impulse by making each group foreign and inaccessible to others. When difference is celebrated rather than remarked, people must think in terms of difference, they must find meaning difference, and this meaning comes from an endless process of contrasting one's group with other groups…and in the process each group mythologizes and mystifies its difference, puts it beyond the full comprehension of outsiders. Difference becomes an inaccessible preciousness toward which outsiders are expected to be simply and uncomprehendingly reverential…I think universities should emphasize *commonality* as a higher value than 'diversity' and 'pluralism' – buzzwords for the *politics of difference*.[8]

In the light of this history of domination under the guise of respecting cultural difference, and resistance to that domination in terms of the politics of equal dignity, perhaps we might begin to understand the anomaly that, in spite of its popularity in the intellectual circuits of Europe and North America, multiculturalism and multicultural education have not become major issues for debate in South Africa.

Perhaps, to put the point in an exaggeratedly sharp way, we can say that South Africans have had a century of experience of the politics of difference, and they didn't like what they saw.

Multiculturalism and social stability

South Africa needs to escape from the dark clouds of its history, and one of the most threatening clouds is that both colonialism and Apartheid emphasised difference in a way in which coercion and manipulation became the main means of maintaining social stability.

A main problem in the 'new' South Africa is how to discover social cohesion that is not dependent on manipulation, threats and force, and in a political context in which some of the major trends of our history have generated an assumption of mutual cultural incomprehension and antagonism, fragmentation and division. We have to discover and maintain a shared meaning for 'we', a sense of community that is a necessary condition for democratic politics. And, at present, the politics of equal dignity looks like a more promising route than the politics of difference.

But perhaps even to pose the issue in this way, as if it is a matter of a *choice* between alternative routes, is misleading.

It is noteworthy that debates about multiculturalism and multicultural education do not seem much in evidence in, for instance, Somalia, Chechnya, Burundi, Bosnia or Rwanda, or other countries that attract the attention of Amnesty International. The debate flourishes in Western Europe and North America, and countries like Australia that participate in the same intellectual circuits and, significantly, in public institutions, especially educational institutions which, in spite of self-understandings of conflict and division, enjoy broadly accepted legitimacy and a stable existence.

To put it in what might turn out to be a crude formulation, debate about multicultural education takes place against a backdrop, typically unarticulated, of social stability. The phrase 'social stability' is hardly transparent, and I shall try briefly to indicate what I am referring to.

People living in the countries of the north enjoy a degree of social and personal security that is hardly imaginable in large parts of the world. In such countries there is substantial affluence and economic stability, and a framework of political traditions and institutions, which are a product of historical developments over some centuries, and which provide a structure within which political and social conflicts are only abnormally resolved by resort to machetes and AK47 rifles.

Mass schooling systems are well established in such societies; it can be assumed that at least the vast majority of the children of the society not merely have access to regular schooling, but that pupils and teachers actually attend school on a regular basis. And, in spite of skepticism in some academic circles, the value of schooling is broadly accepted; by and large it is believed that public educational institutions contribute to the amelioration of gross social inequality and enable people to fulfil their potential. Furthermore, such social and institutional stability is underpinned by what we might call deep moral agreement, although whether 'moral' is the right word to refer to this underlying condition is a moot point[9]. Agreement at this deeper level is neither bland moral consensus nor an inflexible republic of virtue; it is more like a deeply embedded assumption about how it is appropriate for human beings to relate to each other, even if they disagree profoundly about some significant issues.

These features of the countries of the north that I am describing in broad and generalised terms here can, typically, simply be taken for granted in such societies, and anxiety about the perceived 'problems' – such as the fate of 'marginalised' groups in some urban centres and rural backwaters, the levels of domestic and other violence, a 'rising tide' of drug abuse and teenage pregnancies, and the difficulties of 'minorities' to flourish in public institutions such as schools – can be seen as reinforcing the point I am making. To see such issues as 'problems' is to assume agreement about what is 'normal'.

The achievement of this degree of social stability is, at least in large measure, an outcome of the persistent pursuit, since the European Enlightenment, of the politics of equal dignity. This form of politics arose in opposition to what were seen as the injustices of a social order based on difference, and what it emphasises is the ways in which human beings are similar to each other. It is a kind of politics for which impartial treatment is the central regulative ideal. It is 'difference blind' in respect, for example, to schooling. All children, irrespective of the social status of their background, deserve an equal opportunity for schooling. Much of the history of schooling in such societies, over the past, say, two centuries, is a history of attempts to achieve more and more adequate implementation of the ideals of the politics of equal dignity. As cracks show, we try to repair them.

It is against this background of social stability that the politics of difference emerges and can flourish. The politics of difference is logically and historically parasitic on the politics of equal dignity; it arises in a historical context that has been shaped by a tradition of the pursuit of the politics of equal dignity. If this claim is true, then it is likely that not only will the politics of difference find it difficult to gain a foothold in a society that does not have an established tradition of the politics of equal dignity, but it might be unwise and risky to try to introduce it in such a society. It might have the effect of simply tearing such a society apart. The high moral tone of much of the discourse of multicultural education has a hollow ring to it, if it is the harbinger of social disintegration.

Teacher Education in South Africa and the politics of equal dignity

Let us now turn our attention to Teacher Education in South Africa. South Africa does not (yet) have the kind of social stability I have tried to describe above; it does not have a strong tradition of the pursuit of the politics of equal dignity. For the majority of the people in this country, sheer survival is a constant challenge. Many do not have even adequate nutrition and drinkable water, never mind basically decent shelter or healthcare, and reasonable security from the high levels of violence that are 'normal' in some sectors of the society. At the same time, human and financial resources are stretched to a limit, and economic recovery is high on the development agenda.

The schooling system is in tatters. As is typical of many 'developing' countries, school-age children constitute a much higher proportion of the population than they do in richer countries, but significant numbers of children have no access to schooling at all, and the majority attend schools that are in deep disarray, with little by way of established routines and even less in terms of a shared sense of the significance of systematic learning. We might polemically ask what purchase multicultural education might have in such a situation.

The education struggle in this country has left us with a legacy of widespread cynicism about the value of learning, a deep suspicion about the ideological underpinnings of educational authority and idealistic views about the democratic governance of schools. In spite of the 'miracle' of the general election of April 1994, fundamental moral agreement is not securely established. Social cohesion is fragile, and it is not merely alarmist to suggest that South Africa runs the ever-present danger of becoming another Somalia or Bosnia of the world.

These social conditions have direct implications for Teacher Education in South Africa at this time. The schools, and thus the teachers who teach in them, are a critical locus for the regeneration of South Africa, and such regeneration depends crucially on the fostering of social cohesion. But this implies a particular agenda for Teacher Education. At the heart of this agenda stands the politics of equal dignity.

We might fill in some of the details as follows. Given our experience of the ugly lines of segregation, a high priority for teachers, and thus for Teacher Education, in this phase of our history, is to contribute to the generation of a unifying and deep moral agreement; a shared meaning for who 'we' are. This will be achieved not so much by lectures in moral philosophy or political exhortations to patriotism or national pride, but in the details of teaching practice. Teachers need to resist the moral blandishments of the politics of difference, and develop a procedural commitment to ignore the historically constructed differences between learners – to be colour and gender blind – and to treat and respect all learners equally. Teachers need to learn the difficult skills of exercising impartiality in their professional relationships and educational judgement, and using forms of assessment and evaluation that are strictly 'difference blind'. They need to cultivate a stance of equal expectations of all learners, and to overcome the matrix of demeaning, patronising or condescending, and ultimately disempowering, attitudes that have historically shaped human relationships in South Africa.

In addition, and in line with the traditional attempts to achieve the ideals of the politics of equal dignity in countries with a long history of striving for this end, Teacher Education needs at this time in South Africa to retrieve a belief in the value of systematic learning, and to foster in teachers a proper sense of their responsibility to contribute to the maintenance of regular institutionalised schooling – conventional in countries of the north – characterised by standard routines, regular class attendance and 'normal' standards of progress through the system.

And, underpinning all of this, there needs to be a reassertion of what it means to be a member of a profession with a vital public role in society. In Teacher Education there needs to be a strong emphasis on the fostering of a proper sense of professional responsibility to contribute to the improvement of society by being an initiator of social cohesion in gestation, an exemplar and practitioner of the politics of equal dignity, against a historical backdrop that has corrupted these ideals.

This sketch of the main agenda for Teacher Education in South Africa at this time would rightly be regarded as deeply conservative in an affluent society characterised by dynamic social cohesion. But my point is that South Africa is not such a society.

The reconciliation between the politics of equal dignity and the politics of difference

But perhaps the politics of difference is a warning shot across our bows. South Africa is, after all, a highly plural society.

Perhaps the kind of emphasis I have placed on the centrality of the politics of equal dignity in the main agenda for Teacher Education in South Africa at this time is simply an assertion of a different form of monocultural Teacher Education to replace the forms traditional in South Africa. Perhaps, in my attempts to emphasise the historical contextualisation of debate about multiculturalism, I have not been sufficiently sensitive to the real diversity of South African society. Perhaps we need to take more seriously the implied warning from the north that the politics of equal dignity turns out to be self-defeating in the end.

Perhaps, too, the sketch I have given of social conditions in South Africa is too pessimistic. While it is true that much of the schooling system is in disarray, some of it is in very familiar good shape, and while social cohesion might not be as robust as it is in more settled and affluent societies, it is, paradoxically given our history, not so fragile as to be at the point of imminent breakdown. And we need, too, to take into account the increasing intrusion of international moral conviction, and the extent to which either mode of politics in its pure form is likely to become increasingly unstable in a globalising world. As Charles Taylor remarks, 'there are other cultures, and we have to live together more and more, both on a world scale and commingled in each individual society'.[10]

In the section above, called 'Multiculturalism and social stability', I raised doubts about the idea that the politics of equal dignity and the politics of difference offered alternative routes between which we had a choice. The argument was that historically and logically the politics of difference is parasitic on the politics of equal dignity, and until the politics of equal dignity has done its work of establishing social cohesion, the politics of difference can have no real purchase, and might indeed pose a threat to social cohesion.

In this section I shall explore a different way in which it is misleading to suggest that the two modes of politics present a *choice* between alternatives. I shall reconsider the incompatibility I have assumed between the two modes of politics, and then, in a concluding section, introduce some modifications to the sketch I have provided of the main agenda for Teacher Education in contemporary South Africa.

The incompatibility I have assumed arises in the following way. The politics of equal dignity is procedural; it claims to be culturally neutral, to be able to provide a public space in which differences between citizens will be ignored, where all citizens will have equal dignity, rights and entitlements as citizens. The politics of equal dignity claims to provide a neutral ground on which people of all cultures can meet and co-exist.

Against this, the politics of difference argues that the politics of equal dignity, with its seminal 'difference-blind' principle, subtly perpetuates inequalities of life chances. It is not true that the politics of equal dignity ignores all differences between people. Why, for instance, does this mode of politics favour the idea that it is the young of the society who appropriately attend primary and secondary schools, or that only those found guilty by the due processes of law should be confined in prisons? In effect, what the politics of difference claims is that a range of differences is already acknowledged by the politics of equal dignity as relevant to different treatment, but that the range is too limited. In order to achieve its overarching goal of an equal society, the politics of equal dignity needs to take on board additional differences, such as cultural and gender differences. In other words, it needs to expand its view about which differences are relevant.

The politics of equal dignity understands human dignity to consist largely of respect for individual autonomy, the potential of each person to determine for themselves a view of a good or satisfactory life for them, and the capacity, given the opportunity, to construct their own identity in the light of that view. But the politics of difference objects that this understanding of individual autonomy is based on the fantasy that each individual human being constructs their own identity in a cultural vacuum, as it were. It ignores the ways in which individual identity is not a free, monological construction but is formed by, and in, cultural contexts, and is essentially dialogical. Recognition and respect from those who understand one's project are key factors in the construction of identities.

Ignoring cultural differences in schooling, failing to recognise or respect them, as is recommended by 'difference blindness', is said to massively and persistently disadvantage pupils who come from a cultural background different from the hegemonic culture of the school, and it hinders their access to education. No politics can be as culturally neutral as the politics of equal dignity claims to be, and its claim to provide neutral ground is a fraud which, in effect, simply perpetuates inequality.

But let us now see whether there is some *modus vivendi* between these two modes of politics, some reconciliation between them. Two examples can help us in this task.

The first is the example of affirmative action, or reverse discrimination. At first glance, a policy of affirmative action looks like an affront to the politics of equal dignity, an obvious example of the politics of difference. But this is not the case.

Affirmative action is a response to an acknowledgement of systematic historical disadvantagement. But it is conceived of as a temporary strategy, a *provisional* recognition of specific, historically produced differences in order to 'level the playing field' so that the politics of equal dignity can resume its normal operation.

In this way a policy of affirmative action is quite different from multiculturalism and multicultural education. These stances require the *permanent* recognition of difference as a ground for special treatment. Indeed, the object of multiculturalism is to perpetuate and maintain differences, especially cultural differences, and to defend them against being watered down and losing their distinctive identity in interaction with other cultures.

The second example is of the 'mainstreaming' of children with special needs, children previously regarded as requiring special treatment, perhaps special classes and – in some cases – even special schools. The policy of 'mainstreaming' seems to be opposed to the politics of difference, and a strong appeal for the recognition of equal dignity. But a more nuanced interpretation is to say that what this policy implies is that mainstream schooling runs on too narrow a conception of 'normality'.

Mainstream schooling already accommodates significant forms of diversity, but the demand is that it become more accommodating and tolerant of diversity, to expand its notion of what kinds of differences are compatible with a politics of equal dignity, to modify its modes of operation, including its traditions of teaching, to accommodate additional learner diversity. The key point here is that the institution cannot be regarded as a 'given' to which learners simply need to adapt. This is, in effect, a challenge to an inflexible implementation of the politics of equal dignity[11].

These two examples take us towards reconciliation between the two modes of politics, but we need concessions from both. The politics of equal dignity must abandon its claim to be culturally neutral and 'difference blind', and acknowledge that it is not purely procedural but itself a particular political and cultural project; the politics of difference must disconnect itself from its attachment to its presupposition that difference is permanent and necessarily of value. The politics of equal dignity needs a more expansive and inclusive conception of rationality; the politics of difference must abandon its adherence to epistemological and moral relativism and, in this way, distance itself from most of what we find under the blanket of multiculturalism and multicultural education.

In the concluding section I shall supplement my suggestion for the main agenda for Teacher Education in South Africa at this time with two lessons drawn from reconciliation between the two modes of politics.

Additions to the agenda for Teacher Education in South Africa

South Africa is a plural society with its schools becoming more heterogeneous by the day. The responsibilities of schoolteachers are likely to become significantly more challenging, and Teacher Education is obliged to take increasing diversity on board.

I shall here suggest two supplementary additions to the main agenda already outlined in a previous section. These additions are complementary to that agenda, and not in conflict with it.

The first arises out of a consideration of the conception of culture, which is one of the dark clouds of our history, and is also embedded in debates about multiculturalism and multicultural education. In this conception culture is sacred, and it might have its roots in a conceptual link between culture and religion. Mercifully, religious differences do not stand at the centre of South African diversity.

If we think of culture as sacred, then we are likely to go on to think that reverence is the appropriate stance towards culture, that cultures are inviolate and that their differences should be regarded as sacrosanct. Furthermore, if our background is in one of the monotheistic religions such as Christianity or Islam, we are also likely to think of cultures as having unequal value and embodying incommensurable values.

I do not have a recipe for how it might be done, but I do think that an important item on the agenda for Teacher Education in South Africa at this time must be to enable teachers to develop a different conception of culture. At the heart of this conception is the view of culture, at least living cultures, as continually being modified. In the profane world in which we live our lives, there are no 'pure' cultures and cultural forms are in continual interaction with each other. One way to generate a different conception of culture in a Teacher Education programme might be to consider critically the fate of culture in the modern world of unprecedented mobility, rapid transportation, transnational markets, and the burgeoning of more and more available globalised electronic information and communication technologies.

But, however it is done in practice, South African teachers at this time need to be operating with a conception of culture in which cultural difference can never provide an excuse for a romantic and sentimental refusal to engage in respectful dialogue, and one which acknowledges that the interfaces and mutual enrichment between existing cultures provide the most promising node for the generation of the social cohesion we need for our survival.

The second supplementary item on the main agenda underpins the first. Teachers need to overcome a stance of moral and intellectual relativism, which can sap their confidence by inducing anxiety and guilt about the very practice of teaching. Moral and intellectual relativism is one of the dark clouds from which we need to escape, and a lesson we do not need from much of what is said about multiculturalism and multicultural education in societies in which such debates are not a matter of life or death.

From the security of an affluent society it might seem reactionary, but I think that a main task for Teacher Education in South Africa at this time, plural as the society may be, is for teachers to develop a supple and resilient conception of rationality, and to implement it as the regulative ideal of their practice of professional educative teaching.

Notes

1 This essay was originally published under the title 'Teacher education and pluralism in South Africa' in Maurice Craft (ed.), *Teacher Education in Plural Societies*, London: Falmer Press, 1996, pp. 95–107. It is reproduced here with the kind permission of the publisher. The essay benefited from conversations with Charles Taylor, Rosalie Small, Susan Meyer, Nelleke Bak, and Sigamoney Naicker, but none is likely not to disagree with some of the conclusions I reach.

2 The phrase 'rainbow people' was put into circulation by Archbishop Tutu, the Chancellor of the University of the Western Cape.

3 The oustanding example here is Jan Christian Smuts.

4 An example is Professor J Chris Coetzee in 'The theory of Christian-National Education' reprinted in B Rose & R Tunmer (eds), *Documents in South African Education*, Johannesburg: AD Donker, 1975.

5 The seminal expression of this view is to be found in Frantz Fanon, *The Wretched of the Earth*, Paris: Maspero, 1961.

6 Steve Biko, *I Write What I Like*, London: Penguin Books, 1988.

7 Paulo Freire, *The Pedagogy of the Oppressed*, Harmondsworth, Middlesex: Penguin Books, 1986.

8 S Steele (1989), 'The recoloring of campus life. Student racism, academic pluralism and the end of a dream' as quoted in Fernand Ouellet, 'Education in a pluralistic society: Proposal for an enrichment of teacher education' in Kogila A Moodley (ed.), *Beyond Multicultural Education*, Calgary, Alberta: Detselig Enterprises, 1992, p. 296.

9 A wonderful discussion of this view, characterised in terms of the classical Greek notion of *nomos*, is to be found in Martha C Nussbaum, 'The betrayal of convention: A reading of Euripides' *Hecuba*' in *The Fragility of Goodness: Luck and Ethics in Greek Tragedy and Philosophy*, Cambridge: Cambridge University Press, 1987.

10 Charles Taylor, 'The politics of recognition' in Amy Gutmann (ed.), *Multiculturalism and 'The Politics of Recognition'*, Oxford, N.J.: Princeton University Press, 1992, p. 72. This paper by Charles Taylor is the source of my key contrast between the politics of equal dignity and the politics of difference and, in general, had a major impact on my argument.

11 The University of the Western Cape has developed an 'open admissions' policy that combines the two kinds of considerations – affirmative action in relation to those historically excluded by the policy of Apartheid from university study, combined with an attempt to transform the university and its practices to accommodate students who would previously have been seen as standing outside of the boundary of 'normal' university students.

10 *Multicultural education in South Africa*

(First published in 1998)[1]

Social justice…requires not the melting away of differences, but institutions that promote reproduction of and respect for group differences without oppression.

Iris Young, *Justice and the Politics of Difference*

The politics of difference

Over the past decades in the liberal democratic world there has been a growing emphasis on the recognition of social diversity. This emphasis is evident in debates in political and social theory and, of course, education, but it is also reflected in the forms of protest that have become prevalent in liberal democratic societies. By now it seems to have become a commonplace that modern societies are 'plural' or 'multicultural' and that their public policy should 'recognise difference', perhaps especially in the field of education in the form of multicultural education.

Advocates of multiculturalism typically understand these developments as a critique of liberalism, and its reproductive wing liberal education. Although this critique takes a variety of forms, central to it are the allegations that liberalism homogenises society, it ignores some of the crucial differences between people which are basic to their identity and its formation, and that the self-understanding of liberalism as 'neutral' is fraudulent. Liberalism is characterised as a form of normalising oppression – more insidious than other forms of oppression due to its benign 'neutral' face – and liberal education is vilified as one of the prime instruments for the maintenance of that oppression.

Defenders of liberalism are, understandably, shocked by such allegations. In its self-understanding, liberalism has always thought of itself as the primary opponent of oppression, including those forms of oppression that rest on a denial of difference. The ideal of autonomy is one of the defining features of liberalism, and this has been expressed in terms of not merely a tolerance of individual differences, but their celebration and promotion as well, especially in education. Liberalism was always committed to the 'recognition of difference' but, say the critics, it was not the right kind of difference that was recognised.

According to critics, a major flaw in liberalism lies in the way it prioritises individuals in its conceptions of difference and identity. Liberalism is socially homogenising, not because it does not acknowledge differences between individuals, or that it is committed to doing so is one of its defining characteristics, but because it does not acknowledge or recognise in its public policies and practices, including education, significant differences between the groups which compose the population. To conceive of identity in individualistic terms, as liberalism does, not only ignores the sources of identity, but also involves 'abstracting' individuals from the group membership that specifically defines and maintains their identity.

The politics of difference focuses not on differences between individuals, but on differences between groups; it refers to what are called 'collective differences'. On this understanding, to talk of a 'diverse' or a 'plural' society is to be referring not to the truism that any society is composed of individuals who are obviously different from one another in a potentially huge variety of respects, but to differences between the groups that compose the society. The argument is, then, that to fail to recognise collective differences in appropriate ways in public and educational policy is a form of oppression because collective identities are primary. Individual identities, it is claimed, are products and reflections of collective identities, so that to fail to respect collective identities in education, for example, is to undermine the vulnerable individual identities of, particularly, members of traditionally marginalised or oppressed groups, and to fail to provide a nurturing environment in which those identities can develop and flourish.

Considered from the point of view of these debates, South Africa exhibits social diversity in the starkest possible terms. Most of what have been claimed to be salient 'differences' (differences which demand public recognition) in liberal democratic societies are found in South Africa, and frequently in an extreme form. South Africa is the home of a breathtaking range of different languages, religions, ethnic groups and cultural traditions and practices. The phrase 'the rainbow nation' has been used to highlight this rich and colourful diversity. From this observation the conclusion can be drawn, so it is thought, that South Africa should enthusiastically embrace the politics of difference and build multicultural education into the heart of its system of public education. South Africa is socially diverse; therefore it ought to favour the politics of difference and foster multicultural education.

This is the argument I set out to explore in this essay.

Similarities between Apartheid and multiculturalism

It is understandable why South Africans will approach this argument with some ambivalence. South Africa is a product of an embrangled history of Eurocentric colonialism and its stepchild, Apartheid, and bitter struggles against these harsh forms of oppression. A defining feature of both colonialism and Apartheid was the identification and maintenance of separate groups in the population. Both the defence of and the struggle against these regimes have deeply entrenched these group differences. Contemporary South Africa, we might say, is not so much 'socially diverse' as 'socially divided'; it is more in need of a 'discovery of commonality' than it is in need of a 'recognition of difference'.

But there is also a more theoretical kind of reason South Africans should be anxious about embracing the discourse of the politics of difference and multicultural education. We think of colonialism and Apartheid as so thoroughly unjust and evil that it is difficult for us to imagine that they could once have been plausibly defended, and by some people of good will. A constant theme in the official justifications for these oppressive regimes was the need to recognise and respect the differences between the different groups that compose the society, and to protect and perpetuate group integrity. At least in respect to thoughts like this, the discourse of the politics of difference and multicultural education is uncomfortably similar to the discourse of colonialism and Apartheid.

Intellectual apologists for Apartheid would have had little difficulty in agreeing with the statement from Iris Young, which I quoted at the head of this essay, and they would have had few problems about agreeing that it is the shortcomings of liberalism that require us to develop a different political philosophy more appropriate for a plural society. They would have agreed that one of the worst forms of oppression is the domination of one group by another, but would have added that this form of oppression is, in practice, impossible to avoid when such groups occupy a common political and geographical space. The only way to avoid such domination and oppression, they would have said, is for groups to be segregated and provided with the opportunity autonomously to nurture and perpetuate their own distinctive cultures, in their own institutions.

The segregationist position is not unique to Apartheid, as anyone who knows about racial problems in the United States will know. Over the years, the defenders of Apartheid pointed to the examples of Ireland, India and Pakistan, and the former Yugoslavia. In Africa itself, there have been ongoing problems about the 'artificial' colonial boundaries. Nigeria and Rwanda provide brutal examples of the kinds of problems that arise when cultural differences are ignored in public policy. In general terms, the problem in all these cases is how to maintain a peaceful and coherent society in a situation of cultural diversity.

The charge that the discourses of Apartheid and multiculturalism are similar to each other is one that the defenders of multiculturalism will find deeply disturbing; their natural response will be to deny it passionately. But what can be their grounds for such a denial? That they see Apartheid as morally obnoxious and multiculturalism as morally virtuous is not sufficient. They need to be able to point to some more substantive differences in order to provide grounds for these moral judgements.

They might, first, think in terms of contrasting goals. Apartheid, they might say, was driven by the goal of oppression; multiculturalism is driven by the goal of alleviating and undermining oppression. But this does little to advance the argument. Here, as elsewhere, good intentions are not enough. I have already indicated that there were some defenders of Apartheid who argued that the goal of the policy was to avoid oppression. Putting aside the suggestion that they were simply lying, we might say that the historical record shows that they were deluded. But if they were deluded, then, given the apparent similarities between the two discourses, perhaps the defenders of multiculturalism are similarly deluded. To rebut this suggestion, the defenders of multiculturalism still need to point to substantive differences.

Differences between multiculturalism and Apartheid

In this rebuttal, there are two closely linked possibilities: one in terms of the underlying theories of social groups, the other in terms of the socio-political policy of segregation.

Apartheid was founded on an essentialist account of cultural groups; multiculturalism might be able to reject this account. For Apartheid, each cultural group was conceived of as homogenous and self-contained, as having a distinctive and essential nature that needed to be protected from contamination, preserved for the sake of current and future members of the group, and perpetuated by means of education. The roots of the view in 19th century evolutionary biology and European racism are clear, and it provides a classical example of the reification of social phenomena. Cultural groups are conceived of on the model of biological species; like species they can suffer extinction or degeneration, and although they can develop gradually over time, such development is guided by a kind of internal dynamic which, if it is ignored, will lead to the disintegration of the group with the dire consequences of demoralisation and the loss of the natural integrity of the group, which is the principal ground of the identity of its individual members. Individual members of a cultural group might, through blindness or ignorance, lose sight of the seminal importance, for their own identities and the significance of their own lives, of maintaining group integrity. This is why group differentiation has, if need be, to be imposed on people for their own benefit, as a matter of political policy.

Multiculturalism might be able to reject the organic metaphor that lies in the roots of such an essentialist account of social groups. The origin and formation of social groups is to be explained in terms of historical, as opposed to organic, processes. For some versions of multiculturalism, social groups arise out of the social processes of differentiation and affinity and, once formed, they shape how people understand one another and themselves; they become, in short, sources of identity for their members. Social groups come into being as an outcome of social encounters and interactions. Thus, the concept of a social group is relational as opposed to essential. In the words of Iris Young, 'Groups are an expression of social relations; a group exists only in relation to at least one other group'[2].

This provides one way of distinguishing between Apartheid and multiculturalism, and it leads towards another.

Apartheid insisted that traditional cultural groups needed to be segregated from one another not only to avoid irresolvable conflict, but also to ensure the integrity and continued survival of distinctive cultures. In clear contrast to this, multiculturalism holds the view that diverse social groups all need to be accommodated in the same geographical, political and institutional spaces. Indeed, the very description of a society as 'plural' or an institution as 'multicultural' implies that the members of diverse social groups share, or should share, common public spaces. Multicultural education implies a form of education that accommodates a variety of cultures in a mutually respectful environment in common institutions.

A policy of segregation harmonises with an essentialist view of social groups and, paradoxically, in the light of what happened under Apartheid, one might say that it draws one strand of its inspiration, in the South African context, from a genuine, if paternalistic, concern for the fate of indigenous cultures under the destructive impact of Eurocentric colonialism. Apartheid attempted to minimalise the interfaces between cultures as much, its defenders would have claimed, for the sake of the integrity of indigenous cultures as for the sake of social peace. Multiculturalism is opposed to segregation; it stands for the idea that politics and institutions should generously accommodate culturally diverse groups while avoiding any overt or covert bias in favour of any particular cultural group.

At a formal level, this provides a second distinction between the discourses of multiculturalism and Apartheid but, to ground this distinction, we still need to know how multiculturalism can respond to the segregationist claim that it is not possible to maintain social peace and stability without cultural domination, in a situation in which diverse cultural groups inhabit common public spaces and institutions. To distance itself definitively from this view, a defence of multiculturalism has to reject a basic theoretical presupposition of the segregationist stance.

Cultural relativism

The segregationist stance, that group domination is unavoidable where diverse cultural groups occupy common political and institutional spaces, presupposes cultural relativism. This is the view that cultures are incompatible with one another, and where they come into conflict there can be only victories and defeats. Cultural relativism is a theory with definite consequences for political and educational policy and practice. If we allow cultures to live together, either some will be lost or destroyed as others achieve dominance, or they might all lose their integrity in a kind of bland cosmopolitan homogeneity. Mutual accommodation between cultures is a form of cultural impoverishment and, far from being desirable, is simply another way of expressing the loss of cultural integrity and a decline in cultural diversity.

Cultural relativism claims that cultures are incommensurable with one another; they each have their own forms of life and there is no way of 'translating' between cultures. Each culture has its own internally coherent form of rationality, rational deliberation is possible only *within* cultures and there can be no such thing as culturally neutral rational deliberation; rationality does not cross cultural boundaries. The idea that there could be culturally neutral institutions or practices, which can accommodate rival cultural groups, is seen either as an illusion of liberalism or a fraudulent attempt by one cultural group to maintain cultural and political domination, or perhaps both at the same time. Unless it is merely a form of politically naive and optimistic romanticism, multiculturalism must oppose this view.

To distance itself definitively from Apartheid's segregationist stance, multiculturalism has to reject the theory of cultural relativism on which it rests. In order to defend its non-segregationist stance, the claim that cultural diversity can be accommodated in common public space without cultural domination or irresolvable conflict and social chaos, it has to commit itself to the view not only that cross-cultural communication is possible, but that there must be some forms of dialogue and deliberation in terms of which cultural conflicts can be resolved or dissolved.

Multiculturalism is incompatible with the kind of dogmatic antagonisms that are a practical consequence of the theory of cultural relativism. Its defence thus requires the rejection not only of the theory of cultural relativism, but also the kinds of practice underwritten by that theory. Multiculturalism is necessarily committed to the idea that there must be some forms of shared practice which, whatever their origin, are not limited to specific cultures or cultural groups, and which are robust enough to generate mutually acceptable resolutions of intercultural incompatibilities and conflicts.

Multiculturalism and liberalism

In distinguishing between multiculturalism and Apartheid we have had to give an account of multiculturalism as having specific characteristics. Multiculturalism needs to be based on a non-essentialist theory of social groups and a rejection of the theory and practice of cultural relativism. There are two important consequences of this result.

One is that this account excludes some accounts of multiculturalism that lead a flourishing life in contemporary populist and polemical debate in this field. Any account of multiculturalism that underplays the socio-political sources of the formation of social groups, or implicitly or explicitly presupposes cultural relativism, is guilty of the charge of being a fellow-traveller in the discourse of Apartheid. In spite of self-righteous attempts to distance themselves from Apartheid, any defenders of 'multiculturalism' who support the ideas of the intrinsic goodness of cultural diversity, the desirability of ensuring the long-term survival of cultural differences, or of pre-emptively demanding equal respect for all cultural achievements, are probably entangled in either an essentialist understanding of cultural groups or cultural relativism or both. Cultural ecology is a contemporary expression of the continuing power of organic and biological metaphors in our social and political theories.

Another is that to the extent that multiculturalism is characterised in terms of a non-essentialist account of social groups and a rejection of cultural relativism it draws closer to liberalism. It becomes more like a variation within the discourse of liberalism than like a competing discourse. Multiculturalism can still be distinguished from orthodox liberalism in terms of its focus on groups and collective identities rather than on autonomous individuals and individual identities, but in other respects it now emerges as a development within liberalism as opposed to a rival to it.

With this understanding of multiculturalism in hand we can now proceed with the exploration of the argument that because South Africa is socially diverse it ought to favour the politics of difference and foster multicultural education. We need to think more directly about multicultural education, and then take into view two major historical characteristics of contemporary South Africa: it is a modernising society engaged in trying to transform itself into a democratic society, on any account a difficult process.

The practice of multicultural education

Bhikhu Parekh[3] usefully points out that the debate about multicultural education originated in a contrast with what was called 'monocultural education'. Mainstream education in liberal democratic societies was accused of being a form of cultural imperialism, monocultural and Eurocentric, which put members of minority cultures at serious social, personal and educational disadvantages. Monocultural education was seen as a form of education which, in its 'nature, aims, contents and ethos', consolidated students in one particular culture by implicitly assuming the superiority of that culture and ignoring or marginalising others, or representing them in superficial, uncomplimentary or demeaning terms.

From an educational point of view, monocultural education has serious shortcomings. It is unlikely to awaken students' intellectual curiosity about other cultures or to develop their moral imagination by exposing them to alternative forms of life and enabling them to enter into the spirit of different visions of a good life for human beings. Monocultural education is likely to stunt the growth of students' critical capacities and to breed cultural arrogance, insensitivity and racism.

On this understanding, the schooling systems inherited by postcolonial societies were monocultural, as was the schooling system of Apartheid. Under Apartheid, with its separate schooling systems for different cultural groups, what we had was a set of monocultural schooling systems. But we can now add, as Parekh does, that some forms of multicultural education are, paradoxically, monocultural; they are '…no less monocultural, and no better, than Eurocentric education'[4]. Multicultural education, which draws its inspiration from an essentialist theory of cultural groups and cultural relativism, turns out to be *de facto* monocultural. The insistence that various cultures should be accommodated in common institutions is a trivial difference from Apartheid.

Discussions about how we might 'Africanise' the curriculum of South African schools have an important role in the future development of education in South Africa. However, to the extent that they are based on, or move towards, the idea of recommending 'Afrocentric education' to replace 'Eurocentric education' they are simply another form of the monocultural education deeply ingrained in our colonial and Apartheid heritage, and suffer from the same kinds of shortcomings from an educational point of view.

Forms of multicultural education that are, in effect, monocultural, foster educational practices that defeat the ideals of multicultural education. To the extent that, in practice, various cultures are merely studied rather than brought into critical dialogue with one another, to the extent that cultures are treated as if they are hermetically sealed from one another and beyond criticism, we have in view a form of educational practice that subverts the real promise of multicultural education.

But running through the whole of this debate, and reinforced by the supposed contrast between monocultural and multicultural education, is a misleading assumption about education. Education is understood as embedded in and existing to reproduce and subserve specific cultures. All education is assumed to be a more or less subtle form of indoctrination, which recruits new members for specific cultures.

In opposing this assumption we need to avoid committing ourselves to an unsustainable ahistorical theory of rationality, which is a legacy of pre-Enlightenment religious belief. We need to understand rationality as the practice of reasoning. The practices of reasoning and education are not confined to any particular culture, while nonetheless being in the realm of culture, with all that that implies about how their very existence and their flourishing, corruption or degeneration is intimately tied to historically variable patterns of theories, institutions and practices. Reasoning is a practice that assumes that no practices are immune from criticism; it is the platform for cultural critique and provides us with the basis for recognising the inevitable partiality and shortcomings of any specific cultures.

As Parekh claims, 'Education cannot transcend the realm of *culture*, but it can and ought to transcend specific *cultures*'[5]. That form of multicultural education, which rejects cultural relativism and an essentialist view of cultures, is committed to a view of this kind. This has implications for both curriculum content, which is the focus of most of the debate about multicultural education, and for the practice of education, namely, teaching. Multicultural education needs to be underwritten by a characteristic kind of teaching which might, in fact, be even more important than curriculum content.

For multicultural education to be a live option it needs an educational practice that undermines the temptations of cultural relativism and enables students to become participants in the practices of reasoning. Such a practice is difficult and hazardous; it needs to be porous without becoming merely shapeless. It disrupts the traditional 'cultural' authority of teachers and focuses sharply on their professional judgement. The professional judgement of teachers committed to multicultural education needs to avoid the inauthenticity of pre-emptively favourable judgements of worth, but at the same time to be unusually sensitive to possible cultural differences. In this view, the teacher is neither a demagogue nor a 'non-judgmental facilitator'; neither a propagandist for a particular culture nor passively 'neutral' between cultures. The professional judgement of a teacher in multicultural education needs to be guided by a positive commitment to fostering the practices of reasoning, and this requires some ironical distance from any particular cultures.

Provided that we interpret it in this way, South Africa must foster the practice of multicultural education, and not merely for the reason that it is a diverse society. Thus interpreted, multicultural education is a kind of education that effectively promotes the capacities, talents and virtues which characterise what it is for a person to be educated, as opposed to being merely trained for specified tasks, activities or occupations, indoctrinated into the sentiments or beliefs of a specific culture, or blindly socialised into particular sets of habits and practices. This kind of education disembeds students from myopic immersion in the settled practices of a particular culture and its traditions, and encourages the development of a shared identity across cultural boundaries. The promise of multicultural education is that it can powerfully contribute to such an achievement.

But the argument about whether South Africa should foster multicultural education also needs to take into view an important feature of contemporary South Africa: it is a society on the trajectory of modernisation.

Multiculturalism and modernisation

Apartheid can be seen as a comprehensive attempt to stem the tide of modernisation but, even during the darkest days, economic developments compelled at least partial modernisation. Modernisation erodes traditional cultures and the stable identities associated with them. Given that Apartheid was based on a commitment to the integrity and continued survival of distinctive traditional cultures, it was right to try to block the processes of modernisation by, amongst other things, protecting traditional cultures in monocultural education systems.

Some of the catalysts and features of modernisation, which Apartheid tried to control, are urbanisation, the circulation of printed matter and the increasing penetration into everyday life of mass media and new technologies[6], all of which shrink space and time and disrespect traditional geographical and cultural borders. Such developments expose people to a strong mix of disparate cultural influences and images, increase mutual dependence between people and require the increasing coordination of their various activities.

One of the main deficiencies of monocultural education is that it traps students in a traditional culture and, thus, fails to contribute to their access to the modern world; it provides, at best, only limited opportunities for students to develop the talents and virtues needed to cope well in that world of diversity. According to Parekh, multicultural education enables '...the student to accept, enjoy and cope with diversity'[7], and being able to do this is at the heart of what is needed to handle the diversity and lack of certainty that characterises a modernising society. This is especially true in the case of South Africa, where the processes of modernisation were kept under such a tight rein during the previous half century in which modernisation increased apace in much of the world.

Modernisation and multiculturalism are two sides of the same coin, and multicultural education is a form of education that provides access to modernisation and develops the mobile intellectual and moral capabilities needed to survive and flourish in the modern world. This provides a further reason for South Africa to foster multicultural education.

The politics of difference in an emerging democracy

We can now refocus our attention on the argument that because South Africa is a diverse society it ought to favour the politics of difference and foster multicultural education. The upshot of the arguments of the previous sections of this essay is that, provided we understand multicultural education in a particular way, South Africa should, of course, foster multicultural education. It is now time to turn our attention to the politics of difference.

The account of multicultural education developed in this essay asserts that multicultural education and the politics of difference are not the close relatives they are commonly assumed to be; in fact, they pull in opposite directions. The argument in support of fostering multicultural education in South Africa is not at the same time an argument in support of the politics of difference. I shall conclude this essay by arguing that there are good reasons to oppose the politics of difference in South Africa, especially in educational institutions.

A liberal democratic society is one premised on the view that perfect social justice is unobtainable in the real historical world. Thus, we need to establish a polity that, without coming apart at the seams, remains open to constant attempts to remove injustices that unexpectedly appear. A liberal democratic society '…makes authority accessible without dissolving it, [and opens] such authority to future deliberation and critique…'[8].

The politics of difference is a confrontational style of politics that presupposes an established political order and a shared identity. The politics of difference emphasises differences between groups with a view to removing injustices in a political dispensation which is, broadly, just. The risks of the politics of difference are that by generating group hostilities and antagonisms it might lead to social, institutional and political disintegration.

It is significant that the politics of difference has emerged specifically in well-established liberal democratic societies, in which there is at least some sense amongst their members of a shared identity, a sense of belonging to a common political community. Acknowledging this point, Iris Young writes that, 'Group identification arises, that is, in the encounter and interaction between social collectivities that experience some differences in their way of life and forms of association, *even if they also regard themselves as belonging to the same society*'[9].

The politics of difference is a product of societies that have well-established procedures for resolving conflicts without violence, (relatively) stable public institutions, (relatively) robust traditions of the practice of public deliberation about common interests, (relatively) low levels of poverty and destitution, (relative) social peace and lack of civil disorder. For those brought up in societies with such characteristics, the bitter political compromises and patient collective efforts of which these historical achievements are the outcome are hidden from view and can safely be ignored. The inevitable shortcomings of such historical achievements can be emphasised in the politics of difference with a view to overcoming them and can be treated as a consensual backdrop for the dramatic performances of the politics of difference. The politics of difference is a centrifugal force, parasitic on established institutions and practices.

But South Africa has only very recently emerged from a history of oppression underwritten by radical social division. It is in the midst of the difficult process of trying to rebuild itself as a just society; it is thus too early for the renovators to move in. Many of South Africa's public institutions are fragile and tainted with the too easy accusation that they are parts of the historical legacy from which we need to extricate ourselves. The democratic practice of public deliberation about common interests is far from being a well-established tradition, and it is vulnerable to being subverted and distorted by convictions about democracy forged in the abnormal furnace of struggle and shaped by assumptions about structurally induced group hostility and antagonism. South Africa is characterised by high levels of poverty and destitution and plagued by violent crime and a lack of civil security.

Education has an important role in the building and consolidation of a just and cohesive society. South African education and its institutions were dangerously over-politicised during the time of Apartheid education and the protests it evoked. These stances eroded the authority of the professional judgement of teachers and educational institutions. The politics of difference, imported from well-established liberal democratic societies, aspires to replace these stances but it is, in effect, merely a continuation of them. It is a corrosively anti-educational force in contemporary South Africa, undermining the professional judgement of teachers and the educational authority of institutions to the detriment of the education of students.

South Africa, in short, has not yet achieved the kind of secure framework, such as that characteristic of established liberal democracies, in terms of which to accommodate the politics of difference with any equanimity. In the historical context of South Africa, the politics of difference is more likely to hinder the achievement of a just democratic society than to contribute to its realisation.

At this time in South Africa, the politics of difference is likely to reinforce traditional divisions, rather than to enable us to discover the social cohesion of which we were deprived by colonialism and Apartheid. By contrast, multicultural education (as characterised in this essay) promises to contribute to the fostering of the shared identity across the divisions of our history. And this is an important dimension of the task of building a just and democratic society to begin to overcome the oppressions of the past.

Notes

1   This essay was originally published in W Morrow & K King (eds), *Vision and Reality*, Cape Town: UCT Press, 1998, pp. 232–244. A revised version is reproduced here with the kind permission of the publisher.

2   IM Young, *Justice and the Politics of Difference*, Princeton: Princeton Univesrity Press, 1990, p. 43.

3   Bhikhu Parekh, 'Education for a culturally plural society' in *Papers of the Philosophy of Education Society of Great Britain*, March 31–April 2, 1995.

4   Parekh, in *Papers of the Philosophy of Education Society of Great Britain*, p. 7.

5   Parekh, in *Papers of the Philosophy of Education Society of Great Britain*, p. 7.

6   Albert Hertzog, the Minister of Posts and Telegraphs during the early 1970s, bitterly opposed the introduction of television in South Africa.

7   Parekh, in *Papers of the Philosophy of Education Society of Great Britain*, p. 10.

8   Stephen G Salkever, ' "Lopp'd and Bound": How liberal theory obscures the goods of liberal practices' in RB Douglas et al. (eds), *Liberalism and the Good*, London: Routledge, 1990, p. 182.

9   IM Young, *Justice and the Politics of Difference*, p. 43 (my emphasis).

11 *The politics of difference in South African education*

(Based on a paper prepared for Kenton Conference, 1996)

> ...then we shall have advanced a little in the process of what Raymond Williams has called the 'unlearning' of 'the inherent dominative mode.'
>
> Edward Said, *Orientalism*

In this essay[1] I am concerned with moral high grounds, with education and democracy and with our collective survival. I am going to explore these issues in terms of the politics of difference. The politics of difference has played, plays, and is likely to continue to play, a key role in education in South Africa.

The shape of my story is as follows. I say what I mean by the politics of difference, then focus on the main problem in contemporary South African education and pose the question whether the politics of difference might contribute to its solution. I argue that it does not, and is likely to be a hindrance to our survival in the global village. This essay puts forward *arguments* in defence of this claim, and challenges those who disagree with its unpopular conclusions not merely to reject – but to *refute* – them.

The politics of difference

At the root of the politics of difference is the demand for special treatment on the grounds of membership of a group claimed to be different. But this demand begs the question: different in respect to what? There can be various answers to this question; some of the currently fashionable ones are in respect to culture, gender, sexual preferences, ethnicity or nationality. But why should special treatment be accorded to a member of a group so specified? In general terms, the answer to this question is that members of this group are claimed to be in some way systematically 'disadvantaged' by certain prevalent rules and practices. However, the politics of difference is in conflict with what I shall call, following Charles Taylor[2], the politics of equal dignity.

The politics of equal dignity arose in opposition to pre-democratic forms of social organisation characterised by sharp distinctions between the power, rights and privileges of social groups. Against such pre-democratic social forms, as we in South Africa know all too vividly, the politics of equal dignity insists on the principle of universal equality, on the impartial treatment of all people, irrespective, particularly, of to which social group they happen to belong. For the politics of equal dignity, all people, in terms of their common humanity, should have the same powers, rights and privileges, because all have fundamentally the same needs and basic aspirations, and all are assumed to be (at least potential) participants in the discourses of reason.

The principle of non-discrimination stands at the heart of the politics of equal dignity and, from its point of view, the politics of difference violates this principle. The politics of difference insists on discrimination in favour of a specified group; it demands that the prevalent practices and rules should be suspended or modified in the case of this group. For the politics of equal dignity this looks like an obvious reversion to a pre-democratic social order. But the politics of difference will deny this, and claim that it is in fact *more democratic* than the politics of equal dignity. The argument could run along two significantly different lines.

In one version, the politics of difference concedes that although it is demanding discrimination, it is not the kind of discrimination that characterises a pre-democratic social order but is 'reverse discrimination' – the kind that has as its purpose to 'reverse' the historical disadvantage suffered by members of a particular group. This kind of discrimination must be conceived of as temporary, a strategy to 'level the playing field' so that the politics of equal dignity can resume its 'normal' operation. In this version, the politics of difference is not intent on changing the game but on establishing the conditions for fair participation in the game. In places such as the USA or the UK this is called 'affirmative action'.

But in another version, the politics of difference, in claiming that it is precisely the cherished principle of non-discrimination that it wishes to defend, turns this principle against the politics of equal dignity itself. The politics of equal dignity is accused of itself being highly discriminatory in forcing people into a homogenous mould that is untrue of their authentic identity. Prevalent rules and practices should be not temporarily suspended, but replaced with a new set that acknowledges that group membership is at the basis of personal identity and, accordingly, provides different rights and privileges to people according to their group membership. In this version, the politics of difference is intent on changing the game. The underlying argument for this position is that group diversity is a good that should be protected and perpetuated.

We in South Africa might at this point get a shock of recognition – this sounds suspiciously like Apartheid. But in other parts of the world and, perhaps, increasingly in our country, under the influence of Euro–American intellectual fashions, it is called 'pluralism' which, in manifesting itself in various forms of multiculturalism, feminism, or other kinds of the politics of difference, sees itself as occupying the moral high ground in respect to debate about democracy. But, ignoring our history, let us see how the position might be defended.

The issue of identity introduces a new and powerful dimension into the rivalry between the politics of equal dignity and the politics of difference. For someone to lose or fail to discover their identity is for them to lose or fail to discover what is central to their life as a human being. Each person has their own original way of being, which only they can discover and pursue, and any political or educational regime that hinders or distorts this project is perpetuating disadvantagement of a particularly insidious kind. But both modes of politics can agree about this, as they can both agree that identity depends, to a significant degree, on recognition that identity is not monological but dialogical[3] or relational, an ongoing project of which recognition by others is a key component.

However, on this selfsame ground we can expose a major fault line between the two modes of politics. The politics of equal dignity sees identity in terms of the rational autonomy of individuals, which underpins its understanding of the principle of non-discrimination. Against this, the politics of difference (as did Apartheid) argues that individual identity is dependent on group identity and asserts that this is something the politics of equal dignity fails to acknowledge. For the politics of equal dignity to ignore group identity is for it simply to maintain the power of currently hegemonic groups, and so to hinder the development of democracy.

This line of argument might be reinforced by some kind of appeal to relativism, or to a story about the collapse of the 'grand (universal) narrative'. The Enlightenment ushered into the world a conception of rationality, which it mistakenly conceived of as being, among other things, linguistically and culturally neutral. It was this conception of rationality that was a catalyst for the development of the politics of equal dignity, which simply overrides the obvious and profound diversity of human beings and their forms of life. Such forms of life are incommensurable; each has its own horizons of significance and standards of judgement and, contrary to the pretensions of Enlightenment rationality, there is no neutral ground in terms of which to adjudicate between them, there is no 'view from nowhere'. But the politics of equal dignity, according to the politics of difference, is committed to this presupposition and is, in this way, profoundly discriminatory and anti-democratic.

With this understanding of the politics of difference, and its claims as a background, let us turn our attention to the main problem in South African education.

Educational collapse and the tradition of resistance

Contemporary South African education is confronted with a widespread collapse of what has been called 'a culture of teaching and learning'. Whether or not we use this label, it is now acknowledged across the political spectrum that many of our schools and universities are close to a point of breakdown, and that – if we regard education as important – we are in serious trouble. The question I want to pursue in this context is whether the politics of difference offers us a way of addressing this main problem in South African education.

Some symptoms of our malaise are the lack of regular attendance at the places of learning by both teachers and learners; deep cynicism about the significance of learning, a cynicism that generates an impoverished view of certificates issued by the schooling system as nothing more than tickets to status and privilege; the prevalence of corrupt and fraudulent practices in the schooling system; and dissolution of traditional structures of educational authority, sometimes in the name of democracy, which has given rise to a lack of established orderliness and an increase in violence and other forms of tyranny in many educational institutions. This bleak catalogue underwrites the widespread conviction that we urgently need to improve the quality of teaching and learning in our schooling systems. Although this conviction points in an appropriate direction, unless it is generously interpreted, it might divert our attention from what has unravelled at a very basic level, and how we might work for a renaissance of the cultures of teaching and learning.

I think most of us will agree that the causes of this breakdown have been political. One obvious candidate here is the evils of Apartheid schooling[4], but another, this time perhaps not as readily acknowledged, is the traditions of resistance to Apartheid schooling, and the ways in which those traditions politicised education in a particularly virulent way. It is here, rather than with multiculturalism, that we come to the politics of difference in South African education.

Consider, briefly, some characteristics of resistance. Resistance is engaged in by those who see themselves as victims of some transparently and overwhelmingly unjust regime. Opposition to such a regime is seen as, without question, morally good, and we can understand how those who engage in such opposition can come to regard themselves as occupying the moral high ground. The central strategy of resistance is to put forward demands, backed up not by reasons but by threats and the power of refusal; the underlying rationale for resistance is deep distrust of 'the oppressor' and an entrenched conception of necessarily antagonistic interest groups. Problems and difficulties, real or imagined, are projected on to the external agency, and the purpose of resistance is to destroy or dismantle the evil regime in order to solve the problems and eliminate the difficulties. Resistance is constitutionally hostile to institutions and established structures of authority, which it conceives of as the tools of the regime and, thus, has no interest in the maintenance of institutions as the locus of potentially enabling practices.

A prevalent stance, which might have arisen from traditions of resistance in contemporary South African schooling, centres around the concept of 'academic exclusions'. Academic exclusions are conceived of as illegitimate, as in the same category as other forms of exclusion that lace our history, and as a perpetuation of the injustices of the past. Academic exclusions revolve around the issues of assessment and failure in schooling.

This stance is expressed in the slogan 'Pass One, Pass All', and in constant disputes about examinations and examination results. Failure is seen as illegitimate because (to paraphrase the views of some university students) failure simply further disadvantages students who have already been massively disadvantaged; failure is a denial of the identity of the learner; failure is 'disempowering' and thus in contradiction to the principle that education should 'empower'; and failure is a violation of the principle of equality.

Before we focus on interpreting this stance as a form of the politics of difference, let us remove two possible distractions. The first is that failure is not a necessary feature of schooling. We could, quite easily, adjust our scales of assessment so that C, for example, is the lowest ranked grade, and everybody would, in effect, pass. This might be one of the lessons we could learn from the USA where, in many schools, less than A++ seems to have come to be seen as a cause for despair. But, of course, this doesn't solve the problem; it merely moves the goalposts.

The second is that there *is* room for a great deal of legitimate debate about forms of assessment of educational achievement. For example, although in some cases they might be the fairest test of students' educational achievement, there is nothing sacrosanct about three-hour written final examinations. But, of course, this merely changes the subject; again, it does not solve the problem.

Might this stance usefully be interpreted as a form of the politics of difference?

Establishing the conditions for fair participation in the game

Consider, first, that version of the politics of difference called 'affirmative action'. In this version, prevalent practices and rules should be suspended in respect to an identified group, but only *temporarily*, until historically induced disadvantages have been overcome and we can return to the 'normal' operation of the politics of equal dignity. The key problem, of course, is what we mean by 'temporarily'.

We can begin by noting the common distinction between the practices of teaching and the assessment of learner achievement. Good teaching necessarily starts at the present level of the learner in relation to what is being taught. The teacher of a language, as much as the teacher of motor car driving or gymnastics, must start teaching from the current capacities of the learners in respect to what is being taught, whether language, motor car driving or gymnastics.

This teaching, obviously, attempts to bring the learners to some *improvement* in their current capacities in respect to what is being taught. Knowing whether this task is proceeding involves assessment of some kind, no matter how formal or informal. But the assessment of improvement is necessarily based on interpersonally agreed standards; it ceases to be assessment to the extent that it degenerates into merely personal or subjective judgements, no matter how self-possessed and comfortable ('empowered') they might make the teachers or the learners feel. Furthermore, assessment is not something that takes place only at the end of a teaching programme; it is woven into the practices of teaching. The tasks of teaching cannot be understood if they are disconnected from their constitutive achievements.

The distinction between the practices of teaching and the assessment of learner achievement thus masks the conceptual connection between them. Using different terminology, 'process' and 'product', in the case of teaching, cannot be conceived of independently of each other. The same point applies equally to 'procedures' and 'outcomes', 'modes of delivery' and 'exit criteria' or any other terminology used to advert to this distinction.

What this implies for the problem of what we mean by 'temporarily' in thinking about affirmative action in education is that, although there are many interim points at which a sympathetic teacher can and should allow 'affirmative action' considerations to affect her assessments of learner improvement (this is simply a redescription of good teaching), if such concessions do not have a terminal point, she is not engaging in this version of the politics of difference.

But that is not all. There are certain points at which schooling systems publicly recognise educational achievement in the form of certificates. In our case, for example, we can think of 'matriculation certificates', 'national diplomas' and 'degrees' of various descriptions. These certificates are assumed to have uniform significance and to have value as a form of currency. A BSc degree, for example, is supposed to have a standard currency no matter which university awarded it, and irrespective of whom its recipient is, especially with regard to which group or groups she happens to belong. In respect to publicly recognised certificates (and we can acknowledge that they are conventional but that does not affect the argument), a policy of affirmative action must at some point either acknowledge that it has reached a limit or become self-defeating.

To get a feel for the force of this argument, consider how demeaning it would be for someone to be told (or even to think) that they had been awarded an 'affirmative action' matriculation certificate, that they had been awarded a BSc because they are a woman (the university is trying to improve its record of the proportion of women awarded BSc degrees!), or that their PhD had been awarded to them because they are black or come from the 'third world'. (There are some 'universities' and colleges in the USA and the UK that are suspected of awarding special degrees and diplomas to 'third world' students!)

Affirmative action at these admittedly conventional, but nonetheless crucial, points would undermine the assumption of the uniform significance and value of such certificates and, thus, deprive them of their 'normal' currency, thereby subverting the purposes of affirmative action. At these points, benevolence and sympathy are self-defeating; students awarded certificates that did not have normal currency would be seriously disadvantaged.

There are further dimensions to this argument that relate to the ways in which academic qualifications are not only perhaps tickets to jobs and status, but are supposed to signify the attainment of particular capabilities. This is a very obvious point, which we can concretise in terms of the issue of the certification of schoolteachers.

There are many dimensions to the kinds of deprivation suffered under Apartheid, but one stands out in this context. Apartheid Education generated and perpetuated cycles of epistemological deprivation, that is, it deprived many learners in our country of a fair opportunity to gain access to the kind of knowledge that is supposed to be distributed in formal schooling.

The mechanisms of this deprivation were of many kinds, but a key element was teachers ill-prepared for their professional responsibilities. As in the case of poverty, the key question is at what point(s) one might begin to break the cycles. In the case of cycles of epistemological deprivation, at least one key point is in respect to the licensing of schoolteachers. If we apply affirmative action at this key point, we are likely to be contributing to the perpetuation of cycles of epistemological deprivation.

Underlying this argument is a question about who the beneficiaries are of an affirmative action policy: whose interests does it serve? The central demand of the politics of difference is that a *group* must be given special treatment in order to enable it to overcome historically induced disadvantage. In the particular case of the licensing of teachers, the interests to be taken into account include those of the communities that those teachers will subsequently serve, and those communities are hardly likely to be benefited by licensing teachers ill-prepared for their professional responsibilities.

But a defender of the politics of difference might at this point catch on to phrases like 'professional responsibilities', 'epistemological deprivation', and the 'normal significance' of the certificates issued by the schooling system, and charge the previous argument with missing the point. These phrases presuppose and reinforce, it might be said, the currently hegemonic academic culture. When students say that failure is illegitimate, they are demanding not neo-paternalism in the form of 'affirmative action', but a radical rejection of the prevailing academic culture, including its concept of quality.

Here we move to the second version of the politics of difference, that version which demands not a temporary suspension of prevalent rules and practices, but their replacement by a new set that discriminates on the basis of group membership.

Changing the game ('transforming' education?)

In order to be able to take this suggestion seriously we have to assume that we can overcome a problem that infects the whole of the project of the politics of difference. This project assumes that group membership is relatively clear-cut and stable, that all the possible differences between people will line up neatly in clear sets. But this assumption is open to serious doubt.

In the first place, as we in South Africa know all too well, the boundaries between social groups are porous and unstable. In spite of its best efforts, Apartheid never found criteria in terms of which to harden these boundaries[5]. In the second place, any individual person, especially in a modern urban environment, belongs to a variety of diverse social groups. It is problematic to know what to make of a concept of clearly bounded and homogenous groups or cultures in such a context. In the third place, social group membership is neither static nor stable, and this is increasingly the case in the modern highly mobile world with its rapid transport systems and burgeoning cross-boundary information and communication technologies. Group membership is, and is increasingly, volatile and inchoate, and the notion of stable and static group membership is a kind of nostalgia for a previous age, in which human interaction was essentially in situations of co-presence, which, perhaps even in a pre-modern world, was much more fragile than it is imagined in retrospect.

But, even assuming we can overcome or avoid this problem, what would this way of changing the academic game imply? The first question we would need to ask is whether we could still talk of *the* academic game, or whether we would need to talk of a variety of academic games each recognising the distinctive group membership of the participants.

One way in which the latter possibility might be defended is to appeal to two of the fashionable concepts of the politics of difference: 'identity' and 'empowerment'. Starting from the idea that individual identity is dependent on group identity, and adding to that the idea that education has to do, amongst other things, with the development of identity, it might be argued that the only genuinely non-discriminatory system would be one in which there was an academic game for each of the distinctive groups.

But against this we can say, first, that schooling is not *the* only source of identity, and second, that the dimensions of identity with which schooling is concerned are not global, but have to do with the development of a specific range of capacities. Schooling has to do, for example, with a person's identity as a 'literate person' or as someone who is able to do arithmetic.

This might be conceded, but it does not yet take on board the argument from empowerment. I am skeptical about whether talk of empowerment has a useful role at all in thinking about education, but let's see how the argument might go. Education, it might be said, is supposed to empower the learner and, if we are serious about doing that, then we need to acknowledge that failure to respect the group membership of the learner will undermine that project, and disempower her.

I am doubtful about whether this argument is cogent but, assuming it is, what is the concept of empowerment that is at play here? Is to be empowered to have a particular feeling, to be in a particular affective state? This must be incorrect. A viable concept of empowerment must, therefore, refer to something like actual effectiveness in the world. But, if it is education we are talking about, then we must be referring to effectiveness in respect to those kinds of things with which education is concerned – such things as learning how to think systematically.

At this point, someone defending the politics of difference might say that the phrase 'thinking systematically' is a virtue in only one possible kind of academic game; there might be others in which it is not regarded as a virtue. Or perhaps there are different conceptions of 'thinking systematically', each of which underwrites a different academic game.

But we do not need to follow the argument into this whirlpool of relativism as we can again pose the question of the public recognition of achievement. In a system in which there were different academic games for different groups, what certificates would be issued? If different certificates are awarded in each of these games, they would either have no currency, or conventions or rules of equivalence would develop. This would be like living in a country that had a variety of currencies in circulation and that would need to establish exchange rates (which might fluctuate dramatically) between them in order for ordinary commercial activities to be possible.

But, however we managed to figure out how such a system might work, it would deprive us of the uniform significance on which the current value of educational certificates depends. Perhaps it might now be said that we should not be too impressed with this merely practical problem, as what we really need to do is to reject the current value of educational certificates. I will pick up this suggestion in the next section; I want here to summarise my response to the question of whether the politics of difference offers us a way of addressing the main problem in South African education.

I think that the considerations I have brought forward in this and the previous section will at least have highlighted limitations, if not yielded a clear-cut negative answer to this question. Given the deep way in which our schooling system has unravelled, the politics of difference seems most unlikely to be able to provide us with ways of addressing the problem. If a car is going, we might be able to steer it; but if it is not even going, then the most we can do is to pretend to steer it.

I will here make a short detour to bring on board some of the broader considerations that are at stake. Arguments about the politics of difference need to be contextualised in our historical context. We need to take account of the degree to which the social fabric of our society has unravelled.

The politics of difference flourishes in societies with relatively secure institutions and a relatively widely shared sense of justice that provide the frame for political and moral disagreements. In such societies, this background can simply be taken for granted in debates (for instance, about multicultural education). But, as Partha Dasgupta remarks, 'What is uttered makes no sense unless we have an understanding of what has not been spoken'[6].

The politics of difference is a centrifugal force that depends, for its moral appeal, on there being a centre of some kind. If 'the centre cannot hold', then a situation such as in Ireland, Bosnia or Rwanda is the likely prognosis; differences will be noted with a view to identifying whom to kill.

It is a commonplace that the 'centre' can be one of two kinds. Either it is a coercive centre, one backed by suppression of difference, the imposition of raw power and lack of respect for persons, and characterised by guns and other traditional weapons, high levels of surveillance and the closing down of spaces for the free exploration or exchange of proscribed information or ideas. This option, vigorously and powerfully enough pursued, can bring a certain degree of social stability and even economic wealth, as the example of Singapore demonstrates. We don't need to look very far in either space or time to remark that this is indeed a live option.

Or it is a centre of a different kind, one founded on a *shared* sense of how we should relate to each other as persons, a regime of mutual trust, a shared moral discourse that underpins the possibility of both agreement and disagreement, and is based on the central ideal of democracy, namely to resolve (or perhaps dissolve) conflicts and disputes by reasoned discussion rather than by reaching for our wallets, knobkieries or other instruments of violence.

A main problem with the politics of difference is that it creates and succours the idea that society is made up of hostile groups, either dominating or dominated. It is inhospitable to the Enlightenment ideals of a common humanity and a shared rationality. In those societies which have an established centre, the politics of difference can be like the 'conscience' of society, reminding it of the ways in which it falls short of its acknowledged ideals.

But in our society we do not (yet) have a secure centre, and references to, for example, 'the currently hegemonic academic culture' are little more than rhetoric that has lost its substance in its translocation from other historical situations to ours. If anything is 'hegemonic' in our educational institutions, it is the widespread lack of understanding of the value of systematic learning and the conditions for it to be possible.

If we are going to avoid the coercive option, we will need to work to establish an alternative kind of centre. Schooling is one, but only one, site at which this work can proceed. The politics of difference in schooling seems more likely to undermine than to contribute to this work. The (mostly American schooled)

Pied Pipers of the politics of difference are dangerous in our situation, even if they present themselves as occupying the moral high ground.

Discrimination in education

The politics of equal dignity, we can recall, assumes that each person is a (potential) participant in the discourses of reason, insists on the principle of universal dignity – on the impartial treatment of all individuals – and is deeply committed to non-discrimination. In trying to work out an alternative way of changing the academic game, we can use as our stalking horse the suggestion that failure in education is illegitimate because it is a violation of the principles of equality and non-discrimination.

Prevalent rules and practices underwrite the situation in which some students fail (or at least are awarded lower grades than others). If we are really serious about our commitment to non-discrimination then, it might be said, all students should get the same grades and no students should fail, and we need to change prevalent rules and practices to accomplish this end. What drives our project here is our thoroughgoing commitment to non-discrimination as well as our democratic opposition to the stratified and hierarchical forms of organisation that anchor prevalent discriminatory practices.

But, although democratic schooling, in its commitment to an ideal of a common humanity, is opposed to discrimination on the basis of the social group membership, wealth, race, gender, religion, and countless other differences between people, *unless it discriminates on the basis of progress and achievements in learning, it has ceased to be education.* If it is education we are talking about, then discrimination between learners in terms of their learning achievements is inevitable; without something like this, some scales of assessment of improvements in learning, it is difficult to know why we would call any process a process of education.

There is, in short, a form of discrimination that is essential in education; this form of discrimination constitutes this sphere of our collective life. To reject this form of discrimination would be to reject education. There is a further argument that flows out of this, an argument about the necessarily stratified form of organisation needed for a project of public education. But, due to space constraints, I can't here and now develop that argument[7].

The argument that there is a form of discrimination that is necessary in education does not depend on the claim that schooling is culturally or politically neutral or impartial in its goals. Schooling is a particular cultural and political project, and it is one of the major access routes to the modern world. It is in the democratic business of opening up that route for as broad a range of our people as possible, of providing access to the kinds of knowledge and other capacities that are needed for participation in modernity.

Societies that already enjoy the benefits of modernity, such things as the availability of adequate drinking water, nutrition, shelter and other basic conditions for sustainable human life can, perhaps, afford to concentrate on the shortcomings and damaging consequences of modernity, including the ways in which it marginalises some people, but their collective survival is not so immediately at stake. They can indulge themselves in the luxuries and anxieties of postmodernity, and agonise on the internet, but only because they have lost sight of what it took to establish the conditions that make these indulgences possible. The route from pre-modern to postmodern society cannot be accomplished without a 'detour' via modernity.

Discrimination in education in South Africa

Prevalent rules and practices are not written in stone and, as we painfully try to drag ourselves out of our past, we need critically to scrutinise our current rules and practices. But, unless we do not care about education at all, we are going to have to avoid losing sight of the form of discrimination that constitutes the sphere of education; we are also going to have to guard against its corruption by demands for group entitlements, especially those that present themselves as occupying the moral high ground.

This characterisation of the programme for the transformation of education gives an indication of the difficulties we face. In practical terms, it is far from easy to distinguish clearly between the kind of discrimination that is constitutive of education and other forms of discrimination. We in South Africa need no reminding of that.

There are forms of feminism and multiculturalism that are located in the evolving traditions of the politics of equal dignity. What they are calling for is not special treatment on the grounds of membership of groups claimed to be different, but a firmer commitment to a recognition of the rational autonomy of individuals. A problem is how, in practice, to distinguish between these forms of feminism and multiculturalism and those that pursue the politics of difference[8].

This is a general problem. We need, in the details of practice, to distinguish between the form of discrimination that constitutes the sphere of education and those forms that are a violation of the ideals of the politics of equal dignity. We cannot solve this problem by demanding either the abandonment of discrimination altogether or the introduction of additional forms of discrimination that corrupt the sphere of education.

Without having the space here to argue for it, I shall indicate what these conclusions imply for how we might address the main problem in South African education.

A priority in education in South Africa at present must be to try to establish some forms of orderliness, to prevent the further unravelling of our social fabric. The politics of difference is unlikely to help us; the politics of equal dignity, with its commitment to the presumption that all people are potential participants in the discourses of reason, to its understanding democracy as a procedure for resolving conflicts by reasoned discussion, looks like an appropriate place to begin, at least. The very idea of 'reasoned discussion' embodies a substantive view of the appropriate form of life for human beings, and it is underpinned by its opposition to the belief that certainty is an attainable goal. It is a way of trying to unlearn the inherent dominative mode.

But a pragmatic condition for being able to achieve and maintain a form of orderliness, based on reasoned discussion in our educational institutions and other public sites, is the establishment of appropriate structures of authority and a commitment to institutions governed by rules that discriminate impartially on appropriate grounds. If we fail to establish these conditions, then our infant democracy is in jeopardy – either from degeneration into a new form of coercive regime or from our project of securing our collective survival in the global village in which our traditional special pleading is a diminishing resource.

Notes

1   Saleem Badat, Nelleke Bak, Rosalie Small and George Subotzky responded in detail to an earlier paper, 'Teacher Education, pluralism and the ugly lines of segregation in South Africa' (on which Essay 9 is based), and their illuminating comments have valuably contributed to my argument in this essay.

2   Charles Taylor, 'The politics of recognition' in Amy Gutmann (ed.), *Multiculturalism and 'The Politics of Recognition'*, Oxford, N.J.: Princeton University Press, 1992. This paper by Taylor was a significant catalyst in the argument I develop in this essay.

3   This phrase, and the distinction it makes, comes from Taylor, in Gutmann (ed.), *Multiculturalism and 'The Politics of Recognition'*.

4   Although I try to maintain a distinction between schooling (as institutions whose formal aim is to promote systematic learning, including tertiary institutions such as colleges, technikons [now known as universities of technology] and universities) and education (as a regulative ideal in our collective lives), I am not sure whether I do so successfully throughout.

5   J Chris Coetzee in 'The theory of Christian-National Education' reprinted in B Rose & R Tunmer (eds), *Documents in South African Education*, Johannesburg: AD Donker, 1975, reveals this problem. In Wally Morrow, *Chains of Thought*, Johannesburg: Southern Book Publishers, 1989, I am much concerned with it. See, especially, the paragraph on the lower half of p. 39 and the section in 'The voice of the people?' called 'The ownership problem' pp. 27–31.

6   Partha Dasgupta, *An Inquiry into Well-being and Destitution*, Oxford: Clarendon Press, 1995, p. vii.

7   The argument is developed in Wally Morrow, 'Stakeholders and senates: The governance of higher education institutions in South Africa' in *Cambridge Journal of Education*, Vol. 28 No. 3, 1998.

8   See Martha Nussbaum, 'Review of M Antony & C Witt (eds), *A Mind of One's Own: Feminist Essays on Reason and Objectivity*' in *The New York Review of Books*, 20 October 1994, pp. 59–63, and the subsequent discussion in *The New York Review of Books*, 6 April 1995, pp. 48–49. See also Susan Haack, 'The best man for the job may be a woman…and other alien thoughts on affirmative action in the academy' in *Manifesto of a Passionate Moderate*, Chicago: University of Chicago Press, 1998.

12 *The rubber hits the tar*

(WCED – Provincial Education Conference, 23–24 March 2005)

Preamble

In March 2005, the Western Cape Education Department (WCED) held a two-day conference, attended by some 500 people, including local teachers, members of school governing bodies, departmental officials and other people interested in how we should carry schooling forward 10 years after the transition to democracy. This conference was not an academic conference; it gathered together not those whose main focus is on research and theorising about education, but those whose professional tasks are the conduct of schooling on a daily basis, the point at which the rubber hits the tar.

The formal purpose of the conference was to provide an opportunity for public critical discussion of the WCED strategic plan for the coming decade and a half but, given the date of the conference, it also became a critical reflection on what had been achieved, or not achieved, in the first post-Apartheid decade in South Africa. This essay is my comment on the first day of the conference, presented at the start of the second day.

The style of this essay, and its manifest location at a particular historical moment and place, sharply raise the question of whether it belongs in a book, alongside the other essays in this collection. There were a number of issues to be considered.

One was whether the essay should be left in its original form, or whether the names of particular individuals and the specific time references ('yesterday') should be removed. However, to have made changes of this kind would have altered the whole tone of the essay, and turned it into something it was not intended to be. On balance, it seemed better to leave the text in its original form. Unlike most other essays in this collection, it is conceived of not as a theoretical discussion but as an engagement with those directly involved in the daily practices of our attempts to achieve the transformation of schooling in our country.

Another issue is that the essay covers a range of topics, some of which are not addressed in other essays in this book. For example, the HIV and AIDS pandemic and the profound impact it will have on schooling is seldom even mentioned in earlier essays; the idea of 'social capital' is not previously mentioned at all; and, although the issue of equality is what undergirds the importance of the distinction between formal and epistemological access, equality and inequality are not explicitly discussed in any of the previous essays.

However, some of the main themes that emerge out of the previous essays are reflected in this essay, embedded in a direct response to real-life thinking by people trying to cope with contemporary challenges.

The opening section of this essay, 'Democracy and discussion', shows in what ways the struggle with relativism in Essays 8, 9, 10 and 11 touches the heart of what we understand by democracy. The section entitled 'Access and quality' implicitly shows how the distinction between formal and epistemological access (Essays 1 and 3) is reflected in concerns about the insufficiency, in striving for 'transformation', of thinking simply in terms of the material conditions of schools. In addition, this section contains a direct reference to the argument of Essay 4, that the main purpose of basic education is to provide access to the modern world, and that a key to such access is basic print literacy. The section on 'Demography' can be seen as a reflection on the issue of the increase in student and pupil numbers while resources remain limited, the issue addressed in Essays 1 and 3.

The section on 'Teachers as social workers' provides the opportunity to think in practical terms about what it would be to move away from the traditional model of a school. In the introduction to this book I claim that this is 'a major issue for the future of education in South Africa', and I mention it briefly in the final paragraph of Essay 4 and the last two sections of Essay 6, but I do not develop it in these essays. In the WCED strategic plan, and at the conference itself, there was some discussion about the proposal that a range of government departments needs to use schools as the sites for the delivery of their services, and this can be understood as a tentative step – by those directly involved in shaping the schooling system – toward the reconceptualisation of schools, and the functions of teachers within them.

One of the major themes in the previous essays in this book is the ways in which we persistently fail to focus clearly on the practices of teaching, and their centrality to anything that could be called education or schooling. If this essay does nothing else, it brings clearly into the open, in the section called 'Teaching', the way in which we occlude teaching in our public policies.

But one main reason for including this essay in this collection lies in the view that one of the guiding purposes of research and theorising in the field of education must be to contribute towards an answer to the question: how should we go on 'now and around here'[1]? Many of the essays in this book can be seen as attempts to think about this question, but this essay gets closer to the action. Despite their good intentions, many researchers in the field of education either fall to the 'temptations of theory' or are simply 'fact collectors' trying to describe the current situation.

This essay was written for a particular occasion and a particular audience – those at the leading edge of coping with the realities of schooling – in a particular region of our country, soon after the start of the second decade of our democracy. During the first post-Apartheid decade, the Ministry of Education had been exceptionally busy[2] developing education policy and, by the end of that decade, there was a general climate of self-congratulation about what had been achieved in respect to the 'transformation' of education.

But, one year later, by the time of the WCED conference in March 2005, the mood had shifted. The impacts of education policies were beginning to become more visible, and it was acknowledged that in some respects our aspirations had overshot our capacities. This essay plays the role in this book of providing an example of direct engagement with those upon whom the success of the 'transformation' of education in our country is ultimately dependent.

Summary of day one

1 Democracy and discussion

Perhaps the most striking comment made yesterday was that from Premier Rasool: 'We come here not to celebrate (our achievements) but to consider whether we should change course.' Coming near the start of our second decade of democracy this is an important reminder. 'All our analyses are telling us that the majority of our youth do not have hope and a sense of a better future...This conference has been called to issue a wake-up call to the government.'

Yusuf Gabru congratulated the WCED for organising this conference and being prepared to take an honest, and public, look at itself. In various contexts, Superintendent-General (S-G) Swartz emphasised that the main purpose of the conference was to get feedback from the participants about *Education 2020: A Human Capital Development Strategy for the Western Cape*[3]. 'We want the interaction to be as controversial as possible.' And he expressed some disappointment about the decline in the extent of public participation in key policy debates over the past years. 'We need a willingness to participate. People do not take up the spaces provided.'

Comments such as these provide a strong appeal to move away from patting ourselves on the back for what we have achieved in the first decade of democracy and collectively to turn our attention to the realities of our situation, and *Education 2020*, which is the (draft) plan developed to cope with those realities. What is needed is not unthinking acceptance or rejection of the plan, but critical participation in making it as good as we can.

As an observer of the proceedings on the first day of the conference, I was struck by the disappearance of the word 'stakeholders' from the discussions that took place. This word used to be prevalent in the Western Cape, and still has a potent life in other parts of South Africa. Premier Rasool spoke about the need to move away from 'narrow populism' and from the idea that the state should 'retreat' and not intervene too directly in the conduct of schooling. The question is: 'What does the state do for the majority (the "great unwashed")?' He insisted that the state *does* have a role to play but that it needs the advice of those close to the action. But the advice needed was advice not from a narrow or sectional point of view, in protection of the interests of a limited interest group, but from the point of view of what will be best for all of us. This reinforced the S-G's call for *critical participation* in this conference.

To accomplish a shift away from defending the interests of ourselves or our sectional group is no easy task. It has been one of the problems for democracy since at least the time of Rousseau, who eventually came to the conclusion that the only way to accomplish it was to establish a 'civic religion'. Before he lost his head, Robespierre came to the same conclusion. And in South Africa we have a particular problem – one of the pillars of Apartheid was a relativist epistemology that asserted that there is no escape from speaking from some sectional point of view – do you remember '*eie sake*' ('own affairs')? Such views forge a conceptual link between democracy and power, and break the link between democracy and discussion. Democracy should be understood as, at heart, the view that collective decision should be the outcome of open and public discussion amongst all those who will be affected and, if we want to consolidate our democracy in its second decade, we need spaces for public discussion, and to learn the value of critical participation.

Thus, the tone of this conference, as set out in the proceedings of the first day, was to be a re-emphasis on the link between democracy and *critical discussion*. Rasool: 'Teachers are intellectuals; where are they in public debate?'

2 HIV and AIDS

One of the comments from the floor yesterday spoke of 'the complete absence of HIV and AIDS in the document'. This is not quite true. On page 42 of *Education 2020* we see the following: 'By the year 2009…A programme of action is entrenched within the department designed to mitigate the impacts of HIV/AIDS and related diseases.'

However, it is true that the document seems to pay too little attention to the pandemic, and the ways in which it is likely to cripple even the best-crafted strategic plans. Although the HIV-positive prevalence rates might at present be slightly lower in the Western Cape than elsewhere, the virus is no respecter of either provincial or national boundaries, and the net migration of population into the Western Cape is likely to increase the prevalence, at least in the shorter term.

In defence of *Education 2020* it can be said that there is a sense in which we cannot even imagine what the onslaught of the pandemic is going to do to our society and its institutions. We all know from UNAIDS reports that 66 per cent of people living with AIDS, 66 per cent of those newly infected with HIV, and more than 76 per cent of deaths from AIDS-related illness were in sub-Saharan Africa in 2003. The actual numbers we are talking about here are in their millions, but they do little to convey the ways in which the pandemic has shred the very fabric of communities and societies. We are talking not merely about the attrition rate of teachers through death or illness; we are talking about teachers facing the pandemic on a daily basis in their schools and classrooms – an increasing number of learners and colleagues in deep distress and increasingly unable to carry out their normal activities. Public denial is going to do little to help those teachers faced with the roll out of this crisis.

It is not going to help us to get into a panic. We will have to live with this problem for at least the next decade – until 2015 – and one may wonder what the Western Cape might look like by 2020. A 'programme of action…designed to mitigate the impacts of HIV/AIDS and related diseases' might quite soon come to appear a case of sneezing against a storm.

3 Demography

In 1995 I was privileged to attend a conference in Penang, Malaysia. I happened to land right in the middle of a public debate about modifications to the 35-year national development plan (called, significantly, *2020*). One of the elements of this plan, launched in 1985, was that annually a particular town or region was targeted for concentrated development. The resources and attention of the central government would be devoted to that town or region and, according to need, infrastructure would be built, capital investment would be encouraged, and so on. While I was there, the plans were well under way to target a small island to the north of Penang the following year. This was the home of fishermen and small fisher villages. The plan was to organise an international airshow on the island. An airport – with a modern runway – was to be built, hotel chains were invited to come to the party and build hotels to accommodate the expected visitors, etc. Whatever one might think about whether such 'development' was indeed development, it is clear that the island would be launched on a trajectory of becoming a tourist destination for the rich from the north. The plan could not have been expected to have forecast a devastating tsunami almost a decade into the future.

It had also been originally agreed that the plan would be reconsidered at five-yearly intervals, and adjusted as circumstances changed. In 1995, the debate was about whether the targeting of some rural regions should be shifted to towns and cities to which those previously from the rural regions were migrating in burgeoning numbers. The towns and cities were beginning to burst at the seams, and needed urgent assistance to provide housing and other services for their increasing populations. At its harshest, the question was whether it was wise to pour significant resources into rural development when all the projections indicted that their populations were declining rapidly.

Increasing urbanisation is an inevitable accompaniment of development, and it should be no surprise that Professor Bekker's research[4] found that over the past five years in the Western Cape, 350 000 learners have moved from rural areas into towns. This is, clearly, a significant finding in relation to developing a strategic plan for the Western Cape, and especially in relation to education. Deputy Minister Surty rightly noted this finding in his keynote address.

In his opening address Premier Rasool spoke of two (main) challenges: one was the intellectual content of the curriculum; the other was the success or failure of 'diversity management'. After a comment about the 'Grape Trek', Professor Bekker pointed out that as many as 95 per cent of the newly arrived population of the Western Cape were born in the old Cape Province and, in this sense, were not 'intruders' at all.

4 Access and quality

Minister Dugmore, after speaking about the key role of education in fighting poverty, recommended that in the 'second decade of democracy we need to focus on *quality*'. There is a sense in which we all know what he was saying, but the word 'quality' needs to be handled with care.

We are driven by the logic of the word 'quality' as a noun to understand it as the name for something, and then we try to find that something[5]. However, we will avoid being misled if we think of 'quality' as deriving its basic meaning from its use as an adjective or an adverb. This apparently superficial linguistic recommendation has significant consequences in debates about quality. We might refer to a quality cricket bat, or a quality concert. But unless we know something about cricket bats or concerts we are in no position to make an informed contribution to a discussion about the quality of either. Disputes about whether cricket bat A is better than cricket bat B presuppose knowledge about what cricket bats are, and what they are for. And the same comments can be made about disputes about whether one concert was better or worse than another.

Similarly in the field of education. There are constant debates about what 'quality education' is. Some argue that the quality of education can be measured in terms of whether it is producing the skills needed for a flourishing economy, but others and perhaps Yusuf Gabru offers an example here – argue that 'in our mad rush to produce skills' we might fail to produce the 'general critical skills' needed by the citizens of a democracy. My modest point here is simply to draw attention to the fact that arguments about 'quality education' are arguments not so much about 'quality' but about what we mean by 'education'.

In his keynote address Deputy Minister Surty made a few comments about 'transformation'. He suggested that transformation has to do with much more than simply demographics; it has to do with mindsets and attitudes. The question, he said, was how to transform institutions so that they can take account of the impacts of the modern world. I have no idea whether or not this idea is popular – but it has much to commend it. In the contemporary world, one might say, one central purpose of schooling is to enable access to the modern world, and the quality of that schooling can be judged in terms of the extent to which it is successful in enabling such access.

There are, of course, many barriers to such access, many of which we in South Africa are vividly aware, and some of which we have removed since 1994. But there is one barrier that cannot be removed by legislative decision, and this is the barrier that is called (print) literacy and numeracy (which can be understood as a special form of literacy). In the modern world, it is assumed that all people can read and write and handle straightforward computations. This is a necessary capacity for access to the modern world.

It is to the credit of the Western Cape that it undertook Learner Assessment Studies of Grades 3 and 6, focusing on literacy and numeracy[6]. These studies measured progress towards literacy, and what the results show is that despite the undisputed progress made in other dimensions of the transformation of schooling, our achievements in respect to teaching children how to read and write are less than satisfactory. If the quality of schooling is understood in terms of enabling access to the modern world, and if such access depends on literacy and numeracy, then improving the quality of schooling for the majority, and particularly the disadvantaged, still evades us.

These studies reveal one of the starkest realities of our situation. *Education 2020* acknowledges that. On page 29 we find the statement that, 'The development of high levels of language use and numeracy are key to all learning,' and in the section on the introduction of Grade R, there is a reference to '...a high correlation between reading and numeracy performance at Grade 3 level and access to pre-school programmes' (p. 31). The strategic goal articulated in Section 6.8.3 is, 'To ensure that all learners from Grades 1 to 6 read, write and calculate at the level determined by the National Curriculum Statement', and that section spells out a series of goals for the achievement of such levels of literacy and numeracy over the next decade, with regular diagnostic testing to measure progress towards those goals.

This is so obvious that we might wonder why it is not more widely recognised. One possibility is that we are hypnotised by the idea that 'Maths, Science and Technology' are the key to our future. In fact, so ubiquitous is this view that we might refer to it as the 'MST mantra'. Huge resources, both public and private, are devoted to the improvement of teaching in MST. But do we have any hard evidence that this kind of emphasis is going to lead towards a glorious future for all? I recently read an article[7] in *The New York Review of Books* about three books that set out to explain the 'long expansion' of the US economy during the 1990s. All three focus on 'technological advances' as the key explanation. But the reviewer disagrees. There are many reasons why the US has 'flourished' as it has, and one key reason is 'free and widespread education' over a long period of time.

The usual examples are the 'Asian Tigers', and in *Education 2020* I see a reference to the 'Celtic Tiger' (p. 43). But these examples are misleading; what is occluded in both of these cases is that we are referring to societies that have well-entrenched and centuries-long traditions of print literacy. We can agree with David Rose that '…the basis of inequality in the classroom, and hence in the society, is in students' differing capacities to independently learn from reading, which is the fundamental mode of learning in secondary and tertiary education'[8]. We can agree, too, with Tony Ehrenreich when he says: 'This country will be torn apart unless we tackle the issue of growing inequality.' One contribution that teachers at all levels of the system, and in all areas of the curriculum, can make to overcoming inequality is to focus strongly and persistently on developing learners' capacity to read and to learn from reading.

5 Teaching

Both Yusuf Gabru and Professor Fataar noted the lack of an emphasis on teaching in *Education 2020*. Gabru: 'What I didn't see in the report was teaching.' Fataar: 'The document is silent about what goes on in the classroom.'

Professor Fataar elaborated on his comment in terms of the dominance of economic discourses in discussions about education. 'Discourses from outside of education have come to dominate education discourse' and, as a result of this, while we see lots of references to 'developing skills and human capital' in *Education 2020*, we see very little about 'pedagogical issues'. I must confess to having something of an aversion, for some odd reason, to the word 'pedagogical', but I think the point made is correct. The practice of teaching is the essential feature of any education system, and very little is said about teaching in *Education 2020*.

The problem about the ways in which economic discourse has come to penetrate to the heart of our understanding of schooling and education is not limited to the Western Cape, or to *Education 2020*. It is a problem that is prevalent in the whole of the western world, and it has transformed some higher education systems beyond recognition. *Education 2020* talks of all learners in Grades 7 to 9 being provided with a high-quality *general* education (p. 32), and this can be understood as trying to keep the discourse of economics at bay – at least during the senior phase of schooling.

It is no good to ignore the financial realities in terms of which we operate. We can say, if we want to, that, 'We must get rid of school fees in poorer areas,' as Tony Ehrenreich did, but much as we might agree with the sentiment, we would need to know how we are going to fund such schools. Similarly, there are universities in this country that have ignored their financial realities, and some of them reached the stage of virtual bankruptcy, unable to pay their staff for months at a time, unable even to maintain their infrastructure, and dependent on the national government to bale them out with huge handouts.

However, the trick is how to acknowledge the financial realities of schooling and education while keeping those realities at the boundaries of our core business. This is a far from easy path to tread, and there are many higher education institutions and schools that have bought into the language of the 'marketplace' and now talk about, and understand, their core activities in such terms. The practice of teaching is central to anything that could be called education, and that practice becomes corrupted by the adoption of an alien discourse in which to understand it.

Yesterday someone from the floor said '…thank you for reminding us of the child-centred approach…' It was unclear to me who they were thanking. In *Education 2020* I can see very little that might remind us of the 'child-centred approach', and I do not remember anyone talking about it yesterday.

Perhaps what the speaker meant was that a primary defence against economy-inspired ways of understanding education is to understand it in terms of 'child-centred education'. The former focuses on the 'needs of the economy' and asks how we can produce learners to serve those needs; the latter focuses on the learners and their personal development. But, as in the case of the rhetorical contrast between Apartheid education and Outcomes-based education the dichotomy assumed in these cases is false. Child-centred education marginalises teaching, and makes unviable assumptions about what learning is and how learning takes place. Of course learners are at the heart of our educational efforts, and any teaching that ignores the recipients of that teaching is poor teaching. But if that implies that teachers must become non-intrusive facilitators, we have lost the plot. We point our noses in a more promising direction if we speak not of 'learner-centred education' but of '*learning*-centred education'.

6 Teachers as social workers

Conscientious teachers are chronically overloaded. And we aggravate that overload when we describe teaching in terms of the 'seven roles of an educator' put forward in the *Norms and Standards for Educators*[9], and continue to expect that teachers and schools are going to provide the solution to all the ills of society. If we are serious about Johan Stegmann's claim that, 'Good education is a necessary but not a sufficient condition for development', then we need to think seriously about what we are expecting teachers to do.

At its simplest, we can say that the job of teachers is to teach, and that is their distinctive contribution to development. The problem is that to the extent that we expand teachers' responsibilities to include many other functions that might, collectively, be called welfare functions, we make it increasingly difficult for teachers to focus well on their primary professional responsibility.

We have fallen into a trap here. Of course, the young need many kinds of pastoral care – and this is even more obviously the case in conditions of poverty, illness, destitution, mobility and frustration. Such conditions severely disrupt family life and stretch community networks of care to breaking point. But are we sure that it is teachers who need to cope with these social ills? Someone needs to, if we are a compassionate society, but it is not obvious that it should be teachers – whose principal function is to teach.

Perhaps we need to reconceive schools as centres of care for the young, but avoid taking the next step that, therefore, teachers need to be social workers as well as teachers. There is a promising element of *Education 2020* that can provide us with a clue to the development of schools, especially in the light of the looming HIV and AIDS pandemic.

In his opening remarks, Minister Dugmore mentioned the 'Transversal Initiatives' discussed in *Education 2020* (pp. 22–25). 'We expect from sister departments…that they contribute to the process of Human Capital Development…' Nine (government) departments are mentioned – from health to environmental affairs and planning – and for each there is a brief description of how they might contribute.

This opens the door to the possibility that schools could be conceived as the sites for the delivery of a whole range of social services for the young, although not piled on the shoulders of teachers, but rather, in the hands of departments with mandated responsibilities for such services, and people who have been specially trained for such work.

Professor Fataar spoke of teachers spending 'so much of their time on pastoral and social responsibilities that their teaching responsibilities become sidelined'. He is, surely, right about this, and about lamenting the not unconnected 'de-professionalisation of teachers'. The defining task of professional teachers is to teach. If those they are employed to teach lack some of the necessary conditions for learning to be possible – such things as nutrition, parental care, shelter, emotional support, physical security, even clothing or a birth certificate – those conditions need to be addressed. There is no argument about that. But the 'Transversal Initiatives' we find in *Education 2020* provide us with a clue to an alternative way of thinking about how to do that, and to avoid crippling professional teachers with unbearable workloads.

7   *Professional agency*

After mentioning R4 billion available to improve the quality of education, Deputy Minister Surty spoke about the problem of how to retain teachers in 'hardship positions' – that is, less popular teaching posts in geographically remote areas, or in learning areas where there is a shortage of teachers. He suggested the possibility of 'incentives' to retain teachers in such posts. Then he asked the question of whether such incentives should be linked to 'performance'.

We need here to be very careful. The shortage of teachers in some remote schools, and in some learning areas – such as mother tongue in the Foundation Phase, and maths and science – is a genuine problem, and it is more prevalent in other provinces than in the Western Cape. But would 'incentives' solve it? The idea of incentives for some categories of teachers is fraught with difficulties, and has a long and controversial history. One difficulty is that, as all teachers know, if 'performance' is to be measured in terms of learner achievements this can be very unfair. There are some situations in which successful teaching is much easier than in others, and by and large teachers can have little control over such situations. In the UK there was an attempt to overcome this problem by trying to find a way of measuring 'added value', but this attempt ran into insoluble complications about how this might be done.

A much more promising way of thinking about this problem is to think of teachers as members of a profession, whose commitments are shaped in terms of the ideals of the profession. Members of a profession are agents, in the sense that they need to take responsibility for their own professional actions. In the words of Yusuf Gabru, 'Any process of renewal must start and end with the teacher.' Although the idea of a profession has run into difficulties in a world dominated by the idea that at the root of all social arrangements stands the economy, we lose something invaluable if we become too skeptical about the idea of a profession. The case of Steve Biko provides a compelling example. The medical doctor assigned to the case failed in his professional duties, no matter what his views might have been about the importance of remaining obedient to the authorities.

There is a strong contrast between teachers being treated, and having a self-understanding of themselves, as civil servants or as members of a profession. As civil servants, their primary responsibility is to the state, as their employer, and obedience to the dictates of the state is their central duty. There are those who see this as the best way to maintain orderliness in the schooling system, and to accomplish the goals of transformation against the (counter-revolutionary) 'resistance' of institutions and dissident individuals. By contrast, the primary responsibility of teachers as members of a profession is to the ideals of the profession, and they are accountable for their professional actions not to their employers but to their professional peers[10].

Professor Fataar contends that, 'We have been witnessing a diminution of agency in education.' One way of interpreting this is to surmise that he is saying that teachers have increasingly, through exhaustion, despair or perhaps dwindling conviction, given up trying to improve the quality of their teaching; they have increasingly come to see themselves as embrangled in situations over which they have no control, and have lost an understanding of themselves as professional agents whose responsibility it is to act as best they can in the situations in which they find themselves. In effect, they have adopted the stance of dependent victims, deferring responsibility to others or forces beyond their control, and have lost sight of themselves as agents with a professional responsibility to contribute actively to the improvement of the quality of education.

In case we think these are merely the thoughts of a mere professor, we can note that Premier Rasool expressed very much the same thought in terms of his injunction that teachers should be 'navigators of change' rather than being pulled down by feelings of hopelessness and helplessness.

8 Social capital

But it is not only individuals who can be agents. Communities can also be agents and, importantly, agents in their own development. Despite legitimate anxieties about the ideological associations of the word 'capital' – and the very subtitle of *Education 2020: A Human Capital Development Strategy for the Western Cape* can arouse those anxieties – something like this thought can be seen as underpinning the idea of social capital. Our history has induced in us a tradition of dependence, and its cousin, a tendency always to find others to blame for the troubles we face. And the emphasis in *Education 2020* on social capital can be understood, innocently, as an appeal to communities to escape from these historical habits and to become active agents in improving their quality of life.

S-G Swartz spoke of the formation of social capital as a key strategy in the development of the Western Cape, but he also said that he had been uncomfortable with the word 'capital'. Like the phrase 'human capital', it has its home in a discourse that depersonalises people, and treats them as little more than replaceable cogs in a vast economic machine. However, he suggested that we can 'appropriate the concept of capital' for our own purposes, and understand it as implying that the bedrock of all development is active community participation.

Education 2020: 'In general it is agreed that social capital refers to the networks in communities that enable it to take responsibility for, and to take leadership in projects that are designed to improve the conditions of the collective in that community' (p. 16). At the same time, there is an acknowledgement that this kind of bootstrap strategy presupposes viable and fairly stable communities, with the capacity to put energy into their own endogenous development. We cannot make such a presupposition, in good conscience and without qualification, in a situation such as that in the Western Cape. There are many communities that have suffered severe disruption and are effectively dysfunctional, without the collective capacity and coherence to change the trajectory of their lives. And this is why we should approve of the idea of the developmental state – that is, a state which has the responsibility to intervene where communities hardly exist: 'However, where the systems and fabric within communities have broken down almost irretrievably, then government must intervene to help facilitate, grow and develop that social capital' (p. 16).

Professor Bekker yesterday passed a very significant comment that went by perhaps too quickly. He spoke about the relationship between institutions and interests, and said that the common assumption that institutions exist to serve pre-existing interests is at best a half-truth. Institutions not only serve interests but are also a source of interests. The institutions of education – from schools to Further Education and Training (FET) colleges and universities – not only serve independently formed interests, such as the interest in getting a job or contributing to the economic prosperity of the society, but they shape our conceptions of who we are and what we mean by the quality of life. Of course, collectively and individually we have economic interests, but those are not the only interests we have, and our educational institutions are a source of interests that give sense to our lives.

The 'Transversal Initiatives' which are mentioned on pages 22–25 in *Education 2020* are closely linked to the project of forming social capital, and are an expression of what it is for a state to be a developmental state in practice.

9 Inequality

A contributor from the floor said that alarm bells should be ringing for us about the increasing inequality in our society. As noted earlier, Tony Ehrenreich, in more passionate rhetoric, said: 'This country will be torn apart unless we tackle the issue of growing inequality.' There is little doubt that these sentiments are true, but it is also true that two centuries of Enlightenment thinking have not yet provided a genuinely viable solution. Moral evangelism is clearly not enough, and passionate rhetoric does not solve the problem – it merely draws attention to it. In a Marxist mood we can identify 'capitalism' as the main villain, but this mood is difficult to sustain in a world that has seen the collapse of the most thoroughgoing attempts to establish societies based on Marxist principles. Equality has to do with the distribution of the goods and benefits of society, but if there is a reduction in available goods and benefits there is less to distribute, no matter how 'equally'.

It should be obvious that neither *Education 2020* nor the critical discussions at this conference are going to provide the definitive solutions to this mounting problem. But I think we should acknowledge that there are some elements of *Education 2020* that have promise in this regard. What I have in mind is the emphasis on the development of (print) literacy and numeracy, the need to reassert our collective agency in achieving a better future for all, and the idea of the 'Transversal Initiatives', to bring together a full range of government departments in a coherent effort to improve the lot of all our citizens, especially those marginalised from the mainstream and most in need of help.

Notes

1 Bernard Williams, *In the Beginning was the Deed*, Oxford, N.J.: Princeton University Press, 2005, p. xiii.

2 Some might say *too* busy. South African education is characterised by policy overload.

3   Western Cape Education Department, *Education 2020: A Human Capital Development Strategy for the Western Cape*, 5 September 2004. Available at <http://capegateway.gov.za>.

4   Simon Bekker, 'Socio-economic overview: Population dynamics 10 years and beyond', presentation at the conference.

5   The same kind of point can be made about the word 'intelligence' and with it the notorious ideology of 'IQ'. We need only consider the insidious influence of this ideology during the previous century, and the profound impact it had on schooling and the ways in which teachers saw their learners, to appreciate the significance of recommending that this word derives its basic meaning from its use as an adjective or an adverb.

6   Western Cape Education Department, *Grade 3 Learner Assessment Study 2002*, and *Grade 6 Learner Assessment Study 2003*. See <http://www.jet.org.za>.

7   Jeff Madrick, 'The producers' in *The New York Review of Books*, March 10, 2005.

8   David Rose, 'Democratising the classroom: A literacy pedagogy for the new generation' presented at the Kenton Conference, October 2004.

9   DoE, *Norms and Standards for Educators*, Government Gazette #20844, 2000 – which remains the ruling policy for Teacher Education.

10   See Wally Morrow, 'Accountability and the idea of a profession' in *Chains of Thought*, Johannesburg: Southern Book Publishers, 1989.

Bibliography

Achebe C (1988) *Things Fall Apart*. London: Picador

Bak N (ed.) (2000) *Making OBE Work?* Cape Town: Western Cape Education Department

Barnett RB (1994) *The Limits of Competence*. Bristol: SRHE and the Open University Press

Biko S (1988) *I Write What I Like*. London: Penguin Books

Boyd W (1956) *Emile for Today*. London: Heinemann

Bundy C (1989) 'Action, comrades, action!': The politics of youth-student resistance in the Western Cape, 1985. In W James & M Simons (eds) *The Angry Divide*. Cape Town: David Philip

Carlyle T (1843) *Past and Present*. London: Chapman & Hall (reprinted 1909)

Chomsky N (1959) Review of BF Skinner's *Linguistic Behavior*. *Language* 35(1): 26–58

Coetzee JC (1975) The theory of Christian-National Education. Reprinted in B Rose & R Tunmer (eds) *Documents in South African Education*. Johannesburg: AD Donker

Craft M (ed.) (1996) *Teacher Education in Plural Societies*. London: Falmer Press

Dasgupta PD (1995) *An Inquiry into Well-being and Destitution*. Oxford: Clarendon Press

Deacon R & Parker B (1999) Positively mystical: An interpretation of South Africa's Outcomes-based National Qualifications Framework. In J Jansen & P Christie (eds) *Changing Curriculum: Studies on Outcomes-based Education in South Africa*. Cape Town: Juta

De Villiers E (1990) *Walking the Tightrope*. Johannesburg: Jonathan Ball Publishers

DoE (Department of Education) (2000) *Norms and Standards for Educators*. Government Gazette #20844, 4 February

DoE (2005a) *A National Framework for Teacher Education in South Africa*. Pretoria: National Department of Education

DoE (2005b) *An Assessment of 10 Years of Education and Training in South Africa*. Pretoria: National Department of Education

Fanon F (1961) *The Wretched of the Earth*. Paris: Maspero

Freire P (1986) *The Pedagogy of the Oppressed*. Harmondsworth, Middlesex: Penguin Books

Fullan MG (1991) *The New Meaning of Educational Change*. London: Cassell

Gibbs G & Jenkins A (eds) (1992) *Teaching Large Classes in Higher Education: How to Maintain Quality with Reduced Resources*. London: Kogan Page

Gordon P (ed.) (1985) *Is Teaching a Profession?* London: Heinemann

Haack S (1998) *Manifesto of a Passionate Moderate.* Chicago: University of Chicago Press

Hart HLA (1961) *The Concept of Law.* Oxford: Oxford University Press

Hemson C (1995) In defence of content. Unpublished paper presented at the Kenton Conference, 27–30 October

Hofmeyr J & Hall G (1995) *The National Teacher Education Audit: Synthesis Report.* Pretoria: National Department of Education

Hoyle E & John P (1995) *Professional Knowledge and Professional Practice.* London: Cassell

Jansen J & Christie P (eds) (1999) *Changing Curriculum: Studies on Outcomes-based Education in South Africa.* Cape Town: Juta

Kovesi J (1967) *Moral Notions.* London: Routledge & Kegan Paul

MacIntyre A (1981) *After Virtue.* London: Duckworth

Madrick J (2005) The producers. In *The New York Review of Books,* 10.03.2005

Malcolm C (1999) Outcomes-based education has different forms. In J Jansen & P Christie (eds) *Changing Curriculum: Studies on Outcomes-based Education in South Africa.* Cape Town: Juta

Morrow W (1989) *Chains of Thought.* Johannesburg: Southern Book Publishers

Morrow W (1993) Entitlement and achievement in education. *Studies in Philosophy and Education* 13(1): 33–47

Morrow W (1998) Stakeholders and senates: The governance of higher education institutions in South Africa. *Cambridge Journal of Education* 28(3): 385–405

Morrow W & King K (eds) (1998) *Vision and Reality.* Cape Town: UCT Press

Muller J (1995) Knowledge and higher education. National Commission on Higher Education, Taskgroup 2, November 1995

Nussbaum MC (1987) The betrayal of convention: A reading of Euripides' *Hecuba.* In MC Nussbaum *The Fragility of Goodness: Luck and Ethics in Greek Tragedy and Philosophy.* Cambridge: Cambridge University Press

Nussbaum MC (1994) Review of LM Antony & C Witt (eds) A mind of one's own: Feminist essays on reason and objectivity. In *The New York Review of Books,* 20.10.1994

Parekh BP (1995) Education for a culturally plural society. *Papers of the Philosophy of Education Society of Great Britain* March 31–April 2

Pendlebury SA (1991) Luck, knowledge and excellence in teaching. Unpublished DEd thesis, University of the Western Cape

Peters RS (1965) Education as initiation. In RD Archambault (ed.) *Philosophical Analysis and Education*. London: Routledge & Kegan Paul

Peters RS (1966) *Ethics and Education*. London: Routledge & Kegan Paul

Rose B & Tunmer R (eds) (1974) *Documents in South African Education*. Johannesburg: AD Donker

Rose D (2004) Democratising the classroom: A literacy pedagogy for the new generation. Paper presented at the Kenton Conference, October 2004

SAHRC (South African Human Rights Commission) (2006) *Report of the Public Hearing on the Right to Basic Education*. Johannesburg: SAHRC

Said EW (1995) *Orientalism*. Harmondsworth: Penguin Books

SAIRR (South African Institute of Race Relations) (1988) *Race Relations Survey 1987/8*. Johannesburg: South African Institute of Race Relations

Salkever SG (1990) 'Lopp'd and bound': How liberal theory obscures the goods of liberal practices. In RB Douglas, G Mara & HS Richardson (eds) *Liberalism and the Good*. London: Routledge

Schon DA (1991) *The Reflective Practitioner: How Professionals Think in Action*. Novato, CA.: Arena

Shulman L (2004) *The Wisdom of Practice: Essays on Teaching, Learning, and Learning to Teach*. San Francisco: Jossey-Bass

Sockett H (1985) Towards a professional code of teaching. In P Gordon (ed.) *Is Teaching a Profession?* London: Heinemann

Steele S (1992) 'The recoloring of campus life. Student racism, academic pluralism and the end of a dream' as quoted in Fernand Ouellet, Education in a pluralistic society: Proposal for an enrichment of teacher education. In KA Moodley (ed.) *Beyond Multicultural Education*. Calgary, Alberta: Detselig Enterprises

Taylor C (1992) The politics of recognition. In A Gutmann (ed.) *Multiculturalism and 'The Politics of Recognition'*. Oxford, N.J.: Princeton University Press

Taylor N (1999) Getting learning right. Paper presented at the Teacher Development: Connecting Policy and Practice conference, 18–20 May

Taylor N & Vinjevold P (eds) (1999) *Getting Learning Right*. Report of the President's Education Initiative Research Project. Johannesburg: The Joint Education Trust

Trow M (1987) Academic standards and mass higher education. *Higher Education Quarterly* 41(3): 268–292

UNESCO Institute for Statistics (2006) *Teachers and Educational Quality: Monitoring Global Needs for 2015*. Montreal: Unesco UIS

WCED (Western Cape Education Department) (2004) *Education 2020: A Human Capital Development Strategy for the Western Cape*. Cape Town: WCED

Williams B (2005) *In the Beginning was the Deed*. Oxford, N.J.: Princeton University Press

Wittgenstein L (1963) *Philosophical Investigations*. Oxford: Basil Blackwell

Young IM (1990) *Justice and the Politics of Difference*. Princeton: Princeton University Press

Index